Resignation or Revolt?

Resignation or Revolt?

Socio-political Development and the Challenges of Peace in Palestine

CHRISTOPHER PARKER

I.B.Tauris *Publishers*
LONDON • NEW YORK

Published in 1999 by I.B.Tauris & Co Ltd
Victoria House, Bloomsbury Square, London WC1B 4DZ
175 Fifth Avenue, New York NY 10010

In the United States and Canada distributed by St. Martin's Press
175 Fifth Avenue, New York NY 10010

ISBN 1 86064 335 3

A full CIP record for this book is available from the British Library
A full CIP record for this book is available from the Library of Congress

Library of Congress catalog card: available

Typeset in Adobe Minion by Hepton Books, Oxford
Printed and bound in Great Britain by Creative Print and Design Wales

Contents

Preface

More than just rivers of coiled razor wire, or the wide asphalt tarmac that stretches for 300 or so meters between Israeli and Palestinian Authority checkpoints at Erez, separates Gaza from Israel. Gaza is distanced from Israel by years of neglect and repression. It is a contrast that workers who commute from their homes in Gaza to jobs in Israel experience regularly, (at least when permitted to go to those jobs), and it represents a gap that Gaza's Palestinians increasingly doubt the ability of their newly recognized political elites to close.

This book presents a political sociology of accommodation in the Gaza Strip, and discusses the dilemmas of civic development during the interim, not a discussion of Israeli policies toward, or abuses against, the Palestinian population. However, the balance of power underlying the negotiations toward a 'final status,' and the explicit Israeli role in determining the boundaries of the exercise of authority in the self-rule areas, suggest that Palestinian autonomy cannot be understood without at least a brief examination of Israel's strategic position vis-à-vis Palestinian self rule. Similarly, it is perhaps useful to sketch the circumstances which pushed the PLO to accept in the 1990s an agreement similar to proposals that it consistently rejected in the 1970s and 1980s.

The Israeli Labour Party vision of the post-Oslo 'final-status' – consistent with its historic position favouring the exclusion of Arab Labour from the Jewish economy in Palestine – foresaw a separation of the Palestinian and Israeli peoples. As Shimon Perez put it, the goal was to 'get Gaza out of Tel Aviv.' By the late 1980s, unemployment in Israel was rising. New immigration (particularly immigration from the former Soviet Union) reduced the Israeli capital's reliance upon access to a cheap Palestinian labour force and a captive market for Israeli goods in the occupied territories (OT). With the intifada, Israel incurred greater financial, social and political costs associated with expanding the role of the military in quelling unrest and imposing its economic and political suzerainty over the territories. In this climate, corporate and political strategists in Israel began to look for ways of restructuring dependent relations. Labour's response was 'separation.' It seems that the architects of the Labour plan for Palestinian autonomy realized that for such a separation to be viable, Israel would have to give up at least some of its control over land and resources in the OT. Beyond these economic and ideological considerations, the Israelis were brought to the negotiating table by the failure of direct military intervention to deal with the unrest of the intifada. By turning the responsibility for security and administration over to Palestinian elites, Israel reduced the cost of occupation and diverted international attention. The problem was Palestinianized.

We may never know what final status negotiations between a Labour government and the PLO/PA would have resulted in, but the agreements signed as of 28 September 1995 suggest that the final contours of autonomy would have encompassed the apparatus of a bureaucratic mini-state whose control over resources, borders and 'external' security would have been carefully regulated through agreements with Israel. Palestinian sovereignty would have been undermined by Israel's ability to enforce such arrangements at the expense of the PA's ability to regulate and plan with regard solely to the interests of its population. The contours of Palestinian authority would probably have continued to be subject and accountable to many of Israel's fundamental strategic concerns.

The regime change bringing the Likud party of Benjamin Netanyahu to power in Israel has threatened the trajectory of the peace process in ways which may have a decisive impact on the meanings of self rule. Using tactics of delay and obfuscation, Netanyahu's policies seem to reaffirm commitment to Likud's strategic vision of a 'greater Israel.' Furthermore, the Likud government seems to be intentionally breaching both the letter and the spirit of the agreements, provoking instability in the territories in order to justify delays in negotiations and intervention in Palestinian affairs. Such actions have served to induce Palestinian apathy toward the ineffectiveness of their autonomous institutions, while at the same time inciting anger toward Israel. One of the gravest weaknesses of the agreements is that their ambiguity (an ambiguity that was probably intentional in order make them politically acceptable to both sides) also means that they were very dependent on the personal commitments of the personalities who signed them. This gives scope for the Likud government to argue that they do not represent binding contracts of state, and that in the absence of 'final status' talks, any portion of the agreement is subject to renegotiation.

The most discussed example of this is the continuation of 'Jewish only' settlement activity in the West Bank. Such activity is recognized as a violation of international law, as contrary to the spirit of the Oslo Accords, and certainly must be seen as an action which is openly and unapologetically provocative to Palestinians. However, settlement activity is not mentioned in the interim agreement, and that the interim agreement seems to be viewed by the United States and Israel (overwhelmingly the major powers in the region) as superseding previous rulings, claims and international proclamations. While the agreements clearly state that no measures shall be taken that might prejudice 'final-status issues,' Arafat seems to have counted on the personal assurances of Israeli Labour leaders in this regard, and was left vulnerable by the defeat of Perez in the May 1996 Israeli elections.

Unlike Labour, Likud has less problem with the idea of Palestinians migrating to low wage jobs inside Israel. Dependence on jobs in Israel (and within the PA) is an important factor in undermining an activist Palestinian stance. More importantly, dependence on wage Labour in Israel removes human obstacles to direct Israeli control over the land in the OT, and leaves it more vulnerable to confiscation by Israeli authorities. In as much as Likud is willing to accept some degree of Palestinian civil self-administration, autonomy would not preclude Jewish sovereignty over land and resources in the OT. This strategy has been described as 'creeping encroachment.' Without control over resources, land or employment opportunities, autonomy or no autonomy, the Palestinians would eventually be forced to leave, or kept pacified by donor dependence. This is in line with Likud strategy and tactics in the tradition of Begin, Shamir and Sharon throughout the 1970s and into the 1980s. Assuming that the process is carried out gradually, and that Israel manages to keep a stranglehold on the provision of basic needs to Palestinians, Likud might be able to reverse the trajectory of the current peace process, but almost certainly it would have to pay a sustained and exacting price to maintain order if Palestinians rights, aspirations and needs remain unfulfilled. In the meantime, economic dependence on Israel, and the social and political fragmentation of the Palestinian communities in the OT, has hindered sustained and organized Palestinian uprising.

While Palestinian income has fallen drastically since Oslo, the international donors have rather uncritically stepped in to make up some of the difference, thus covering up some of the major structural defects of the process itself, and perhaps undermining the incentive to change it. As this book suggests, the subordination of socio-economic imperatives to the techno-diplomatic framework of the peace process has undermined the ideological content in Palestinian politics, leaving instead a combination of repression, concession and patrimonial pay-offs to sustain a process which is incapable of maintaining grassroots participation with reference to the institutional rights and obligations suggested by 'self-rule.'

At one level, the current transition toward Palestinian self-rule must be considered within attempts by competing national movements to resolve tensions arising between ideological visions and economic and political realities (both global and local). Like Israel, the PLO was forced to respond to realignments in global relations of patronage and international economic incentives as well as to economic trends affecting its respective constituencies. Participation in the peace process afforded PLO elites access to the resources and diplomatic recognition of the 'international community' at a time when previous sources of funding had dried up; and it allowed them to claim a constituency at a time when they were more distanced from their traditional diaspora constituencies than ever before (this is discussed in Chapter 3). Thus it may be argued that current trends in Palestinian society reflect the redefinition of conflict and the reconstitution/rejustification of international patronage networks occurring in the post-Cold War international environment generally. The case of the transition to Palestinian self rule indicates that these trends rapidly trickle down to inform political and social relationships at the local level. This may be especially true in areas such as Gaza where people have been heavily dependent on nationalist and international patronage for survival, and affected by the unaccountable intrusion of external authority upon social interaction. Developments in Gaza should be seen against the backdrop of similar constitutive transitions and the redefinition of conflicts elsewhere on the globe.

For Palestinians, the alleged advantages offered by the 'new world order' came at the time when their institutions were most poorly prepared to take advantage of them. The PLO was an over-bloated and largely ineffectual bureaucracy which had been relegated to exile in Tunis. Distanced from its traditional constituencies (a situation which left the diaspora communities more prone to fragmentation), it was increasingly ignoring its own national institutions in favour of micro-management of the movement by the charismatic figures who had come to personify it. At the same time, the communities of the OT were being purged of their local activist leadership and becoming a less relevant part of the Israeli economy as the Israeli military cracked down harder. During the chaos of the early 1990s in Gaza, the PLO scrambled, using its diminishing ability to provide patronage, to entrench itself in Gaza. As is shown below, these initiatives failed from the point of view of creating real effective social structures. However, they did give Fatah and the PLO the appearance of solid and absolute support which eventually forced Israel to recognize that the PLO was the only viable negotiating partner in the Palestinian community.

Having lost its old patrons in the Soviet Bloc and the Arab World after 1991, the PLO's access to new patrons depended on reaching an accord with Israel. This in turn affected the PLO/PA's client base – switching its attention to events in the OT rather than political manoeuvring in the diaspora. At the same time, changes in the Israeli economy and the socio-economic implications of Israel's de-linking with the Palestinian population in the OT have meant that many if not most Gazans are dependent in some way on the PA for contacts and opportunities to ensure survival over the short term.

By signing the Oslo accord, the PLO was perhaps looking out for its own institutional survival before the interests of the Palestinian people. Cut off from its main sources of funding after the 1991 Gulf war, the PLO bureaucracy sought to replace the lost funds by usurping the role of NGOs in the OT and using that as a rationale and legitimized base for procuring the funding that would allow for bureaucratic survival. The concentration of aid in PA hands is clearly a pay-off for concessions embodied within the Oslo accords, and patterns of patronage 'established in exile have meant that public and private investment are benefiting Arafat's entourage rather than the people of the OT.'[1] According to one PFLP sympathizer:

> They said they would never give up our rights to statehood, self-determination and the rights of the refugees to return. Then they came up with this. They came up with a new logic that we have to rescue what there is to rescue. Oslo is not an agreement, it is a conspiracy in the dark by people who didn't have the legitimacy to do it ... once they try to sell your ownership, they no longer represent you.[2]

The agreement was born not out of the strength of the local or international position of the PLO vis-à-vis Israel, but out of the desperation of a particular grouping in the diaspora. Thus, we might refer to a political economy of accommodation. Netanyahu currently seems to be bargaining that a reversal of the current trajectory is possible based on Israel's overwhelming material power, and on an electoral mandate that many Israeli right wingers would argue indicates a willingness by Israelis to pay the price of creating a 'greater Israel.' At present, the future does not seem bright.

While there is no shortage of proclaimed 'expert' opinion on the peace process in the media, less attention has been paid to the character of the emerging relationship between Palestinians and the Palestinian authority. Similarly, little effort has gone into defining what is actually meant by 'self-rule.' The phrase 'self rule' so neatly avoids the complexities, tensions and contradictions within the process of state-building and the exercise of authority that one wonders whether those who put forward the term are attempting to establish a basis for an 'end of politics.' Certainly, the framework of the peace process seems only with difficulty to account for any political expression from the Palestinian street, and tragically both the international donors and the Fatah leadership seem to be responding as though street activity were surprising and/or illegitimate. If those who would orchestrate social consolidation from above find the institutions of autonomy not up to this task, then opposition will also be encouraged to express itself without reference to such institutions. Without institutional mediation and amelioration, violent opposition becomes more likely.

If Palestine is to be governed, it must be defined. This definition must be manifested in power, institutions and perception. It must be reflected in mobilization. Self-rule as elaborated under current agreements amounts to something else. The diplomatic utility of 'self rule' is apparent: it has the advantage of being one of those concepts that says everything and nothing at the same time. As a solution on paper, it allows an elite to assert a claim to political leadership without the need to legitimize itself through the articulation of a social agenda – and seems to assume that the process of legitimation is a static rather than an ongoing process. It overlooks the internal bases of conflict (witness Nationalist Serbia as of January 1997, or Chechnya and Afghanistan after Russian withdrawal). Another danger of 'self-rule' as invoked in Palestine is the way it can be used (and is being used) to control populations without reference to sovereignty – specifically rights over land, resources and external security. Azmi Bishara, for instance, has argued that 'autonomy means a form of Israeli control where Palestinians agree to define and police themselves as non-citizens.'[3] The ability of the future Palestinian political entity (or state) to stabilize a relationship between people, power and territory – and its ability to govern effectively within institutions – will fundamentally affect the transformation of the Palestinian street's with the PLO elite into identification with a statist status quo.

But as presumptuous and misleading as the phrase 'self-rule' is, in so far as it refers to the internal politics of a particular identifiable group it does help us to isolate certain sets of political phenomena. The political self is defined in terms of interests which are in turn evaluated within a particular political-economic context. Gilen has succinctly noted the interaction between this context and the tactics which are invoked at the grass roots level to cope:

> When people act, their actions cannot be but shaped by the socio-economic environment in which they live. To the extent that this environment exhibits a certain order, the acts must reflect that order, if they are to be successful adaptations to the situations that confront the actors. If acts may be assumed to be rational, insight into the actors' perception of the situation, the deliberations made and the acts performed are indispensable building blocks for analysis.[4]

Sometimes, however, acts designed to ensure short term interests might reinforce an order which undermines longer term interests. We might also apply similar criteria to understanding a group's refusal to adapt once it has found its survival niche in rejection of the new order. In the absence of avenues for civic participation, how might acts of opposition reflect this situation? People must evaluate the possibilities for change in the context of given and potential bases of authority. The crisis of meaning within the current context of interim self-rule thus creates a corresponding crisis in the potential for grass roots mobilization from below, and might mean that political opposition and social frustration can only release itself in violent, disorganized bursts. Meaningful self-rule, by contrast, allows people to participate in a wide variety of organizations and activities that define the public self in ways which might challenge particular parties or political personalities, but not the foundation of the system itself.

Awareness of the extra-institutional framework within which social tensions might be inclined to play themselves out is crucial to an understanding of how alignments might form to challenge the new order from below. If groups doubt the ability of elites to arbitrate in social disputes and represent and promote social interests, then they will challenge these elites. If institutions and political personalities are strong enough to stand accountable to these demands from below, 'self-rule' might accommodate and incorporate such challenges that could then be seen as influencing a dynamic of political order. Inasmuch as existing institutions and processes are able to accommodate or address such challenges without undue violence, then such challenges play a role in testing and consolidating the legitimacy of the order as a whole. So far, however, the new face of authority has proved to be less a reflection of local social self perception than originally expected, and operates in a context where restrictions on social and economic activities are not perceived as balanced by rights, liberties and economic security.

The failure of the current peace process would almost certainly elicit a complex response from Palestinian society in Gaza. On the one hand, there might be relief that a process that seems increasingly unlikely to deliver the promises of national liberation and economic improvement – and instead seemed merely to change the faces which reigned over hardship and repression – has been abandoned. On the other hand, there is a genuine desire in Gaza to end the decades of conflict, but only if issues of human, economic and legal rights are addressed. In lieu of such a development, the failure of the peace process would almost certainly provoke frustration, anger and despair. As of December 1996 leading Fatah figures were publicly distancing themselves from the PA, fearing that any failure of the peace process would severely undermine their personal political fortunes. Such a development is perhaps most ominous in the confusing signals it sends to the Palestinian street, as politicians guard their own positions at the expense of social mobilization. It also encourages doubt about whether Palestinian leaders would be willing to sacrifice on behalf of a peace process that is increasingly seen as incompatible with Palestinian rights and hopes for lasting peace.

Chapter 1 of the book briefly introduces some of the issues and episodes defining Palestinian autonomy and situates them within a broader problematique of political order and civic development. In examining the problem of civic development, the book emphasizes four interdependent variables: (1) conflict, which is here seen as a signifier of participation, and as indicative of attempts to resolve both structural concerns, and tensions within existing social and political institutions; (2) the flow and distribution of resources in society and the degree to which this connotes relationships of production and integration or dependence in society; (3) power, particularly as it is invested in institutions capable of initiating and responding to change and (4) the degree to which the polity as given is seen to offer a meaningful reference point for ideologically motivated action. The notion of a political economy of meaning is elaborated upon and contrasted with models of civil society, neopatriarchy and the 'spectre of superfluous man' as a backdrop against which to evaluate more particular concerns addressed in later chapters.

Chapter 2 investigates the contingencies and trajectories of factionalism in Palestinian political life and suggests why factionalism is and may continue to be a prominent feature of self-rule politics. The historical forces and contingencies that shaped the networks reinforcing a Palestinian identity are reviewed, and their impact on the unfolding situation in Gaza is explored.

In the short term factionalism may compensate for the failure of economic development and job producing growth, but it induces dependence. In spite of the advent of nominal self rule, the essential structural conditions and political contingencies which sustained the relevance of factionalism in Palestinian life remain in place. Indeed, current agreements do little to challenge the structural underpinnings of occupation, and the short term goals of the peace process might be dependent on the relative stability of factional control to carry out current agreements. In other words, factional control may be seen as necessary in protecting the peace process from the instability inherent in broad based mobilizations pressing for structural change and accountability.

Historically the challenge for the Palestinian nationalist elite has been to unite and promote national consciousness among various constituencies of a scattered national community. Now the challenge is to bring a huge exile bureaucracy to bear in governing a local population whose interests and demands might in key areas be different from – and at times even seem threatening to – those at the top. Challenge and confusion arise out of concurrent attempts to shape, to accommodate, and to resist new manifestations of power and authority. There is a struggle to command both the institutions and vocabulary which communicate and infer legitimacy. The Fatah leadership of the PLO/PA faces a difficult task as it attempts to rationalize and consolidate its control over populations within limited autonomy areas while sustaining the fundamental tenets of the nationalist ideology which legitimized its claims to authority in the first place.

Chapter 3 focuses on what might be seen as contradictions exposed in the ideology and social constituencies of Palestinian nationalism since the signing of the Oslo Agreement. Crucial to understanding the significance of these contradictions is an exploration of the apparent incongruity between the social spaces which have traditionally comprised Palestinian nationalism and the uncertain legal/territorial boundaries of proposed 'self rule.' Inevitably, political autonomy will be used as a base from which to represent sometimes competing claims and aspirations. Expectations in the OT of a new condition of liberty can only be unfavourably contrasted with the actual coercive tactics and limitations of PA rule. In the diaspora, the two state solution threatens the claims of 1948 refugees.

The trajectory of this dilemma in Palestinian political development is here discussed in the context of what has become known as the 'inside-outside' dichotomy in Palestinian political life. The stress between 'inside' and 'outside' in Palestinian politics has been nurtured by the Palestinian experience of a variety of legal and economic conditions, awareness of Israeli occupation, and access to international sources of patronage and funding. The failure of the Fatah leadership to appoint prominent figures from the local community to key PA positions, and the removal of local activists from official election lists during the January 1996 elections, have contributed to a mistrust of the new authority.

The economy of transitional autonomy is the subject of Chapter 4. The economic context of the interim period may in fact be undermining the long term economic position of Palestinians by exacerbating dependency and leaving unresolved issues such as: (1) the movement of Palestinian goods and labour; (2) the right of a Palestinian Authority to establish its own fiscal regime; and, (3) the eventual establishment of the ecological boundaries of Palestinian (pseudo?) sovereignty. The uncertain future makes economic planning extremely difficult. It is in the economic sphere that the imbalance of power between the two negotiating parties is most acutely and immediately felt by the 'Palestinian in the street.' While the prices in Gaza's shops and markets correspond to those in Israel, the per capita income of Gaza is a mere 6 per cent of that in Israel. Aid to the Palestinian Authority seems designed to cover up many of the structural imbalances reinforced by current Palestinian–Israeli agreements – imbalances which severely limit the options available to the PA. This facilitates the embodiment of such imbalances within any future status quo, in turn producing long term distortions that leave the Palestinian state aid dependent. This has a negative impact on productive investment and employment opportunities for individual Palestinians. Emma Murphy has succinctly expressed the developmental concerns faced by Palestinians in Gaza:

> No amount of international aid will sustain the Palestinian economy if Palestinian workers are denied employment in Israel over the short term. No amount of support for agriculture will help if the best land is being expropriated. But

then this aid was never meant to stimulate economic development, but rather to sustain a political process in the short term.[5]

A high level State Department official noted: 'Israel's closure of the West Bank and Gaza is Palestine's 'Berlin Wall,' and US aid is a way of 'providing Palestinians with the resources to live with it.'[6]

From the perspective of developing a domestic Palestinian political economy, the approach of giving aid to a regime with few economic powers beyond the ability to distribute aid may in the end only serve to strengthen neopatrimonial relationships which undermine developmental incentives. Given the uphill struggle Gazans already face in terms of productive employment, this could prove disastrous. The donor approach has been to try and devise short term fixes for economic woes in Gaza while bypassing structural and legal issues which, left unaddressed, only serve to effectively reinforce the underlying mechanisms strangling economic development while transferring the responsibility for dealing with the consequences to the PA. So far, the autonomy – by distancing Israeli politicians from directly confronting the impact of Israel's extended embargo against the Palestinian economy – has only served to dramatize Gaza's economic dependence on Israel. Thus, as the deadline for the final status negotiations approaches, the donors buy short term stability for the ruling elites rather than encouraging negotiators to confront and deal directly with these structural problems. Gaza's economic dependence consolidates its political dependence.

The era of self rule has necessitated a fundamental re-orientation of economic coping strategies for individuals and families in Gaza. Given the massive reduction in the number of jobs available to Palestinians inside the 'green line' and the continued ecological and legal restraints on development in the Gaza Strip – not to mention the loss of employment opportunities in the Gulf States since 1990 – factional and international patronage is playing an increasingly important role in individual survival. It has been a primary strategy of the PA to appropriate control over external sources of patronage in order to use it to consolidate its position in the 'autonomous' areas. It is important to note that the signing of the agreement gave the PLO access to new sources of patronage at a time when its traditional funding had dried up. The PA has been using donor funding to cultivate relationships of dependency with strategically located personalities and networks rather than to make investments in developmental infrastructure. Not only does such a strategy fail to address the fundamental structural problems threatening the long term viability of the Gaza economy, it is also unlikely to satisfy short term needs. One overriding concern addressed by this study is the way in which patterns of behaviour established in the name of sustaining 'a process' may condition socio-economic relationships within any future Palestinian state (although at present, the likelihood of any truly sovereign Palestinian political entity remains remote).

Chapter 5 explores the difficulty in identifying a basis of a future PA 'government' (as opposed to mere coercion and administration) given the limitations imposed by the agreements and the emptiness of rituals of legitimacy like the January 1996 Palestinian elections. The chapter centres in on the relationship between limited powers and limited legitimacy, as well as on PA strategies to undermine or accommodate coordinated challenges emerging from below. Conceptually, the chapter sets out to investigate the exercise of self rule with Samuel Huntington's premise that it is less the kind of government than the degree of government that determines political order. It is asserted that limitations on PA power undermine the ability of the administering Palestinian elite to shape the interests of society to correspond with its own.

Since the current model of self rule is based on diplomatic arrangements orchestrated from 'above' rather than arising out of grassroots structures or a socially integrated economic order, it also represents an attempted social de-mobilization from above. The PA is in a position where it will have to legitimize its existence with something more than words or dramatic actions. The types of powers and privileges possessed by the PA will determine the strategies by which it will pursue legitimacy and the consolidation of its control over Gaza. Of course, the goal of any state is to engender compliance rather than forcibly impose it; it seeks to minimize the friction between individual obligations to (and restrictions of) the state and individual interests and aspirations. However, insecurity and weakness has led PA elites to engage in a strategy of reducing the availability of ideological and practical alternatives to the PA itself. This effectively stifles opposition by destroying the viability of dissenting perspectives and the ability of alternative networks to deliver on promises of services or economic benefits. Ominously, opposition to the PA is pushed into the camp of rejection. Opposition is therefore likely to be articulated outside the given order rather than promoting change or reform within it. Perhaps this makes opposition more likely to be violent if it does coalesce and express itself as a viable force for change.

Chapter 6 investigates the possible bases of social mobilization from below and argues that an ongoing crisis of authority in Palestinian life leaves society torn between responses of disorganized revolt and resignation. Current developments may push the Palestinian street to take back the one power it had – the power to disrupt – and bring political opposition openly and perhaps even violently back onto the streets. Israeli repression during the occupation – and the PA's current repression of internal dissent – have decimated the ranks of those who could perceivably coordinate and serve as a rallying point for active opposition. This means that if a new uprising were to emerge, it might be disorganized and violent, a situation which could encourage opportunist and less disciplined elements to take advantage of the situation for personal gain. This chapter examines just what form revolt might take if the interim model of patronage and repression does not prove capable of sustaining worthwhile conditions of life for the average Gaza Palestinian, and raw force does not succeed in pacifying Palestinians under a regime of limited rights and unfulfilled promises.

Acknowledgements

There are several people, apart from the many Palestinians who gave of their time and thoughts, whom I would especially like to thank for the support and encouragement shown to me over the past months of reading, writing and travelling. First, I would like to thank Dr Dan Tschirgi for suggesting that I do a study on the emerging politics of Palestinian self-rule. As this work progressed, Dr Tschirgi was always willing to hear out my ideas and concerns; his comments were especially helpful in distinguishing between what was merely interesting and what was pertinent to the questions under examination. Furthermore, his encouragement and confidence just when I was beginning to doubt my ability to do something interesting with the topic was an important source of sustenance.

Dr Ivan Ivekovic's tips and insights were invaluable in helping me figure out how I would approach the topic in the beginning. Particularly his suggestion that I emphasize notions of 'inside/outside' conflict and civil society have proven useful. Working as Dr Ivekovic's assistant, I was inspired by his insistence on the relevance of theory and comprehensive scope to understanding even seemingly local phenomena.

Dr Walid Kazziha's insights and cautionary notes inspired some improvements in the final draft of this manuscript. Dr Kazziha's experience and participation in, and vast knowledge of, the history of Arab and Palestinian politics, society, and thought make his commendation of my work extremely valuable to me.

Andrew Tabler and Bill Dorman made indispensable contributions to this work by challenging me to clarify my thoughts at the work's final stages and offering me a place to stay (as did Cole Smith and Tom Harding) on several visits to Cairo *en route* to and from Palestine. Taghreed al-Khodary also earns my thanks for making me feel especially welcome in Gaza, and for guiding me on my first tour of Gaza's NGOs and civic organizations. Dr Paul Sullivan gave a re-assuring economists approval to Chapter 4 in the works final stages.

Probably no potential author actually considers the arduous task of writing, much less completing, a first book without having been encouraged by a singularly inspiring mentor at some early stage of academic life. In this regard, I take the opportunity to show my thanks to Dean (Dr) H. Irvin Penfield of Birmingham-Southern College. I hope this work might justify the confidence he showed in me during my studies there. Similarly, I never would have got to the stage of writing this book had it not been for the support of my family in the USA, and, more recently, the support of my wife's family here in Belgium.

Finally, I would like to thank my wife, Karin Voets. This work benefited from her insistence on clarity in thought and structure. Also, her patience in the face my irregular and often nocturnal work habits deserves special appreciation: thanks Karin. Naturally, any errors or shortcomings in this work are entirely my responsibility.

This book is dedicated to Johanne Parker born in October of 1997 (thus, together with this book, representing another first in what is proving to be a productive year); and in memory of my father, George O. Parker, whom I wish had lived to see them both.

1

Problems, Parameters and the Political Economy of Meaning

Thomas Hobbes wrote that 'out of the past, we construct a future.'[1] During the ongoing resolution of Palestinian 'self-rule' in parts of the West Bank and Gaza Strip, rich possibilities and damning constraints suggested by the past and the future have contributed to a crisis of authority in the present. This crisis arises from institutional, demographic, economic, ideological and psychological tensions within the emerging dynamic of limited Palestinian autonomy as established by 'Oslo' and subsequent agreements.[2] It manifests itself in an increasingly unstable and inarticulate relationship between Palestinian authorities and Palestinian society. The resulting impasse, reinforced by the structural and political parameters of the peace process itself, leaves Palestinian society poorly positioned to affect the impact of 'self-rule' on life in the Palestinian street. It deflects popular political and economic energies away from confronting the structural shortcomings of the transitional political economy, and from the building of integrated and effective national institutions. Not least, this impasse undermines the ability of Palestinian society to mobilize and challenge the constraints implied by the continued unaccountable insinuation of Israeli power and interest into Palestinian political and economic life. These conditions essentially reflect a Palestinian powerlessness written into the Palestinian–Israeli interim accords.

This book explores the transition toward Palestinian 'self-rule' as it appears from Gaza. Its central premise is straightforward: the stability of any 'political entity' that emerges in the Palestinian space will be contingent upon its economic viability, its responsiveness to Palestinian needs and aspirations, and its ability to promote cohesion and integration across spatially and socially fragmented Palestinian constituencies. Concurrently, it is argued that the way in which the transitional period accommodates popular attempts to imbue the new order with accountability to broad based Palestinian interests and demands for basic rights will greatly influence prospects for long term stability. The role played by current agreements in perpetuating Palestinian dependence, problematizing Palestinian social mobilization, and planting the seeds of potential future instability is stressed throughout.

The objectives of the study are thus to present a survey of challenges facing Palestinian socio-economic development and political reconstitution as the regime's provisional character is resolved, and to suggest the future character of Palestinian 'self-rule' given the configuration of personalities, powers and contingencies during the transition. The response of Gaza's civil society to the demographic, economic and political transition implied by the new framework of power relations is investigated, as are limitations on the Palestinian Authority's (PA)[3] ability to consolidate its position in Gaza through the execution of positive economic and social initiatives. The notion of a 'political economy of meaning' is elaborated upon to provide a framework within which to evaluate current developments and future prospects.

The conclusions raise serious doubts about the stability of socio-political and economic relationships as they are emerging within the current trajectory. These findings in turn raise questions concerning: 1) the future governability of Gaza given the limitations of the current regime; 2) the conditioning impact of these limitations on future Palestinian socio-political development and 3) the ability of the Oslo process to lead to a status quo that transcends the limitations of the provisional regime and thus encourage long term stability in the Palestinian/Israeli space. Contrary to declarations recognizing a basis for a Palestinian state and the arrival of peace in the region, the future remains uncertain.[4]

Issues and Context

It is out of what we experience and imagine to be significant about the past, and out of expectations and schemes for the future, that we evaluate the present. The ways in which these evaluations manifest themselves in terms of social mobilization and in the exercise of power are of interest to observers of politics. By contrasting popular perceptions with empirical data and by evaluating popular expectations against who in fact gets 'what, when and how,' and by asking 'what difference it makes,' the political scientist hopes to suggest something about the structural underpinnings of a particular socio-political condition and the ways in which the dynamic embodying power and society may affect the future.

This work reveals and interprets tensions between the external demands of the peace process (which now delimit the boundaries of Palestinian rights and powers) and the construction of a stable and sustainable basis of Palestinian 'self-rule.' Unfortunately, the conclusions are pessimistic. The disparity between expectations and dignity engendered in resistance on the one hand, and the prospects for the future on the other, remain great. The current frustration in Gaza reflects economic circumstances. It also reveals a deeper sense of socio-political uncertainty and in some cases even feelings of betrayal at the hands of nationalist elites. The success or failure of the PA will in no small measure depend on its ability to manage socio-economic despair with its limited political powers; and upon Fatah's ability to transcend its tautological invocation of nationalist ideology to justify the regime in the 'autonomous areas.' In fact, the nationalist ideology is challenged by the nationalist elite's acceptance of the status quo. In a political context held together by dependence rather than mobilization to pursue rights and to effect structural change, many Palestinians may find the regime increasingly irrelevant in their pursuit of basic needs, aspirations and rights.

Meanwhile, the media focuses on the progress of negotiations and on the movements of political elites. The major external actors influencing the process seem drawn ever more toward invoking a combination of advanced metal detectors, ritualistic elections and aid as inputs that will determine the boundaries within which Palestinian aspirations may be expressed, and despair ameliorated.[5] The notion of eminent Palestinian 'self-rule' appears to be used to deflect the legitimacy of 'rejectionist' claims that the agreement does not and cannot represent Palestinian historical, legal and human rights. In this context, it is necessary to question the impact of the Oslo agreement – particularly its distribution of political powers and economic benefits – on a society deeply scarred by occupation, de-institutionalization, resistance and economic hardship.

Responses to the ongoing transition of authority in Gaza include disorientation, despair, anger and indifference. At the same time, the current trajectory of self-rule is revealing glaring internal contradictions. The agreement that was supposed to stabilize the Palestinian human social and economic space does not seem to be achieving its goals, nor encouraging strong identification between emerging structures of authority and the Palestinian community. In an August 1996 interview with an Israeli newspaper, Abu Mazen (Mahmud Abbas) revealed that Palestinian frustration with the peace process had led to several attempts on Arafat's life.[6] Why is the transition toward 'self-rule' being accompanied by greater instability and despondency?

On the surface, the answers appear straightforward. Although the Oslo agreements promised relief from rising living costs in Gaza, the economic situation has deteriorated drastically since they were signed, leaving unemployment at rates of above 60 per cent.[7] 'Self rule' has been accompanied by a constriction of economic space and opportunity for the average Gazan. Jobs and markets in Israel have been lost.[8] Delays in the movement of goods and produce over the borders often leave Gaza's agricultural production rotting in the sun before it has a chance to reach Israeli or third country markets. Israel has pursued policies and practices hostile to economic development in Gaza, and at the same time refused to turn over to the PA many of the substantive powers that might allow Palestinians to create or pursue alternatives to Israel's continued economic stranglehold on the OT.

While the agreement promised Gazans territorial autonomy, it left many ecological grievances subject to Israeli veto and vulnerable to loopholes. Israel remains in effective control of 44 per cent of the surface area of the strip (including much of the most productive land area).[9] While territorial control is supposed to include jurisdiction over water,[10] water projects are to be administered by a joint Palestinian–Israeli committee where Israel holds a veto right,[11] the PA may not develop water resources in a way which threatens the quality and quantity of existing Israeli consumption,[12] Palestinian usage is pegged to 'existing quantities and practices',[13] and Israel 'shall assist' the PA in determining the appropriate occasion to drill new wells.[14] This must be seen against a context where previous over-utilization has left most of the water supply set aside for Palestinians (already a small percentage in proportion to population size) unfit for human consumption. While Israeli settlements in Gaza are today still ensured a generous and subsidized supply of fresh water, the crops of Palestinian farmers continue to suffer from the water's high saline content.[15]

Furthermore, as Rabbani notes:

> According to the terms of Oslo II, Israel can – and routinely does – continue with land confiscations, mass arrests, house demolitions, defoliation, prolonged curfews, arbitrary violence, and any other measure it sees fit to impose on the pretext of security.[16]

These issues, together with the historical grievances that sustained the nationalist movement in exile (essentially if not entirely a refugee movement) seem now, with the recent election of Likud, to be as far from resolution as ever.

Beneath these contingencies, the PA seems to be using its security apparatus to pursue coercive strategies of compliance and control, creating a situation in which many Gazans see a mirror image of the Israeli occupation. The generally undisciplined and consistently repressive exercise of authority displayed by the various Palestinian security forces has thus far generated grave concern from within various sectors of Gazan society. Torture and severe beatings have been reported, and critics of the PA seem to have been systematically singled out for harassment by the security forces.[17] As of early February 1997, there have been at least twelve torture related deaths in PA detention centres.[18] Several mass demonstrations against such police excesses have been put down with violence. Palestinians spoken to by the author consistently reported mistrust of the security forces, sometimes referring to them as agents of a new occupation. Even assuming that such behaviour is not absolutely endemic to the personalities and institutions which currently hold the monopoly of coercive force, (in fact, it represents the accountability of the PA's disciplinary force to the demands of the peace process rather than to the security of the Palestinian people), there is a very real danger that it may be institutionalized over time. The apparent ignorance of or lack of concern for human rights and due process shown by Palestinian security forces is a cause of public alarm.[19] Psychologically, repression from the hand of the liberator, (even though not physically comparable with the 'excesses' of Israeli occupation), is proving perhaps more difficult to accept and bear.[20]

Other practices of the PA have further alienated Palestinians from solid identification with the new regime. The PA has been criticized for making appointments:

> ... more on the basis of favouritism and nepotism than on competence and performance. The leadership is thus accused of appointing to sensitive positions a number of individuals personally loyal to Arafat but whose nationalist credentials or general conduct are in doubt. (The preponderance of diaspora Fatah elites within the self-rule institutions) has further stirred resentments among independent groups and supporters of oppositional organizations that have expressed a willingness to serve in apolitical positions. Fatah's perceived monopoly on power has hardly helped shore up national unity.[21]

In interviews with the author, local NGO and international aid workers consistently complained that the PA hiring process was bypassing experienced local expertise in favour of returnees with questionable credentials and no experience of local conditions. Arafat has also been duplicating agencies and functions within the PA ministries in order to create jobs for well positioned 'loyalists.' This practice has led to great insecurity within the PA bureaucratic structure. It encourages bickering between groups within the bureaucracy which are forced to compete for the same funds, and greatly distracts from the task of identifying and addressing issues on the ground. In perhaps one of the most blatant examples of cronyism to date, Arafat fired the board of Makassed Hospital in Jerusalem (which included some distinguished Palestinian Legislative Council members and critics of PA policies) and attempted to install his brother as the president of the institution. When nearly everyone associated with the hospital resisted this move, Arafat used force to take over the hospital.[22]

However, these facts alone do not explain how internal modes of resistance and accommodation to the execution of PA functions will influence the institutional character of Palestinian 'self-rule' over the long term. How will any future Palestinian state established in the trajectory of current negotiations be conditioned by the socio-political forces of transition, and by the socio-economic networks that are set up to facilitate survival and stability under limited autonomy? How are the various structures and ideological orientations, which taken together comprise the rich but unstable tapestry of Palestinian nationalism, being re-shaped to arbitrate between the traditional claims of Palestinian nationalism and the restricted task of limited autonomy over tightly confined spaces and populations in the Israeli occupied territories? Do PA elites have the kind of power that would allow them to shape and mobilize the interests of society to conform with their own? If not, how might Palestinian society in Gaza rise to appropriate for itself the task of defining the boundaries of a legitimate self-rule political economy? Alternatively, is the transitional paradigm established by Oslo capable of supporting a sustainable and stable base of meaningfully autonomous Palestinian political, economic and social development? And what will happen in the absence of such development?

To answer these questions, we must try to understand the ways in which the new arrangements of power and coercion established in the wake of the agreements have been shuffling political, social and economic relationships in Gaza. Reference must be made to trends and perceptions across the broader Palestinian social space. The variety of ideologies, social networks, factional groupings and power relations which Palestinians use to determine and pursue their interests must be investigated. At present, Gaza offers the most geographically integral territorial unit around which to structure such a study. It represents a coherent 'laboratory' within which the peace process as a whole might be evaluated.

The current arrangement contains a bias which almost certainly affects the character of relationships in the self-rule space. It puts an agreement between elites ahead of a social agenda that responds to the problems facing the Palestinian street. The provisional regime emphasizes control – the ability of elites to discipline and manipulate – rather than a frontal attack on the structural roots of social instability. The trajectory toward a 'final status' seems to emphasize the symbolic rather than the substantive features of political process and recognition and seems to assume that 'self-rule' refers to a ritual, tautological exercise rather than a structural dynamic engaging individuals dialogically in the processes through which power shapes their lives. Put simply, the current order does not establish crucial preconditions of associative civic development.

Optimistic observers seem to assume that a meaningfully new set of power relations leading toward statehood have been established – even while there is little power, and increasingly questioned legitimacy – just because internationally recognized name plates and titles adorn the new desks of Palestinian officialdom. Concurrently, the fragmentation of civil society and lack of economic integration in Gaza also tend to undermine the possibility that a concerted response from below might influence the character of self-rule. The severe limitations on effective self-rule powers might mean that the PA would unlikely be able to pursue an integrated social and economic agenda even if it were more inclined to do so. So far, self-rule has not been accompanied by a sense of social empowerment; and attempts from the street to influence the current character of PA rule have been uncoordinated, ineffective and often counterproductive in their desperation. Tangled in a web of diplomatic demands and elitist nationalist politics, Palestinians are being rendered passive spectators to their own worsening situation. The demands on Palestinian civility at present seem much greater than the potential benefits.

Meanwhile, from 'above,' new institutions of authority and the personalities who occupy them work to consolidate their position and protect their interests within a society over which they have been granted limited power, but – so it at times seems – also unlimited responsibility. The PA has accomplished a certain degree of compliance by setting itself up as the only alternative to starvation, but this hardly offers a promising foundation for the building of a strong state–society relationship. Indeed, the PLO hierarchy's dispositions toward autocratic rule, corrupt patronage, and the lack of a clear social agenda – plus the limited scope of effective PA authority and the structural distortions of the local economy generally – suggest the preconditions for a dependent neopatrimonial political regime.[23]

The potential for instability is inherent in the context of sweeping political and social change. However, while the peace process has been set up so as to limit the potential for instability in Palestinian society, this has the parallel effect of excluding the Palestinian street from participation in the construction of the new order. Exacerbating such tendencies, the PA seems inclined by its own political interests to keep Gaza's civil society weak and fragmented in the short-term in order to consolidate its organizational position with external benefactors and 'partners.' The lack of internal economic development means that any future Palestinian state will remain heavily dependent on external patrons for sustaining 'self-rule' institutions. A pattern of institutional behaviour driven by the external demands and limited powers of the transitional period may condition any future Palestinian state.[24] Such a situation would almost inevitably leave Palestinian self-rule subservient to Israeli strategic and ideological interests.

However, to paraphrase de Tocqueville, revolutions and civil wars do not seem to occur in times of increasing hardship and despair. Certainly factors such as expectations, social and ideological cohesion, and subjective perceptions of the possibility for change must be taken into account when considering the possibility of renewed, sustained popular uprising. While economic conditions are worsening, and the resentment and mistrust Palestinians are expressing toward the new authority is increasing, civil war or grassroots revolution is also unlikely in Gaza. This is so primarily because the Palestinian street has no independent economic or integrated political base upon which prolonged revolt might be sustained. It is also due to the increasing ideological disorientation and fragmentation within Palestinian society (abetting a sense of hopelessness and encouraging withdrawal), and the ability of the PA to co-opt and/or deflect open dissent. In all probability, the PA face a disorganized opposition and the prospect of containing scattered but chronic violence both now as the peace process moves from crisis to crisis, and later within any 'final' Palestinian polity within the OT. The failure of transitional autonomy to legitimize and empower openings for the expression of interests in Palestinian society implies that points of intra-Palestinian as well as Palestinian/Israeli tension will be left unresolved, leaving groups to consider violent responses to issues for which civil responses have proven ineffective. Within this framework, the spectre of mass unemployment and popular disillusionment leaves Palestine balancing on a tightrope between revolt and resignation.

The Political Economy of Meaning and 'the Spectre of Superfluous Man'

By suggesting a complex interaction between various socio-economic phenomena and the establishment and reproduction of political order, the notion of a political economy of meaning offers a framework for describing the dynamic of legitimacy operating within a society. In particular, this notion aims to look beneath techno-procedural (e.g. ritualized elections) and/or reductive primordial factors (e.g. language, ethnicity, historical cartography and/or religion) as primary determinants of political legitimacy. By proposing a conception in which a given regime is held accountable to the norms and expectations of the society in which it operates, it suggests a way around the normative tangles that often surround debates concerning phenomena such as civil society and development. The political economy of meaning (as an ideal type) denotes consensus over a framework for conflict mediation, converging attitudes with regard to broad social goals, and last but not least, a congruence between ideological hopes and structural possibilities. Backed by institutions capable of instigating and responding to change, these features bind society into stable configurations of right and obligation, efficacy and acquiescence. In this work, the idea is invoked to suggest that the consolidation and reproduction of a stable Palestinian political order demands alternatives to the politics of dependence, coercion and resignation.

Defining the political economy of meaning

An overall evaluation of the way in which sources of authority are related to the structural forces that have an effect on people determines perceptions of the legitimacy of a given regime – as does an understanding of where the given authority lies in relation to other potential options. 'Systems of meaning shape, and are in turn shaped by, the political and economic contexts in which they occur ... in reality, [however], most studies assume rather than explore the complex and multi-dimensional relationships between the two.'[25] Eickelman continues:

> ... a fully developed 'political economy of meaning' contrives to achieve a balance between concern with the communication and development of complex belief systems and how these systems shape and in turn are shaped by configurations of political domination and economic variations among groups and classes in societies of different levels of complexity.[26]

Of critical interest is how notions of self and society are maintained or reconstructed within apparent historical transformations, such as the current ongoing transition to a new political order in Gaza. How does the new order stand up against the previous epistème (in the Foucauldian sense of knowledge revealing the conditions of possibility manifested within a history)? How might Palestinians derive meaning in the ongoing dialectic between socio-political agency and objective chances? How will political autonomy stand up against economic suffering? We would perhaps all prefer to be oppressed in our own language, but will the Palestinian people be satisfied with the mere transfer of authority to a nominal organ of 'self-rule?'[27] Or might a political economy of meaning be built against the current structural restraints on Palestinian political and economic autonomy? If not, will there be attempts to reconstitute relations of meaning through the use of violence?

The political economy of meaning is by definition founded in phenomenological experience as well as abstract legitimation. It represents a 'trialogue' between these two phenomena and power. If any of these fail to fall fluidly into the experience of society, the political economy of meaning as a recognizable social bonding agent (implying a consensual notion of polity, but not forgetting that consensus is usually made rather than found) will be lacking. As an abstract ideal, a political economy of meaning suggests a context in which the interests of elites and masses – of people here and people there – are generally ameliorable, and sustain themselves without of necessity succumbing to violence or dependence. It is a condition in which society can accommodate and even constructively channel the tensions which inevitably arise between structural realities, ideological goals and moral concerns. The failure of a dominant paradigm to rationalize social obedience and obligation, or to provide material sustenance, or both, suggests the potential for instability.

In the definition suggested here, the idea of a political economy of meaning incorporates concern for the role of social mobilization in consolidating political order (legitimacy). Social mobilization involves deriving meaning from, and attributing meaning to, making things happen. Clearly, what is being witnessed in Palestine today is not the reproduction of the public sphere in the context of a regime transition, but the very struggle to construct and define such a sphere within a distinctly new Palestinian polity. The way in which the new order accounts for social mobilization will influence the ability of the peace process to achieve long term resolution of those issues which necessitated this process to begin with. This will determine whether the process is merely a mechanism for 'pacification' or whether it is a mechanism for incorporating Palestinians into the production of a viable political order.

The significance of the political economy of meaning to our case becomes apparent in the struggle to define the parameters of autonomy, and within the ability of the provisional regime to sustain the identifiable processes of 'self-rule.' At present, 'the peace process' seems to be premised on marginalizing the role of the Palestinian street in defining the rights and spaces associated with life in a distinctively 'Palestinian' polity. The danger is obvious. If the 'peace process' cannot accommodate expression from the Palestinian street, people may express themselves outside of it; perhaps violently. There are several factors and phenomena which must be considered in an evaluation of the emerging political economy of meaning in Palestine, and they overlap and intermingle throughout this text.

Before going on, it would be useful to elaborate on a couple of themes against which a political economy of meaning may be evaluated. First, civil society and neopatriarchy – two models of politics which have been used to describe and evaluate political society in the Arab world – are reviewed and contrasted. These models assist in the evaluation of participation, accountability and control in the state–society relationship. The second theme, borrowing from David Apter, elaborates on the potential for instability associated with economic and political transformations, and warns of 'the spectre of superfluous man.'

The transition now promising a territorial base for Palestinian political and economic autonomy simultaneously challenges existing bases of the transmission and reproduction of systems of meaning within the Palestinian national context. Changing geographic and 'legal' boundaries of authority, economic change and migrations of people, and geopolitical contingencies of power all affect how people understand and interpret the political environment in which they live. By trying to describe the interactive dynamic between forces shaping the relationship between experience and political meaning, the political economy of meaning approach offers a contextual approach with powerful and broadly suggestive implications.

Associational life and the political economy of meaning

The patterns and content of associational life comprise crucial signifiers of a political economy of meaning. While many studies point to the existence of civil society based on the appearance of nominally civil affiliations in society, this work emphasizes that public affiliations must be identified and evaluated in relation to their interaction with, and meaningful impact on, manifestations of power in social and economic relations. Thus civil society should not be invoked to describe affiliation existing in a vacuum; nor does it characterize affiliations based on dependence. This point is emphasized to counter arguments which suggest that the mere presence of affiliation at certain levels between state-like authority and the street effectively constitute civil society. However, as a comparative concept buttressed by theoretical elaboration and case study, various models of civil society help shed light on phenomena associated with political and economic development in Gaza.

Civil society is a concept used to describe the loose web of interests and groupings in society which are interconnected, consciously or not, in ways that mitigate and arbitrate, again consciously or not, between the power of the state and the individual. According to Edward Shils, civil society is that part of the public sphere lying 'beyond the boundaries of the family and clan and beyond the locality, [but also lying] short of the state.'[28] Historically, this idea has been linked with the development of the capitalist, democratic state in Europe and America. Marx saw civil society as intertwined with the development of capitalist modes of production and the corresponding reorganization of political society: 'Civil society as such only develops with the bourgeoisie; the social organization evolving directly out of production and commerce.'[29] Today, however, most observers have extended the notion of civil society 'to include all non-violent associational activity between individuals and the state.'[30] Whether or not we conceptualize civil society as intimately bound to economic development and integration has important implications for how the concept might be applied to the case of Gaza.

Some observers have noted a tendency of Arab (single party, corporatist) states to co-opt and neutralize the potential of civil organizations and associations to mobilize in ways that might influence the exercise of authority.[31] A defensive reflex seems to exist within many regimes which puts the resources of the state into the protection of the statist status quo at the expense of individual groupings. The survival of these groupings in turn comes to depend on the goodwill or patronage of the state.

Is there a potential contradiction between social expectations and demands in Gaza and the political institutions which are (in theory) being set up to eventually service them? Hudson argues that 'civil society interpreted in specifically Western (Lockean, Hegelian, Weberian or Marxist) terms is unlikely to emerge in the Middle East, but this should not exclude the development of other kinds of inclusive solidarity communities.' But how will these solidarities relate to the existence of a state and its given administration? Are the institutions of the state and its personalities one and the same in the PA? And if state–society relations in the Arab world have historically been problematic, what might we expect of society's relations with an authority that is not quite state, but no longer a movement with the fluidity and the ability to be all things to all people as the nationalist movement at least tried to be? Does the Palestinian experience promise to be an exception to the rule in state–society relations in the Arab world? Ultimately, affiliational loyalties will be evaluated on their ability to 'deliver the goods' of personal, group and economic security, and at the same time offer a feeling of extended belonging and obligation. Outside of pure coercion, few models exist which show how social stability and some form of economic sustainability might be culled out of the current conditions. Neopatriarchy and neopatrimonialism, however, suggest how short term stability, (a sort of tactical rather than strategic stability), and predictability might be maintained in a society currently lacking civic integration at the grassroots level, suffering from under- or even de-development, and whose elites lack the power and will to initiate social transformation from above. The answer is through the manipulation of dependence.

Neopatriarchy,[32] and neopatrimonialism (which represents the networks of neopatrimonialism co-opted and serviced by the institutional resources of the state), offer mechanisms for creating stability within a society without having to refer to or maintain solidarity among disparate social actors. Indeed, in order to encourage dependency on the governing regime, vertical lines of authority are maintained. The neopatriarchal/

neopatrimonial state may be inclined to undermine and discourage linkage between various sectors and interests in society in order to ensure its control. Neopatriarchy as a societal formation lacks both the communal attribute of *gemeinschaft* and the modern features of *gesellschaft*.[33] It represents an elitist attempt to make the interests of society coincide with its own, but also reflects an elite's insecurity in its ability to maintain its position and shape interests by staying within the theoretically integrative institutions of a nation-state. Patriarchy is sustained by enforcing mechanisms of dependency – by maintaining a monopoly on access to basic needs.[34] The economic independence of the nuclear family undermines patriarchal authority as it represents a break with dependence on the extended family, clan, subtribe or tribe to ensure survival. Instead, the nuclear family might depend on wage labour or - in urban areas - on buying and selling for survival. The emergence of the nuclear family is related to urbanization and the development of industrialized modes of production. For Palestinians, labour migrations distanced nuclear families from immediate contact and dependency on extended families for economic security or as a check on certain types of behaviour. Also, the greater independence of younger generations engaging in new types of employment has encouraged the rise of the nuclear family as a more prominent social unit. 'In this sense, the prevalence of the nuclear family, and the values on which it is based represent the most serious threat to the existing neopatriarchal formation.'[35] Economic independence is the condition for the overthrow of neopatriarchy.[36]

In addition to the apparent material incentives determining patterns of affiliation, the role of a shared conceptual/cultural discourse might be emphasized as a base of civic awareness. Culture inevitably offers a code for civility and ensures that meanings are transferred across groups and institutions with a minimal of miscommunication or misunderstanding. The political economy of meaning ultimately expresses itself in a discourse of legitimacy. To a certain extent, the discursive paradigm determines expectations, and can be manipulated to satisfy them. Once broadly accepted, solutions are determined from within its framework; within its own *logos*, it finds its own answers. Hisham Sharabi notes that in traditional Arab societies, patriarchy reflected 'a system of values and social practices belonging to a determinate economy and culture.' However, by way of contrast with the efficacious, dialogical political economy of meaning for which a model is constructed here, patriarchy, and its contemporary step-child, neopatriarchy, is maintained by power relations of dependency and a monological assertion of the meaning of authority from above. It reduces to the maximum extent the claims of society to influence and interpret the exercise of authority from below. 'Thus the world of objects and events tends to be reduced to verbal presentations that possess their own system of validation.'[37] This would seem to indicate an attempt to resolve sociological tensions (divergent dualisms in scope of power and problem, materialistic expectations and material realities) without direct reference to 'facts on the ground.' Neopatriarchy will struggle to delegitimize coping strategies not dependent on it or attempt to render active oppositional coping strategies impotent. It thus weakens the ability of society to mobilize to meet external threats and challenge the structural features reinforcing dependency at all layers of socio-economic and political interaction.

In a social order characterized by factionalism and underdevelopment, both of which are conditions associated with neopatriarchy, unresponsive organs of power seem likely to develop:

> Monological speech, in daily practice, rarely produces good listeners, for it aims not to enlighten or inform, but to dominate. The listener or the recipient, the 'other' of the monological relationship (the son, the student, the citizen), is reduced to silence; he or she may outwardly acquiesce, but inwardly turn away ... the world is inhabited by multiple single voices that command and legislate its life from above.[38]

This description hauntingly reflects the experience of many Gazans in relation to self-rule. It is the social structures which sustained such a neopatriarchal discourse in the past that current powers are attempting to re-empower in order to assert control over society today.

According to Sharabi, neopatriarchy represents the distortion of traditional patriarchal relationships within new forms of dependency, half absorbed institutional structures and the intellectual concepts which service them. Neopatriarchy implies the attachment of traditional forms of patrimonialism to modern forms of dependency. It responds to and reshapes the flow of resources that can be accessed in the cause of self perpetuation. Sharabi goes so far as to say that:

> ... neopatriarchal society as a dependent, non-modern socio-economic structure represents the quintessentially underdeveloped society. Its most pervasive characteristic is a kind of generalized, persistent, and seemingly insurmountable impotence: it is incapable of performing as an integrated social or political system, as an economy, or as a military structure. Possessing all the trappings of

> modernity, this society nevertheless lacks the inner force, organization, and consciousness which characterizes truly modern formations ... Thus between ruler and ruled, between father and child, there exist only vertical relations: in both settings the paternal will is the absolute will, mediated in both the society and the family by a forced consensus based on ritual and coercion.[39]

Neopatriarchal society is governed through manipulation and coercion. Power becomes suspicious of independent cleavages emerging from below and attempts to unite groups in society independently and separately to the apparatus of power. Accordingly, Sharabi notes that 'the most advanced and functional aspect of the neopatriarchal state (in both conservative and 'progressive' regimes) is its internal security apparatus, the *mukhabarat*.'[40] The repressive role of the PA's internal security apparatus in Gaza is certainly affecting how people recognize the face of the new order.

Sharabi implies that the ability of society to transcend the stagnation of neopatriarchal dependence demands that society recognizes and organizes to protect its structural relationship with economic and political modernity and thus protect its own autonomy (as opposed to a limited autonomy deferred upon elites by externalized forces):[41]

> The possibility of genuine *rebellion* is the product of the new age. Because modern individuals 'know how to think of, by and for themselves,' they will demand a clear account of what their bosses and rulers are doing for them – and doing to them – and be ready to resist and rebel where they are getting nothing in return.[42]

The Spectre of Superfluous Man

Of all the conditions describing the relationship of the individual to society, utter irrelevance is perhaps the one most unacceptable to the human psychology. One important question is whether Gazans will be able to find PA structures relevant to their needs and ideas of legitimacy. Will the former wage labourer adjust to the different forms of dependency implied by neopatrimonialism? In precisely what ways does 'self-rule' offer a paradigm shift against which Gazans can reconsider the notion of legitimate authority? In the face of mass unemployment and a ruling elite without relevant powers or a social agenda, how might the inhabitants of Gaza respond to the authority which presides over these conditions?

Ultimately, the political economy of meaning is about social relevance, whether it be through clan loyalties or as a citizen in the industrial or post-industrial nation state. It refers to structural and institutional relationships which afford comfort or promise eventual redress in times of hardship. It implies an acceptance of the economic rules of the game regardless of temporary conditions. It offers one a feeling of being in a legal environment which is predictable and just. In short, it is all that sustains feelings of identification with one's community and institutions of political power.

The contrast is irrelevance. When this irrelevance is grounded in widespread unemployment and corresponding economic hardship, groups might form to interpret this condition of irrelevance and offer a counter explanation of the situation which once again gives them a meaningful place (and more importantly a potential survival niche) vis-à-vis the order which has rejected them or which no longer seems to need their input. In the final chapter of his book *Rethinking Development*, David Apter makes a compelling case for analysing 'disjunctive moments' in the relationship between 1) socially binding metaphors and metonymies, 2) a changing political economy, and 3) the institutional and lexical reality of the state–society coincidence as crucial to understanding what might be described as developmental violence and/or instability; (i.e., violence which seems to be a response to fundamental changes in the social and economic base of the state or perhaps a crisis in the relations between civil society and the locus of power within the state). Violence results when the binding myths and structural logic which should (or could) integrate civic development fail to coincide. Apter's model offers warnings potentially applicable to the situation in Palestine.

Disjunctions occur 'when social polarization leads to conflict rather than mediation, government policy exacerbates rather than ameliorates, and differences over the script lead to random violence, extra-institutional protest, terrorism and ultimately revolution. Polarization in this sense involves states versus anti-states in concrete struggles the object of which is to create or prevent a disjunctive moment.'[43] Such changes challenge the myths by which we recognize the legitimacy of states, revealing what Plato described as 'the noble lie.' It tests the ability of competing potential elites to introduce legitimate authority in an atmosphere threatened with ideological dislocation and anarchy. 'A mytho-logic forms when those at the bottom conclude an alliance, linguistic and coalitional, with those at the top', and the gap between the functionally significant and the functionally superfluous is overcome by myth.[44]

The current transition from occupation to gradually increasing self-rule, a transition based on a premise that shatters many socially unifying myths, constitutes just such a disjunctive moment for Gazan society. It challenges obligations defined by past sacrifices. It is one of the premises of this study that awareness of these obligations is structurally determined (even if sometimes this is of necessity expressed in a very round about way) and that current manifestations of social violence result from a failure to place the balance of civil obligations and benefits into an accountable framework, as well as from a climate of economic stress and uncertainty.

In Apter's model, those negatively affected link economic transformations to the discrediting of the existing political order, or the paradigm through which the legitimacy of the regime was declared. Apter refers to a threat of violence as labour becomes increasingly less relevant as a political grouping in a post-industrial age, but the model applies in no small measure to the way a stroke of the pen seems to have absolved Israel from responsibility for the fate of over 100,000 Palestinian labourers and their families. The severity of economic hardship and neglect in the Gaza Strip has been well documented and widely discussed. Apter's model is adapted here to analyse the implications of the coinciding political and economic disorientation in terms of future stability and the potential for social violence.

O'Donnell and Schmitter argue that challenges to the existing status quo might emerge from within 'layers of an explosive society.'[45] Pointing out that even authoritarian societies contain professional associations, intelligentsia, religious groups and other social groupings, they argue that 'exemplary individuals' capable of awakening civil society may arise and encourage these organizations to challenge and exert an active influence on state authority. Schwedler expands on their idea:

> [the] idea of 'layers of an explosive society' suggests the existence of alternative layers of power, which O'Donnell and Schmitter explore only to the extent that they yield remarkable individuals who dare enter the public sphere. The existence of these alternate systems, however, seems to contradict the claim that under authoritarianism, citizens withdraw from, or are forced out of, the public sphere. Instead, what seems to happen is that citizens withdraw from one particular system of power, namely, the public sphere regulated by the state.
>
> Rather than view the public sphere as the only avenue to social mobilization, it is more useful to view it as one of many such channels or systems of power. Likewise, the individuals or groups that enter civil society do not simply emerge

from thin air; instead, they emerge from these alternative systems of power. As Melucci argues, social movements should not be treated as simply empirical phenomena to record. Social movements are action systems: 'Action *systems* in that they have structures ... *action* systems in that their structures are built by aims, beliefs, decisions, and exchanges operating in a systematic field.'[46]

Do action systems capable of channelling frustration into constructive (even if confrontational) and stable bases of dissent exist in Gaza? The most likely place for such alternatives to emerge would be from the potential interaction across the traditional institutions, the new activist groupings, and the service organizations that comprise what might be loosely described as an 'Islamic sector.' However, coordination and cooperation across these components of the Islamic sector seem at present weak (in any case, they are denied by the actors themselves). It remains to be seen whether this sector might coalesce into a unified mobilizational pillar capable of incorporating participation and protecting its constituent base. If so, it will be interesting to see whether the interaction between elites with bases in the Islamic structures and elites with bases in the PA continues in adversarial directions, or whether they eventually strike a bargain, each accepting the other as 'here to stay' and conceding that there is more to be lost than gained in direct and sometimes violent competition. The development of this rivalry may yet exert a decisive influence on the direction of Palestinian civic development.

Perhaps, as Sharabi notes, the spectre of superfluous man might be sparked by a suppressed modernist impulse:

> ... the modernist impulse, simultaneously cultivated and frustrated over the last three generations, may revive and even take political form. And when one remembers that this impulse might not be as tightly bound to conventional revolutionary means as it was a generation ago, a fundamentalist advance may appear much less threatening and more manageable.[47]

This might prove especially true within a proletarianized society which has been exposed to many of the modernistic features of Israeli productive relations and patterns of consumption.

Conclusion

Simmel noted that the apparent resolution of a conflict 'lowers the energy which guarantees the energy of the group; and the dissolving forces, which were always at work, gain hold.' It disorients the act of opposition which allowed society 'to prove [its] strength consciously and only thus [gave] vitality and reciprocity to conditions which, without such correctives, we would withdraw at any cost.'[48] Fouad Ajami has observed that

> ... the exhaustion of the nationalist fervor generally signals the coming to the fore of economic issues and demands, of problems that do not lend themselves to solo performances, to the magic touch of charisma, to the spectacular and psychologically gratifying performance of a Nasser, a Nkrumah, to the theatrics of a Sukarno, to the flair of a Nehru. Less colorful leaders whose links to the nationalist struggle are often tenuous are the ones who have to satisfy the new needs. The romantic phase of nationalism is then over – words and symbols lose some of their power as societies begin the infinitely more difficult search for ways of putting a domestic order together.[49]

While Arafat maintains a level of nationalist legitimacy, confusion is created as he has unilaterally announced a solution to the national question in a context where many people are suffering ever greater economic hardship and alienation from forces and ideas around which they could once organize coping strategies. People are groping to articulate responses to the new realities. On some levels, Arafat's 'solo performance' is dominating the stage of Palestinian transitional autonomy. However, Palestinian viewers seem less and less likely to interpret the story as being about them, and given the web of external interests (the directors of our solo performer?) which must be satisfied if self-rule is to be consolidated with the current personalities staying on the stage, the script is becoming increasingly complicated — (if not even creating schizophrenic demands on the soloist).

As Ajami implies, within changing politico-economic contexts, new demands and new expectations are created. Civil society should probably be expected to reorganize itself accordingly. Ajami's statement suggests what are perhaps the fundamental questions underlying this investigation of authority: how is civil society responding to the construction of a new political order? What phenomena can be identified within this new context? What are the material and psychological constraints facing the Palestinian order as Palestinian elites attempt to entrench themselves in a stable regime of 'self-rule? how will individuals survive in this order? How will authority and stability be defined in the new order? This book examines the tools, the machinery and the mechanics of the new basis of authority and finds them lacking.

Salah Abd al-Shafi argues that 'if the PLO sets about creating genuine democratic structures in the new authority, structures which should be staffed by and utilize Palestinian expertise and professionals, then maybe something could be salvaged. If, on the other hand, its aim is to duplicate the structures that exist in Tunis or that existed in Lebanon, then the agreement will be a disaster.'[50] Salim Tamari has noted the crux of the challenge: 'the legitimacy of the Cairo and Oslo agreements, and the provisional regime that they gave rise to, are unavoidably linked to Arafat's ability to establish a political apparatus that can govern Palestine.'[51] Will Palestinians accept a paradigm of administer and control – as opposed to a civil discourse and execution of governing sovereignty – as the boundaries of a new political economy of meaning?

At this point, the question is not so much whether there will be conflict in Gaza, but rather what the intensity and character of that conflict will be. Sara Roy has summed up Gaza's basic predicament:

> The crux of the problem in Gaza is that people see less and less contrast with the political and economic order they fought so hard to dislodge. As a result, two seemingly contradictory trends have arisen: a simmering rage and an impenetrable passivity. The former could, over time, erupt into a rebellion against the authority that will be very violent if it occurs. The latter could diminish the possibility for constructive action at the individual and collective levels.
> Palestinian fear is profound. People cannot think clearly when they are hungry or when their children are hungry. In the continued absence of hope and future, there could very well be a popular retreat into violence as the only haven from confusion, loss and abandonment. Without meaningful change and real reform, the prospects are grim.[52]

2

The Dynamics of Factionalism

The roots of factionalism run deep in Palestinian life, and have been shaped and reshaped by various experiences of power, patronage and immediate needs over the past hundred years. This chapter outlines the historical contexts and structural contingencies within which the dynamic of Palestinian factionalism has been defined, and assesses this dynamic's chances of producing long term stability in the context of autonomy. Of particular concern are the ways in which various occupying powers, seeking to protect their own interests, promoted the conditions of deinstitutionalization and underdevelopment that allowed factionalism to flourish. The ways in which the PLO used the factional framework to insinuate its interests into the OT are also investigated. Ultimately, it is argued that the PA is utilizing its access to the donor supported administrative resources of autonomy to create 'new',[1] but still essentially factional, bases of control in Gaza.

The general concerns of this study include the impact of 'self rule' on the trajectory of affiliational life, and the ability of new associational frames of reference and power relations to offer alternatives to current socio-economic limitations and hardship. An understanding of factionalism and its potential consequences in the context of autonomy is therefore imperative. The persistence of factional politics into the context of limited Palestinian autonomy reflects the continuity of structural limitations and weak institutionalization within Palestinian political economy. It also aggravates a dilemma in Palestinian political and social development. While enhancing the relative position of one particular Palestinian grouping, and sustaining the peace process over the short term, the factional political dynamic tends to reproduce and entrench the dependent conditions upon which it is based, limiting the ability of Palestinian autonomy to sustain itself without reference to external patronage. In precluding sectoral, class, and other bases of social integration, factionalism undermines the ability of Palestinian society to mobilize in ways that might challenge the structural deficiencies of the 'interim' order.

Identifying a Rationale: Structure and Dynamic in Factionalism

Factionalism does not necessarily reflect the limited demands and aspirations of Palestinian society. On the contrary, its entrenchment in Palestinian life highlights the peculiar circumstances of Palestinian nation building. Muhammad Muslih has neatly outlined the complex relationship between Palestinian associational life and manifestations of authority in the OT:

> First, the Palestinians have not had a national government in the twentieth century. Since 1967, the Israeli occupation apparatus has functioned as the de facto authority in the West Bank and Gaza. The Palestinians consider the Israeli military regime illegitimate, and their goal is not simply to undermine its control or to temper its arbitrary effects, but to dismantle it altogether.
>
> Second, prior to the signing of the Israeli-PLO Declaration of Principles (also known as the Oslo Agreement), Palestinians in the occupied territories accepted an external actor, the PLO, as their 'state,' clandestinely cooperating with local PLO representatives to sustain a network of institutions through which the PLO sought to exercise political power in competition with the Israeli military regime. With the signing of the declaration and the exchange of PLO and Israeli letters of mutual recognition on 9 September 1993, the PLO has become an internal actor that aspires to replace the authority of the Israeli occupier in the West Bank and Gaza ... *The behaviour of the PLO toward its constituencies in the occupied territories will have an impact on the organs of civil society in these territories.*
>
> The characteristics of society in the occupied territories also influence Palestinian associational life. The essence of social organization is a network of *hamulat* (extended families) as well as village, neighbourhood, and religious solidarities.[2]

In general, the social characteristics outlined by Muslih have contributed to a lack of integration in Gaza society that obstructs the potential of civil society to work collectively to influence authority. In the absence of a responsive civil authority, however, factionalism at least offered a limited arena in which to pursue economic and personal security. Historically, Palestinian elites were forced to pursue political interests in an environment where they were effectively excluded from the official organs of decision making. This insulated them from accountability for hardship on the ground, but also left them with few political tools for pursuing legitimate self interest, or, alternatively, for implementing an agenda promoting change. Reflecting an insecurity that is perhaps inherent in attempts to maintain a political position under such conditions of de-institutionalization, they used the factional framework to undermine independent or alternative socio-political initiatives. This was the case during the British mandate, where a Palestinianized civil service or military bureaucracy never emerged to produce an elite positioned to institutionally integrate national aims (unlike in other colonized contexts – Egypt for example), and in Gaza during the Israeli occupation, where mass political organization was prohibited by Israeli authorities.

After 1948, external relations – that is relationships with non-governmental organizations (NGOs), nationalist institutions, and occupying military forces – in many respects had a more determining impact on affiliational formation than immediate, on the ground structural bases of social mobilization in Gaza. Political and social organizations were more dependent on outside patronage for survival than on success in addressing immediate local concerns. As a result, groupings tended not to overlap or grow into each other. Horizontal integration was both structurally and politically discouraged. This reinforced vertically stratified dependent relations since groups or individuals were unlikely to find opportunities or coping strategies by seeking cooperation with like-minded groups in society.

During Israeli occupation, an indigenous leadership that might have arisen to bridge several groupings was discouraged by both repressive Israeli occupation policies and by PLO practices. While factional politics succeeded in sustaining identification with the Palestinian national movement under conditions of dispersal and extreme social and economic stress, it is perhaps less suited to building a political order capable of standing up to the challenges which face Palestinian society in the wake of the peace process. The factional context encourages subordinate groups to enhance their political positions even at the expense of other ostensibly like minded groups. The low level of elite consensus inherent in factionalism tends, furthermore, to generate instability over the long term.[3] Factional organizational incentives thus leave national structures in constant danger of disintegration. As it transforms itself into the PA, the Fatah bureaucracy has no interest in changing a system that has ensured its control of the PLO.[4] However, control over the PLO and affecting national reconstitution out of an uncertain interim order represent two different tasks.

The PA's current attempts to superimpose PLO bureaucratic imperatives over the framework of autonomy are in some respects similar to corporatist strategies of control and stability pursued by regimes elsewhere in the Arab and third world. In a corporatist model of political organization, 'the dominance of the state is made possible via the deliberate deconstruction of class mobilization ... Interests are negotiated and incorporated into the state's decision making process through internal mechanisms rather than through external challenges.' The single party, supposedly representing:

> the victory of the classless, national society, [becomes] the intermediary between the state and interest groups. The absence of alternative political parties, and the division of class interests between established incorporated interest-based organizations, [prevents] the growth of class-based institutional challenges to the state.[5]

The corporatist model describes a strategy used by post-colonial counter elites (who usually originated from within the colonial military or civil bureaucracy) to consolidate their control over the means of production, and use that control to affect political consolidation. The neopatrimonial model on the other hand, more closely approximating current developments in Palestine, is more overtly grounded in dependence. Christopher Clapham describes patrimonial politics as a system 'held together by the oath of loyalty, or kinship ties (often symbolic and fictitious) rather than by a hierarchy of administrative grades and functions.'[6] By extension – in neopatrimonial politics – public office represents

> ... an important mechanism of private rent seeking; state resources [and the state's ability to shape resource flows] are used to lubricate patron-client networks. At the same time, the state's ability to extract resources and regulate behaviours creates conditions under which the supply of, and access to, scarce goods can be manipulated – the fundamental foundation of the power of patronage.[7]

Inasmuch as neopatrimony represents the connection of modern state-like institutions to the quasi-traditional patriarchal framework (the state utilizing local patronage networks and sectional rivalries in its distributive system), the promotion of patriarchy might also be seen as a way of relieving a state with limited resources of the responsibility for providing welfare for its citizens.[8] Brynen argues that a neopatrimonial 'small carrot and big stick' approach to consensus building reflects the organizational possibilities and limitations on the PA at the present time. It is seen as one of the few tools available for overcoming the break in national consensus following the Oslo Accords. However, the inherent vulnerability of the model in times of regime transition or structural reform also suggests a Palestinian autonomy premised on crisis management rather than effective government. As Ehteshami and Murphy note, attempts at reform within such a system tend to degenerate into overt authoritarianism:

> As the state seeks to build a wider political base in support of [new, often externally mandated] economic policies, it is itself responsible for the breakdown of the corporatist structures which have provided political stability. The political protest and challenges to the regime which result ultimately cannot be contained without resort to the authoritarian assets of the state ... The corporatist state is [thus] transformed into an overtly authoritarian state.[9]

The PA's neopatrimonial use of its resources to hold together a dominant political order or coalition today is dependent on the interests of external donors in sustaining such a situation. Stability is thus contingent upon external factors rather than inherent to the neopatrimonial polity. Embedded in the framework of nationalist ideology, corporatism and neopatrimonialism might be described as pseudo-consensual.

Both corporatist and neopatrimonial regimes are built upon vertically stratified – i.e. factionalized – social networks. In his study of Palestinian factionalism in the last decade of the mandate period, Izza Khalaf makes a useful distinction between structural and political factionalism. Structural factionalism is grounded in politico-economic conditions which contribute to the 'fragmentation, fragility, and vulnerability of ... social structures and organizations at all levels, but particularly at the lower levels.' Accompanied by conditions of structural unemployment and economic hardship, individuals are pushed to rely on the intervention of a patron or patronage organization to meet basic needs. Political factionalism refers to the conflict between elites 'over power and leadership.'[10] It is most likely to appear in an environment lacking in contestable institutions capable of initiating change. The fragmentation of society at the grassroots, and the economic conditions which precipitate it, make it difficult for an elite or activist seeking political influence to appeal to a broad constituency. The predicament is intensified when this appeal is necessarily made without access to governing institutions which are capable of implementing the mobilizing agenda or confronting these structural concerns.

A society factionalized and engaging in essentially non-productive competition with itself poses less of a threat to established power relations (in this case, both intra-Palestinian relations and the relations of domination and control manifested under Israel's occupation of Gaza).[11] The factionalized social base leaves society vulnerable to coercion and manipulation from above. Individual actors are left with few alternative channels of meaningful social engagement and the groupings which elsewhere serve as the foundation of civil society don't engage political institutions in civil dialogue either due to intimidation, extreme alienation, and/or dependency. In other words, because they have become so dependent on the administrative apparatus for survival and privileges, civic activism seems either worthless or counterproductive to short term interests.

Thus, as Sharabi has argued, 'factional ethics are simple and reductive ... *allegiance is not expressly ideological but rooted in basic needs.*'[12] Factionalism seems certainly to have undermined the role of social ideology in Palestinian politics.[13] Instead, the competition to access external funding encouraged groupings to take politically correct stances vis-à-vis the patron often at the expense of working with constituencies on the ground. Hilal has elaborated on some of the attendant problems:

> The partisan and patron-client relations within the (PLO) bureaucracy seriously interfered with the effective management of public services. This was combined with the incessant struggle between the factions, which intervened to determine administrative action at local and national level – for example in the implementation of the political, organizational and financial resolutions of national bodies. Factionalism, which sometimes took the forms of 'clannishness' and 'localism', posed a serious problem, since it characterized administrative action at the highest level of the hierarchy as well as lower down. This factionalism found some nourishment in the geographically and socio-economically fragmented class structure.[14]

In an environment characterized by acute economic hardship and isolation, basic needs are easily politicized. Coercive force and petty administrative privilege represent the current limits of what the PA has to offer society by virtue of interim autonomy. To distribute these limited benefits, and thus ensure control and stability, the PA must co-opt the tips of the factional icebergs. It is forced to do so because it lacks the scope of sovereign powers that might orient interests toward, and thereby sustain identification with, the authority. The individual, whose relations with authority/power are mediated not by the institutions of the state but rather by the factional sub-elite, tows the line or keeps quiet simply because there are no alternatives. Arbitration and mediation is personalized and pushed outside of the visible self-rule institutions. To engage in oppositional political activity is to risk losing access to fundamental sources of security and survival. Accordingly, the dynamic which sustains factional compliance might be described as the political conditionality of basic needs. Factionalism served to keep a confederative nationalist movement singularly dependent on a leadership distanced by exile from local contingencies and direct accountability. For the time being at least, this set-up might be all that stands between relative stability and the collapse of the current order.

Factional Structures in the Context of Autonomy

Talking with young people in Gaza these days, one encounters many former activists who feel alienated from the old factional structures. Given its subservience to the imperatives of implementing the peace process 'from above,' politics is no longer seen as serving any purpose. Arafat is indeed bypassing the old PLO factions. Haydar Abd al-Shafi argues that, 'the political factions have lost credibility with the people and can no longer motivate them.'[15] With the factions stripped of their ability to mediate amongst and 'deliver the goods' to a population hard-pressed to make ends meet, people have no choice but to turn elsewhere. Regardless of the many shortcomings of the PLO factions, an important base of potential social mobilization has been neutralized with their increasing irrelevance.[16] The PA leadership continues to undermine the position of potential 'mid-level' activists whether they be in human rights organizations, Islamist groupings or remnants of the left-wing political factions which had their heyday in Gaza during the late 1970s and early 1980s.

Azmi Bishara goes so far as to argue that Palestinian political society is collapsing in the territories with the ongoing implementation or the Gaza–Jericho formula:

If you look at the PLO factions, you will see an exodus of members from them. The Palestinian political map is changing ... [the factions] are still acting as though the PLO exists and it doesn't. And unless they adapt to the changed circumstances brought about by Oslo they are going to disappear from the scene. [The vacuum created by their disappearance seems likely to be filled in the near term by] two alternatives. First, we are seeing the revival of the traditional tribal structures of Palestinian society, or what is known as the *hamula* or extended family structures ... There are very real signs that the PA is reviving the old *hamula* structures to serve as its main political ally in the autonomy. [The second alternative seems to be] the institutional transformation of the PLO's remnants into the PA's police and security services.[17]

Bishara argues that such conditions constitute reactionary bases of PA power and are likely to produce conditions of 'archaic despotism plus an Islamic opposition.'[18] They also suggest new bases of factionalism. If members are streaming out of the old PLO factions, where are they going? The options are withdrawal, which poses no immediate threat to the security of the regime, or the seeking of efficacy and promotion within the social structures which do exist – mainly the family, which represents a depoliticization of authority. In the latter case, personal and economic security are defined within the recognizable obligations and opportunities outlined by dependent factionalism. In either case, political authority is not openly questioned or actively challenged, and Palestinian society is poorly positioned to defend the boundaries of future rights and 'self-rule' from external or internal challenges. Indeed, as the peace process moves from crisis to crisis, the poverty (if not actual irrelevance) of autonomous institutions has forced Palestinians into street protest as the only public act capable of representing their concerns or pressing for change.

Other social divisions may also be used to promote the 'divide and rule' dynamic of factionalism. Sara Roy reports that:

Arafat is playing on the very pronounced social divisions and tensions that now exist between Gaza's refugee and indigenous communities. After decades of disparity and discrimination, the refugees feel that they are entitled to greater reward than their indigenous counterparts who are not seen to have suffered as deeply or as consistently. Refugees constitute an important source of support for the PA and are a perceived lever against future competitors.[19]

The *hamula* and the Palestinian security forces, discussed below, offer examples of how administrative resources can be channelled into the building and manipulation of factional structures to neutralize potential internal bases of opposition.

The Hamula

Studies on the *hamula* offer a precedent illustrating the group dynamic and power relations of dependent factionalism, and suggest how they might be manipulated in the new order. Traditionally, the *hamula* has been defined as a 'network of patrilineal kinship ties,'[20] or even more vaguely, as 'clan or lineage.'[21] However, more recent research emphasizes the fluidity of the *hamula* structures in response to changing social and political imperatives. While typically conceived in terms of lineage, Abner Cohen

> ... referred to the *hamula* by the more appropriate term of *patronymic association* rather than *group* in order to emphasize better the flexibility inherent in the cultural principle of *hamula* and its frequent lack of sharp principles of exclusion in social practice ... in practise, *hamula* identity was based on a complex web of patrilineal, affinal, and matrilineal ties, neighbourliness (most *hamula* households were located in the same section of the village), and sustained cooperation in political, economic and ceremonial activities.[22]
> Due to a set of interconnected socio-economic and political factors, Cohen argued, the role the hamula played in the political life of the village fluctuated from one period to the next.[23]

Significantly, *hamula* should not be seen as establishing the only basis for social networks: 'friendship, patronage and common economic and political interests served equally as bases for unity and cooperation.'[24] Here, however, it is argued that there is a high coincidence between these factors and what has been described as *hamula* affiliation. The apparent 'authenticity' (a pre-existing awareness which only needs to be defined according to the contexts in which it is invoked) of pseudo-primordial associations such as the *hamula* offers an attractive retreat for the individual in times of hardship, uncertainty, and reduced alternatives. Cossali and Robson observe that:

> The conservatism of Gaza is rooted in the strength of the extended family and under occupation the family has become the major buffer between state and individual. Nobody in Gaza lives outside their family framework ... While the family provides and cares for its members, it can also apply powerful sanctions

against anyone who would challenge its authority ... Certainly the family provides services which should be the government's responsibility, such as mental health care, unemployment benefit, educational grants and so on. But more than this, the preservation of the extended family reinforces the strict male dominated hierarchical nature of Gaza society.[25]

At the same time, we must not underestimate the impact on family structure of widespread migration and immigration, a generation of Gazan youth who spent time in Israeli prisons, the inability of family structures to ensure safety from the intrusions of Israeli force, and the greater involvement of women in economic and resistance activities during the intifada. Contact with wage labour for example has meant that 'lots more young people are now [middle 1980s] independent of their parents financially which gives them the courage to stand up to their fathers.'[26] This situation however has changed in the 1990s with greater unemployment and other factors which tend to extend or 'string out' coping strategies.[27] As a structure bound with patriarchal tendencies, the *hamula* can be mobilized through manipulations from above to serve the interests of power in keeping society divided.

In a 1975 study, Nakleh sought to explore:

the persistence of inter- and intra-*hamula* conflicts in Arab villages in spite of the political, cultural and economic threat generated by the new Israeli regime ... [his researchable question was] 'Why does the political behaviour of Arab villagers in Israel manifest an almost total absence of a level of political consciousness higher than personal utility, the utility of the kinship group, or the utility of the sectarian organization?

He concluded that:

Arabs are encouraged by various agencies of the government to maintain their struggles within the boundaries of the village, or to follow any principle, only so long as that principle does not unite them as a political collectivity vis-à-vis the government.[28]

But Nakleh falls short of discussing the ways in which the overall economic and political circumstances reinforce each other so as to make Palestinians vulnerable to such manipulations. Is the PA pursuing a similar strategy in Gaza today? How might relationships between local institutions in Gaza and the nationalist diaspora organizations have formed in ways which left Gaza society conditioned by and generally prone to ruling strategies which reinforce fragmented and factionalized social responses to authority? While several excellent studies have argued that the intifada represented a culmination of modernizing associative trends in politics in the OT, it is important to emphasize the structural limitations that have always constrained collective action across social and sectoral cleavages in Palestinian life. Associative models of civil society are probably of limited utility in discerning the implications of current developments within the autonomy.

Discussing developments in the OT during the 1980s, Lindholm Schulz argues that 'political parties and factions came to replace village and clan structures as bases for loyalty.'[29] However, it might also be argued that villages and clans attached themselves variously to political parties, factions and other networks of patronage and mediation. A case study presented by Robinson notes that *hamula* organization often coincided with the organization of the popular committees and local self help structures which emerged during the intifada. He suggests that grassroots organization was more effective when it coincided with *hamula* configurations.[30] Thus, beneath the seemingly 'modern' leadership base of much of the uprising, the politics of basic needs and 'primary solidarities' still characterized society at the grassroots structural level. The resilience of such forms of social organization and loyalty should not be surprising considering that conditions in the Gaza space have responded to basically the same contingencies over the past fifty years. Alternatives promising security and a mode of existence where individuals are not compelled to daily consider the tasks of meeting basic needs have not arisen. Robinson, in spite of this case suggesting the contrary, also argues that the intifada 'modernized' the leadership of these local movements and social structures, and as such represented a progressive step toward nation-state building mass integration.[31] It was perhaps over optimistic to assume that reconfigurations at the most visible layer of civil society reflected any fundamental socio-political reorientation.[32]

Thus, while factional structures coalesce in response to immediate needs and to a breakdown in the broad structures of arbitration and authority, they are also prone to manipulation from above in ways which undermine the development of autonomous and sectoral bases of social mobilization. Nation-building and regime legitimation are thus stripped of any socio-economic or developmental character. Politics remains rooted in basic needs. Structures are factionalized and personalized. This problem is exacerbated by the insecurity of the PA, and the lack of alternatives available to Gaza society in general.

The security forces as a factional power base

One of the main mechanisms for enforcing factional discipline under autonomy is the control over access to donor funded employment both in the PA's burgeoning bureaucracy and in shorter term employment initiatives. Perhaps the most striking example of this trend is within the rapidly proliferating Palestinian security forces. The factional control of these forces becomes even more significant when one considers that they are the branch of authority most substantially endowed by current agreements. The implications and dynamic of Arafat's control over the security forces are suggested by Graham Usher's discussion of the subject:

> The myriad of forces gives Arafat enormous scope for political patronage. Since Fatah's Hawk and Panther wings were disbanded in September 1993, former cadres have been steadily absorbed into the PSF (Palestinian Security Forces), making for an increasingly nominal distinction between Fatah and the PSF ... The same logic holds with Arafat's incorporation of the PLO's old diaspora military forces into the PA's new security structures ... Prominent [diaspora] Fatah officials are likely to be appointed to leading posts in the PA's existing security apparatuses or, in the case of 'big chiefs' like Zaki and Hasan, via the establishment of new ones. This pays them a wage and affords them a status commensurate with their former leadership roles. It also serves to erode any lingering political opposition they might harbour toward Oslo.

> (T)he absence of a clear chain of command between the police and the intelligence forces facilitates one of Arafat's oldest methods of rule ... The various police forces compete and conflict with each other for the spoils of political, social and economic power ... The fact that Arafat acts as arbiter in all disputes serves yet another end: by allowing tensions to simmer between the various forces, he fragments them and forestalls the coalescing of alternative power centres. This is important not just because of the dissensions Oslo threw up within Fatah but because such tactics weld together the divergent class, regional, and generational constituencies from which Fatah's 'non-ideological' brand of nationalism has evolved ... Finally, the proliferation of forces has given Arafat maximum leverage in his dealings with Palestinian dissidents, since it allows him to alternate between playing good cop and bad cop against them.[33]

The PA security branches seem to be organized around single personalities whose primary credentials have been loyalty to Arafat (for example, former Palestinian Liberation Army (PLA) commanders such as Colonel Nassir Yusuf and Major General Abdel Razzaq Majaideh). Most security faction heads, like their subordinates, have traded in PLA uniforms for those of the PA.[34] Furthermore, local security force recruits have tended to come from the ranks of the Fatah strike forces, which towards the end of the intifada were increasingly organized along personalized lines becoming gang oriented and self interested. Many old rivalries may have thus been transplanted into the new context. Several witnesses told the author of confrontations between Palestinian security factions in the streets of Gaza where two sides faced each other with guns pointed and grenades in hand, pins pulled and arms cocked. However, at the time of writing, significant violence between security factions has been avoided as their attention has been turned toward suppression of the Islamists.

The security forces are also entirely donor-funded (apart from graft). The fact that they are not accountable to 'taxpayers', but to the donor community, further reveals the security agenda's detachment from the notion of serving the population within which it exercises power. This facilitates (and perhaps even demands) Arafat's subordination of grassroots accountability to factional interests. Arafat becomes a mediator between the security forces and international donations and demands, not between society and its street level security needs. Continued funding of the PA depends on protecting the peace process, and the security forces are used accordingly. Factional control tends to isolate the security forces from public opinion and demands. As later chapters suggest, this phenomenon should not be surprising since it is the combination of patronage and broad powers related to 'internal security' that constitute the effective boundaries of PA power. This combination constitutes a grave danger to the future rights of Palestinians.

Beyond this use of PA coercive powers, administrative functions and employment as instruments of factional discipline, the PA has also assumed direct control over about 40 per cent of the land in the autonomous areas of Gaza. This control over land in many ways mirrors the mechanisms of traditional patronage (building land in post-Oslo Gaza has sold for as much as $2 million per dunum, even though prices are now declining as the peace process seems less and less likely to deliver on economic expectations). Also, reports suggest that Arafat is receiving a ten per cent kickback on all major business contracts concluded with the PA. The presumed result is a fund controlled exclusively by Arafat which is used for 'reconstruction projects,' payment of surplus PA employees, to pay for 'items which have not received the approval of the contributing states,' and as a contingency fund in the event of the dissolution of the

PA. *Ha'aretz* reported in early 1997 on the existence of such a fund in a Tel Aviv bank which, 'according to an internal document of the International Monetary Fund ... is not monitored or controlled by the Palestinian treasury office.' If true, this would dramatically highlight the shortcomings of the patrimonially-based political economy.[35]

While Gazans have been subject to and have actively resisted a high degree of political authoritarianism from a variety of regimes, circumstances forced the populist response to depend on alternative authoritarian structures for sustenance and coordination. Therefore, ironically, authoritarian tendencies coexist with strong anti-authoritarian attitudes in Gaza's collective psyche. Chapter 6 considers the implications of the resulting tension in a context where authorities are themselves in crisis.

Trajectories of Palestinian Factionalism: An Historical Overview

Traditionally, Palestinian elites penetrated daily Palestinian life through landholding, influence in religious institutions, and clan ties. Crushed under despotic taxation, peasants would often place themselves and their lands under the protection of the local notable, who mediated between the peasants and the governing authorities.[36] Reinforcing the position of a family patriarch or village notable as arbiter within such circumstances was the fragmentation of land inherent under Islamic inheritance laws. This encouraged a system of collective land ownership known as the *musha'a.* During the British mandate period, as much as 40 to 50 per cent of the land of Palestine was subject to this kind of collective ownership.[37]

However, the economic dislocations associated with the incorporation of a largely peasant Palestinian society into the world economy – a process which for Palestinians was largely determined according to the strategic needs of the British and subject to the disruptions of Jewish colonization, land purchase and the establishment of a largely separate Jewish economy – had a profound effect on the economic livelihood of Palestinian peasants and the relevance of traditional modes of social arbitration. Even as the economic challenges facing the majority of Palestinians were in rapid transformation during this period, the British mandate rulers continued to base their political control on traditional structures. Their aim was to contain the social pressures that built up in the process of transformation rather than to pursue policies which might channel these pressures into social and political development. And while Palestinians were increasingly forced to orient their activities toward the presence of the colonial state, the state itself excluded Palestinian participation. Furthermore, features of the Ottoman *millet* system were incorporated into the mandate, allowing the various religious communities to obtain permission to administer their own religious, cultural and educational institutions. While such a situation had obvious implications for factionalism, it also precluded the legal recognition of a politically distinct *Arab* community.[38]

Jewish land purchases were not the only factor alienating the Palestinian peasantry from traditional livelihoods and mechanisms of mediation. Changing consumer preferences and economic imperatives made wage labour increasingly important as a supplement to subsistence farming. The vacillating nature of Britain's economic interests in the region encouraged policies which drew peasants off the land to work in, for example, defence-related industries. The eventual removal of these employment opportunities left Arab workers structurally unemployed. The result was a frustrated lumpenproletariat, 'floating' from city to city in search of employment. Loosened from their bonds with the traditional notables, but without sustainable employment in the industrial centres then emerging on the coast, this group was to provide the bulk of active participation in the Arab revolt of 1936–39. While Palestinian labour organizations did mobilize parallel to their Jewish counterparts, these incipient structures were undercut by British policy, by the weakness of the economic base on which their common interests were based, and by attempts of the traditional notability to co-opt them into the factional structure. The most prominent nationalist leader of the time – the Grand Mufti of Jerusalem Haj Amin al-Husayni – in particular sought to undermine the inclusion of labour elements as an independent force in the emerging nationalist movement. The connections of the traditional elite to the peasantry was in crisis, and the interests of Palestinian elites were under siege.

Nationalism was therefore increasingly invoked by the Palestinian notables to reassert themselves into the political arena of the 1930s and 1940s. While the coastal Palestinian bourgeoisie also involved itself in the nationalist politics of the day, it lacked connections to the countryside. In the absence of broad participation by Palestinians in the mandate bureaucracy (civil or military), a 'modernizing' nationalist middle class with access to the institutions of government did not emerge to play an integrative role in relating national ideology to structures with broad powers to govern.[39] The mass of the Palestinian population in the countryside was thus left to identify with the largely Jerusalem-based notable elite that, while less able to insinuate its power economically, was still associated with religious institutions and traditional status.

However, infighting between the notables for control of the nationalist movement in the absence of effective power over which to compete reduced civil energies to factional politicking. This competition was typified, *inter alia*, in the struggles between the Husayni-led Palestine Arab Party and the Nashashibi-led National Defence Party, the manoeuvrings of the Grand Mufti Haj al-Amin al-Husayni, and the bickering within the Arab Higher Committee (AHC) during the final decade of the British Mandate.

The final days of the British Mandate in Gaza were to dramatically demonstrate the susceptibility of the factional structure to petty conflicts and external manipulation. Following the 1947 UN decision to support a partition of mandate Palestine into separate Jewish and Arab entities (a proposal rejected by the Arabs), the AHC – dominated by the Grand Mufti – made a last ditch effort to establish institutions on the ground that were capable of executing administrative functions in cities throughout Palestine. National committees were formed, and these made some inroads toward creating Palestinianized institutions of arbitration and regulation which were referred to by the people. However, these committees were not self sustaining when it came to funds. Funding for the committees was controlled by the AHC, in other words by the grand mufti, who was loathe to support those committees that were prone to independent initiative, thus reinforcing the responsiveness of the committees to factional incentives insinuated 'from above.'

The National Committee established in Gaza City was, in addition to the factional incentives imposed from above, limited by pervasive family politics, jealousies and division. The imperatives of clan politics demanded that the Gaza City national committee include fifty-five members instead of the prescribed twenty; and that instead of an elected leadership, there should be a continually rotating chairmanship.[40] The Gaza district commissioner reported on the potentially devastating impact of these divisions:

> In the town there are still no local leaders, and Gaza is a medley of armed men with no plan or organization. The more one sees of the local Arab the more one realizes that a determined organized Jewish operation will play havoc in this area.

Two weeks later, the district commissioner noted:

The greatest danger to the maintenance of order in the district is the lack of control and organization in Gaza town itself, where petty jealousies and *fassad* [corruption or the creation of division by gossip between families or parties] continue to obstruct the formation of an efficient National Committee. Recent *Haganah* [the pre-1948 Zionist Army] Arabic broadcasts containing up-to-date gossip and scandal of Gaza have started accusations and counter accusations of pro-Jewish activity between leaders and followers of the various factions.[41]

With the 1948 Arab–Jewish war and the flight of hundreds of thousands of Palestinians from the areas which were to become the newly established state of Israel, Palestinians experienced a variety of political, legal and socio-economic conditions. The old social, economic and political order, already disrupted by Palestine's attachment to the world economy beginning in the late 1800s and traumatic events such as the Arab revolt of 1936–39, was shattered by the establishment of the Israeli state and the flight of hundreds of thousands of refugees from areas occupied by Zionist forces. The new situation demanded new responses. Still, however, attempts were made to reconstruct the old social order in exile.[42] Previous social formations were reconstituted, reinvented and often asserted in new ways, but were not always able to overcome the transplantation of old rivalries and distinctions. The new national structures which emerged necessarily took into account (consciously or not) many of the earlier forms of socio-political organization and control, and these were used by future occupiers to interfere in local political development.[43]

Following the *nakba* (disaster, condition of misery – a term used by Palestinians to describe the loss of homes, lands and lives resulting from the Zionist victory of 1948), the position of the traditional elites was mixed. The fundamental mechanisms through which they had inserted their interests into Palestinian life – first gradually eroded – were now shattered. Their prestige had been severely damaged by the infighting, bickering and inactivity which was seen by the masses as having contributed to the defeat at the hands of the Zionist forces. Those elites who had their bases relatively intact (social, economic or both) in the Gaza Strip were now forced to balance pursuit of their interests between accommodation to an emerging nationalist elite in the Palestinian diaspora, (an elite with new bases of legitimation), and to the Egyptian administration and subsequently the Israeli occupation regime. In Gaza autochtonous elites were suddenly burdened and politically threatened by an overwhelming refugee majority in the population – refugees without any immediate ties to the local indigenous notables.

Egypt occupied and administered the Gaza Strip after 1948.[44] The traditional elites were not out of the picture, but they were increasingly a marginal force in a chaotic environment. After a brief spell which saw the Egyptians under King Farouk install Haj Amin al-Husayni at the head of an 'All Palestine Government' in Gaza, Egypt gave up all pretence of supporting Palestinian self administration. The flight of refugees into the Strip during and after the 1948 war – into an environment which was cut off from its economic hinterland, overcrowded, resource poor (water and land being the crucial resources in Gaza) and lacking in opportunities for employment – resulted in the formation of two profoundly unintegrated socio-political groupings who were forced to share the same restricted space, the same limited job opportunities, and the same overburdened resource base. Competition for employment and access to the resources which meant survival was especially acute between the poorest of both groups. In fact, the situation was worse for the 'indigenous' poor as they lacked a claim to United Nations Refugee Works Agency (UNRWA) support. The distinction between the two groups was intensified by the refusal of the refugees to assimilate – mostly out of fear of losing their right of return.[45]

While the experience of exile in refugee camps and the difficulties associated with social and economic integration into a new environment encouraged the reconstruction of 'traditional' linkages among the Palestinians who had been forced to take flight following the 1948 war, many politically active Palestinians in the newly formed diaspora were soon drawn to the pan-Arab political movements which were emerging as a political force in the Arab world by the early 1950s. An insistence on the centrality of the liberation of Palestine as a precondition for the modernization and transformation of Arab society in general – a society which they saw as reactionary, sclerotic and incapable of withstanding and resisting imperialist forces intent on keeping the Arab space divided and underdeveloped – was a general theme which unified the Palestinian branches of these movements. They deigned to influence the emerging agenda of Arab nationalism to adopt the liberation of Palestine and the return of Palestinians to their land as a guiding historical mission, uniting Arab land and people. Their struggle was one to collectivize the tragedy, and they saw in Western support for Israel an imperialist strategy for keeping the Arabs weak and economically irrelevant.

Gaza offered one of the densest and potentially most coherent bases of Palestinian nationalism (given its large refugee population and a seeming need for concerted collective action to deal with new economic and ecological stresses). However, while the United Nations and other aid organizations ameliorated the harshest conditions of refugee life, this may have also undermined the need to define and articulate common political interests. A variety of economic, political and social pressures kept various groups, sectors and classes unintegrated. Political and economic pressures facing refugees in Gaza were in many ways different from the challenges facing refugees in Lebanon or Jordan, even though (especially after the takeover of the PLO by the resistance movements in the late 1960s) the ideology of nationalism increasingly offered an analysis of and solution to the situation which united refugees in various locations and circumstances. This trend was to culminate with the creation and transformation of the PLO from the mid to late 1960s.

In Nasser's Egypt, political activity was harshly repressed. Especially in the early and middle 1950s, Nasser cracked down on all forms of organized political activity in Gaza. By appointing Egyptians accountable only to Cairo to key administrative posts in Gaza, Egyptian rule further stifled the development of a political culture oriented toward local possibilities and indigenous leaders. In fact, 'building political structures independent of Egypt wasn't a main priority for most Gazans during the Egyptian Administration because of the popular belief that Nasser's pan-Arab vision would eventually deliver Palestine from Zionist control.'[46] It was not until after Israel's invasion of Egypt with the 'Suez crisis' of 1956, during which Israel occupied Gaza for more than six months, that Palestinians increasingly agitated to be allowed to represent their cause. Egyptian authorities, although worried about upholding their truce agreements, finally consented and allowed elections. A National Union and a legislative council were formed, although with very limited powers. The Egyptian Army also began organizing and training regiments of what was to become the Palestinian Liberation Army (PLA).

Inasmuch as the Egyptians needed to influence actions and attitudes within the grassroots, they did so through the mediation of local notables. As one Palestinian has noted:

> Most of the *wujaha* [traditional notables or leaders] collaborated with the authorities and informers, not because they were un-nationalistic, but because they feared the new generation which was threatening their influence. These were the people on whom the Mufti depended – they worked together against the new current.[47]

The notables, first and foremost concerned with the protection of their own immediate economic interests, were a generally conservative group. (The upper middle class and merchant bourgeoisie later also tended to take a circumspect stance toward direct challenges to Israeli authorities, but these classes were more prominent in the West Bank.) Thus, while the features which had maintained traditional elite roles had been broken down, the basic lack of grassroots economic autonomy remained a structural feature of economic life in the Gaza Strip. This left the door open to tactics and bases for factional enforcement.

The external determination and orientation of what little productive activity there was in Gaza discouraged the integration of economic sectors. This in turn undermined incentives for local elites or organizations to conceive of individual interests within the collective framework. There was economic change without corresponding social change because no single sector had relations or linkages with other sectors, but only with an external political and economic metropole. Such conditions (beginning with the formation of a large lumpenproletariat beginning during the mandate period) tended to restructure neopatriarchal economic organization and mechanisms of social control. The constraints on political activity during both Egyptian and Israeli occupation of Gaza, together with Gaza's lack of an economic base capable of absorbing the refugees who fled to the Strip after 1948, left it without an integrated social, political or economic base. This precluded the formation of a political class identifying with a mass constituency cutting across otherwise powerful social divisions in Gaza.[48]

Following the 1967 war, Israel occupied Gaza City and its surrounding area, the Gaza Strip. The first three or four years of Israel's second occupation of Gaza were marked by a rather disorganized but widespread armed resistance.

The PLO and the Occupation: Patronage and Resistance

The PLO was established by the Arab League in 1964. In practice, during its early phase it was a political organ manipulated by Arab states in pursuing their interests and intrigues.[49] Many observers saw the man chosen by Nasser to build the new organization – the somewhat blustering and bombastic Ahmad Shukayri – as a mere puppet, although he perhaps deserves some credit for establishing a degree of independence for the organization. Arab leaders at least nominally recognized direct Palestinian involvement in resolving the Palestine question.[50] When viewed against the Arab military defeat in 1967, however, the fiery rhetoric of Shukayri only increased Palestinian despair at the inability of existing political institutions to represent their claims and resolve their problems.

The Arab defeat in the Six Day War of 1967 discredited the PLO founding guard. It was shown up as a tool of other states in the pursuit of intra-Arab state rivalries. In 1968, the PLO was taken over by the resistance movements (most notably Fatah) who 'quickly proceeded to determine the movement's affiliations, discourse and tactics; and as such [the PLO] articulated not only the aims and the outlook of Palestinian nationalism, but also the history and contours of Palestinian identity' – an identity shaped not only in conflict with Israel, but increasingly in conflict with other Arab states as well.[51] The romanticized exploits of the *fedayeen*-heightened grassroots appeal.[52] Here seemed to be an elite committed to direct action. Furthermore, Fatah was the first organization to unequivocally view the liberation of Palestine as a Palestinian task, and its early successes played a crucial role in moving the struggle ideologically away from the broader debate over Arab unity and the transformation of Arab society. The 'new' PLO's direct control over funds (largely under the domain of the Palestinian National Fund) allowed it to establish a deeply rooted factional bureaucracy with military as well as civilian wings. But the cost of this rapid growth was a loss of organizational cohesion.[53] The transition from Fatah as an organization built on 'cells' to a mass-based organization also posed new challenges.

In Gaza, the banning of all political activity under the Israeli military occupation, the deportation of many political leaders, and an initial post-occupation period of militant resistance without social content left Gazans politically un-anchored. Institution building became imbued with a contradictory sense of urgency and futility which has yet to be overcome.

> Political opposition [was] severely curtailed by the occupation. The United National Front, a coalition of groups from the Egyptian period, was systematically destroyed by arrests and deportations which it could not survive. It was left to the Red Crescent Society, the three professional associations of doctors, lawyers and engineers, and to some extent the municipal council [Israeli appointed], to provide a political leadership although this was a role they didn't necessarily seek.[54]

Hindered by Israeli force from establishing an on the ground base in Gaza, Fatah attempted to inject itself into the equation through patronage.

This often proved detrimental to the cohesion of existing groups without creating alternatives responsive to structural realities and needs. The contours of the nationalist movement were constrained both by the general political situation in the Arab world, and by the personal inclinations of the Fatah leadership. As Migdal and Kimmerling suggest:

> ... the nature of dispersal and the disdain of Fatah's leaders for traditional party organization – cells, local committees and the like – made it difficult for the group to educate, recruit, or consistently mobilize the larger population. The committee succeeded in coordinating the organization's own actions, less so in infusing Fatah into the everyday lives of the Palestinians. When Fatah did create some rudimentary regional subgroups, it found itself hemmed in by the governing Arab regimes [and of course after 1967 by Israel].
>
> For all these organizational liabilities, the group did capture the Palestinians' imagination, but not in ways that could have been the basis for systems of control and mass mobilization. This remained true after the 1967 war when it built a complex central apparatus, covering areas from financial control to relations with Arab parties. Over the years, Arafat tried to make Fatah (and later the PLO which Fatah came to dominate) into what the Jewish Agency had been for the Jews during the British Mandate – a 'state-in-the-making' – but without the equivalent of political parties and the Histadrut, which had given the Jewish Agency a firm foundation in the Jewish population.[55]

Another factor contributing to the insecurity of the PLO position was that many Palestinian elites in the OT continued to perceive their interests in terms of political orientation towards Jordan and the Hashemite regime. This was especially true of the traditional landed elites (in Gaza as well as the West Bank) who were concerned about the stability of their economic holdings and were not interested in provoking the Israelis and thereby risking the fate of so many of their fellows.

By the early 1970s, however, the PLO had to a large extent succeeded in integrating itself within various Palestinian communities and constituencies both in the diaspora and in the OT. There existed broad recognition among Palestinians that the PLO represented a legitimate representative and normative national leadership. On 28 October 1974, the Arab world unanimously declared the PLO the legitimate representative of the Palestinian people.[56] This gave increased legitimacy and visibility to the PLO's role of reconstituting the links which had been shattered after 1948,[57] and marked the increased independence of the organization at a time when the oil rich Gulf states had a surplus of donor potential. However, while the PLO's control over the factional purse-strings allowed it to maintain its pre-eminent position across wide and varied constituencies in Palestinian political life, the unintegrated attachment of various groups within the same local community to the PLO bureaucracy also tended to undermine the development of locally integrated sectors and institutions. PLO funding of activities in Gaza sought to encourage political compliance rather than to serve as a helping hand or a springboard toward economic independence.

Most Palestinians accepted the right of the PLO to speak on their behalf. However, the structure of the PLO and the scattered nature of Palestinian society were such that consensus on that right was based on the PLO leadership's ability to speak in the broadest and most general terms about Palestinian interests and to take credit for activities which showed a commitment to the pursuit and attainment of those interests. The name of the game was consensus building, giving various groups within the society reason to conceive of their interests as being best pursued within the context of national self-fulfilment. Patronage and dramatic action sustained the vision of a political order promising accountability to their demands.

However, while the PLO had a strong institutional base in many of the Palestinian communities in exile, most notably in Jordan (before the events of 'Black September') and in Lebanon until 1982, Fatah, the leading faction within the PLO, had only a tenuous institutional base in the occupied territories. Cossali and Robson, writing in the mid-1980s, note that 'although Fatah is the biggest faction within the PLO, we found it hard [in Gaza] to find someone who would defend the Fatah strategy and Yasser Arafat's style of leadership.'[58] According to some of their informants:

> Basically Fatah is not a force here. There are plenty of Fatah supporters, but they have no leader and they are split between personal ambitions and the needs of the actual situation. The PFLP [Popular Front for the Liberation of Palestine], although it has fewer members, has more power because it is better organized.[59]
> There are so many different factions all saying: 'We support the PLO.' The result is that the PLO has no clear cut policy. There is total confusion and always will be while the PLO is trying to speak with so many voices.[60]

In general, free of the burden and demands of consistency implied by the need to work with constituencies to address everyday problems, self-preservation and dominance became a primary objective in the context of factional rivalry. 'The result was an odd mixture of ideological purity and political irresponsibility.'[61] Fatah's attempts to be everything to everyone, and its corresponding inattention to organization at the civic level of the neighbourhood and village, in some ways account for the apparent irony between the traditional broad-based identification with the leaders of Fatah and their simultaneous failure to mobilize society effectively toward specific goals in Gaza since 'Oslo.'[62] The nationalist leaders were not held accountable for conditions on the ground.

The United Nations Refugee Works Association (UNRWA) and the occupation civil administration may have also undermined the PLO position by being able to offer services – albeit limited services – and more importantly by providing jobs and aid that encouraged local loyalties. (This becomes more apparent in the current transitional context. The PA threatens the political composition and perhaps the efficiency of these institutions, creating anxiety among the many Gazans who have become dependent upon them.[63] Today, for example, many refugees are afraid of effectively losing UNRWA services if these services are turned over to the PA as is planned; and the 20,000 Gazans who were employed by the Israeli civil administration are, in spite of guarantees within the agreements, afraid of being squeezed out as the PA is pressured to give administrative jobs to outsiders and to strategically located individuals within Gaza).

While the limited social horizons of classes that might potentially have served as a base for national integration promoted conditions that were ripe for factionalism and particularism in Palestinian society, PLO institutions themselves added a new dimension and even legitimacy to these divisions. Hilal argues that the routinization of a well-funded political bureaucracy operating outside any specific societal formation and without accountability for articulating a social agenda allowed the Fatah elite to manipulate the PLO institutional structure to ensure that Arafat and Fatah were the constant reference point of national unity.[64] Chief among the mechanisms that allowed this was the quota system.

> The quota system [where each of the political groups has a specified number of seats in the PNC regardless of its size in the Executive Committee] contained the seeds of the marginalization of national institutions. It gave power to the representatives of political factions, rather than to the representatives of Palestinian communities, associations and trade unions. In other words, decision-making remained in the hands of the leadership of those political groups affiliated to the PLO, with special powers for the controlling group. This was accentuated by the centralized command structure operating in all the groups of the PLO, reflecting its paramilitary origins and the varying emphases of its affiliated groups

on armed struggle. Rivalries and differences in political outlook among left-wing groups, as well as the willingness of each to enter into direct deals with Fatah to enlarge its representation, were used by the leadership of Fatah, along with other tactics, including the control of PLO funds and appointments, to maintain and entrench its control.[65]

The PLO's factional base beneath a highly centralized command structure encouraged battles over access to increased representation and patronage rather than responses to popular concerns.[66] It should be remembered that inasmuch as this dynamic was influencing political organization in the OT, it was largely covert and subject to Israeli reprisal. At the same time, the relative wealth and diplomatic scope of the PLO made dishing out positions around the world easier than developing a constituency in the OT.

Political developments in Israel were also to have a decisive impact on social development in the Gaza Strip. In the mid 1970s, Menachem Begin assumed power and began to introduce the 'Milsonian' strategy of trying to wean local elites from identification with the PLO using traditionalistic patriarchal patronage networks.[67] Menachem Milson, a right wing historian, first came to public attention after writing that the PLO had come to power in the OT municipal elections in 1976 through fraud, bribery and intimidation. He argued that it was possible to cultivate a pliable indigenous leadership to counter the PLO in the territories.[68] With what was known as operation 'Iron Fist', the Likud regime repressed PLO sentiment in the OT with renewed vigour using physical violence reinforced by collective economic and social punishments. The population was increasingly economically and politically isolated, and conditions deteriorated. On 1 November 1981, Milson was appointed to head a new civil administration in the occupied territories.[69] In early 1982, Israeli authorities ousted the pro-PLO mayors and violence erupted. In a foreshadowing of things to come, Israeli soldiers fired on stone-throwing youths and Jewish settlers joined in the violence.

Meanwhile, the PLO was housed in a sprawl of offices on the Beirut waterfront and was 'developing many of the appurtenances of a governmental bureaucracy, complete with an army of sorts, a finance ministry, and departments to deal with Palestinian internal and external affairs. It built hospitals and paid pensions to the families of Palestinian martyrs.'[70] According to Brynen, the PLO bureaucratic network, centred in Lebanon, employed about 8,000 civil servants and commanded 'a budget in the hundreds of millions of dollars, three-quarters of which went to support the PLO's administrative and social programmes.'[71] Adam Zagorin estimates that by the late 1980s approximately $233 million were at the disposal of the Palestinian National Fund. Over a third of that went to support a standing army.[72] However, the presence of quasi-state institutions within another state had a destabilizing impact on the Lebanese political situation. This instability was exacerbated by lack of real PLO accountability to fixed constituencies and the degree to which its institutions were used as a basis for patronage. Brynen asserts that 'overall, the strong neopatrimonial dynamic of Lebanese politics reinforced this tendency within the Palestinian movement.'[73] Furthermore, the imperatives of national unity and international recognition meant that rather than responding to the needs of specific sectors in society, the PLO leadership responded to factional demands and international possibilities.

The different institutions and components of the Palestinian national movement, rather than being used as a springboard for integrating social structures, became 'political fronts.'[74] These organizations were set up to be financially dependent on the central leadership of the PLO. The PLO had great problems transforming itself from an organ of political mobilization to a bureaucracy with the task of organizing the provision of basic services.

By 1978, Arafat found himself in the position of being responsible for reining in unruly elements in Lebanon.[75] Arafat always sought with his decisions to encompass the widest spectrum of Palestinian views even if this demanded vagueness.[76] At the same time, his tendency to appoint to influential positions cronies and loyalists charged with cowardice and incompetence added to growing confusion in the ranks, and created conditions which greatly undermined the ability of the PLO to respond to grassroots concerns.[77] The crisis is illustrated by the leadership's response to the criticism of PLO dissident Abu Musa, who accused the Fatah leadership of turning the PLO into 'a rotten bureaucracy dedicated only to self preservation' and at one point led an open rebellion within the movement. They tried to pay him off.[78] The impact of successive defeats in Jordan in the early 1970s, in Lebanon during the civil war of the second half of the 1970s and early 1980s, and finally the Israeli siege of Beirut in 1982 and the subsequent flight of the PLO to new headquarters in Tunis, fragmented, and thus increased factionalism within, the Fatah movement itself. Moreover, these changes and upheavals, most notably the PLO expulsion from Lebanon, reduced and in some cases obliterated the PLO's access to the socio-political space upon which it had once relied as a basis for social mobilization. The result was a shrinkage of the effective spatial political geography of the Palestinian movement without any corresponding reform in the PLO's bureaucratic structure. By the mid-1980s, the PLO's presence and prestige in Gaza was under serious challenge.

By involving itself in the increasing chaos and factionalism of Lebanese politics,[79] and undermined by opportunism and cronyism in its own ranks, the PLO was increasingly distracted from its mission of engaging Israel through focused military and diplomatic initiatives. In light of the loss of direction, the likelihood that the PLO would ever realize its existential mission seemed less and less realistic. Concurrently, corruption and incompetence in the ranks of the PLO's factionalized bureaucracy were undermining the effectiveness of the services which they had been providing in the diaspora communities, particularly in Lebanon.[80]

In the occupied territories, on the other hand, activists were generally more realistic about the challenges Israel posed to national integration. But the PLO's reliance on external sources of funding insulated the leadership from changes within the various Palestinian communities. The PLO was increasingly operating outside any real societal formation. It was becoming a political movement with less and less to offer its constituency. While the PLO concentrated more on empty sloganeering and patronage, political awareness and politico-economic structure in Gaza was responding to the institutions and lack of institutions of occupation.

The organizations which the PLO created and nurtured in the diaspora were not necessarily compatible with those which were developing in the OT. Hilal has argued that while the PLO was the initiator of structures and institutions that were designed to recreate a Palestinian identity in exile, the organization was forced to adopt a more reactionary mode toward building its relationships in the OT, grafting itself onto pre-existing structures and distorting the sectoral character of embryonic institutions in a society already susceptible to factionalism.[81]

Grassroots Movements in Gaza: Clients versus Constituency

By the late 1970s, the context of the Camp David Accords signaled to elements within the PLO, specifically the left wing factions, the need for a new resistance strategy in the OT. The left-wing PLO-affiliated organizations began to establish grassroots and professional voluntary organizations in the territories; this had the impact of drawing wider social strata actively into the Palestinian movement as the new structures began to attract cadres and local leaders from the working and lower middle classes as well as from rural areas. Women and students played an increasingly visible role.[82]

The Israelis placed various obstacles to the effective formation and functioning of various professional and sectoral associations.[83] Still, representatives of the left-wing factions ruled the day in associational elections in the late 1970s. The inability of the professional and sectoral associations to act as effective bases for social mobilization, however, pushed activists toward the humanitarian Palestinian Red Crescent Society as an organizational core. Work committees were set up to compensate for the lack of public services, to disseminate information, to support education and health care, to lend labour to families whose houses had been destroyed, to organize women's groups and more.[84] The relative success of the left wing reflected the changing attitudes and imperatives of Gazan society in general after occupation. Gazan labour was 'proletarianized' by contact with the Israeli economy, creating new socio-economic demands and perspectives. These trends also changed the composition of the nationalist movement in Gaza by providing a base for greater lower and working class participation.[85] But the emergence of a class structure has been 'complicated by conflicting forces':

> The original residents of Gaza still dominate the area politically and economically and the bulk of the refugee population work as labourers alongside Jewish workers. These Gazan workers, because of their national struggle with Israel, do not feel a class alliance with the Israeli workers, yet they still remain excluded from the political stage in Gaza and exploited by the capitalists of Gaza. The issue of class is subordinated to the need for national unity and opposition to Zionism. Also, the primary loyalty tends to be to the family, which is the provider and protector, rather than to a class.[86]

While the reference to 'the capitalists of Gaza' sounds a bit exaggerated, the statement bears some points worth noting as we try to understand the failure of the popular committees and grassroots organizations to develop into integrated self sustaining structures rather than politicized patronage networks. Before the intifada, the lack of an economic base for local political much less national integration was apparent within the social divisions of the urban petit bourgeoisie class. The strict division of even members of similar classes along the lines of social origin was reflected in elections in the municipalities and local chambers of commerce:

... where refugee and 'native' candidates had to be balanced delicately in each opposing slate ... despite significant integration and intermarriage since the war of 1967, (divisions based on origin) continue to be a primary obstacle to the social homogeneity of the middle strata in Palestinian urban society. They contributed significantly to the relative withdrawal of town merchants from active participation in the national movement until the eruption of the uprising in December 1987. One outstanding achievement of the uprising has been a noticeable decline in the social impact of these divisions ...[87]

In the late 1970s, the leftist factions began to pursue a strategy which saw social reform as a prerequisite to liberation. They promoted neighbourhood organizations, women's groups, built the trade unions and encouraged a system of home production and other tactics of economic nationalism to break the economic grip of the occupation. Fatah, on the other hand, played a much more conservative role while lending its resources to support mobilization, preferring to concentrate on connecting itself to traditional elements of local authority in the OT.

Throughout this period [up through the early to mid-1980s], Fatah, the hegemonic movement within the PLO, maintained an uncomfortable working relationship with the Jordanian regime in an attempt to retain some of its influence in the West Bank. [This relationship was formalized under the auspices of the Palestinian–Jordanian Joint Committee (PJJC) which oversaw Arab funding in the OT].[88]

Contrary to the grassroots approach of the leftist factions, Fatah's initiatives through the PJJC were directed toward the conservative and more traditional institutions such as the charitable societies, universities and municipalities.[89] Brynen reports that:

By some estimates, as much as a half a billion dollars was injected by the PLO into the territories between 1977 and 1985. Although much went to support needed infrastructure projects in areas such as housing, agriculture, and education, this period saw 'a sizable amount of handouts in the form of patronage money to nationalist institutions and personalities.' Fatah – which had the greatest access to funds – was the primary beneficiary of this, using it to counter the grassroots organizational challenge posed by the left.[90]

Much of this support was imperative for the daily functioning in Gaza as,

... according to Israeli military law, municipal governments had no legislative authority to generate revenue. They could not introduce new taxes, fees or rates without approval of the authorities, which was sometimes given. Consequently, municipal governments depended heavily on donations for capital and development expenditure.[91]

However, it can be argued that PLO funding of the municipalities in Gaza during the 1970s absolved the Israelis of their responsibility to provide basic services, and served to deflect the purposiveness and urgency of popular action. As Locke and Stewart noted in 1985:

Many people in Gaza were angered by seeing PLO money absolving the Israelis of their responsibilities ... (Also,) there is concern that money coming from the outside leadership is being used to buy and reward political supporters in the occupied territories, and that it is difficult to make political decisions without approval from outside. The situation has resulted in political paralysis. There is a growing feeling in Gaza ... that the relationship between the outside leadership and the Palestinians inside should be redefined to allow the latter a greater say in forging a strategy for opposition to Zionism.[92]

Hilal notes that while Israeli oppression played an important part in the breaking apart of the popular committees that had sprung up in the late 1970s and early 1980s, factional co-optation also played a crucial role:

While competition among the PLO groups was an important factor in building grass roots organizations, the fact that this competition was confined to political issues and that social issues were relegated to marginal positions hindered the process of building national institutions capable of functioning independently of political groups. In the place of the popular committees, factional committees were instituted that lacked two of the former's novel and vital features: their openness, and their democratic structure. In other words, those at the centre of the political system could not adjust to a democratic and organizational innovation as represented by the popular committees.[93]

Social issues were pushed to the side in favour of political issues, thus hindering the development of social structures independently capable of providing for social needs. Factional committees replaced the popular ones and subverted the openness and democratic character of the earlier structures. Much of the factional conflict of the 1980s could be viewed on right–left lines (see the case of the attack on Red Crescent Society below).

There is also a great deal of money which is being poured by Saudi Arabia into the hands of people who are also fighting the Left. They are trying to buy people in every way – by providing jobs and work. Money makes a lot of difference and they have money.[94]

It seems that Fatah did not openly come down on one side or the other, but through its tendency to view its own interests in terms of its factional control and its alliances with traditional elements in the OT, it undermined the effectiveness and appeal of the popular organizations and promoted factionalism. One Gazan woman activist argues that Fatah supports 'the negative, sexist elements in Palestinian society because it suits them. They don't want anything more than small changes.'[95] Other activists have noted the shortcomings of the PLO's tendency to frame the Palestinian movement in terms of the leaders against the Israelis rather than the Palestinian people against the Israelis, attacking Arafat's tendency to 'try and grab headlines and excite people without really trying to start a popular movement at the level of ordinary people.'[96] When factional coping strategies played such a strong role in determining short term interests in Gaza, the lack of unity on the 'outside' made it difficult to promote unity on the 'inside.'[97] In the final analysis, these trends may have deadened the potential for collective action which seemed so promising at the beginning of the intifada. Together with Israeli arrests and repression, such tendencies certainly neutralized any sincere efforts of left wing and progressive forces towards broad-based collective institution building. Tamari sums up the shortcomings of the attempts at institution building in the OT:

Two main institutional failures which can be mentioned here were the inability of the 'popular education committees' to create a sustained alternative network to formal schooling (schools had been closed by the Israeli authorities) and the failure of the 'agricultural committees' and the 'domestic production committees' to create the much heralded system of home production, based on cottage industries.[98]

Tamari also comments on the effect of the PLO's increasing concern with enforcing its control over the events of the uprising and turning the focus away from the activities in the territories and toward the international diplomatic arena:

It was the inability of the popular committees to create this alternative power base that was now seen as the essence of crisis in the leadership of the uprising.

In effect, the diplomatic initiatives of the PLO to enter into a negotiated territorial settlement were seen as the new alternative strategy which would circumvent, rather than supplement, the political gains of the uprising.[99]

Recent analyses taking into account the PLO's struggle to consolidate and legitimize its new position and powers in Gaza during the intifada further question the real strength of the intifada's 'embryonic' structures of civil society. The failure to translate the various structures associated with the intifada into stable self rule structures/institutions highlights this.[100] According to Haydar Abd al-Shafi, 'the leadership failed to make benefit of the intifada by failing to provide the needed organization.'[101] Ziad Abu Zayyad has argued that the leadership began to disengage from events on the ground and spend more time cultivating other political relationships and imperatives, noting that 'one of the failures of the intifada was the fact that the masses were neglected.'[102] PLO affiliated structures were finally sustained more on external patronage designed to co-opt rather than on the articulation of a strategy to deal with the issues of economic hardship and human rights that initially fuelled the uprising. The pressure on inside activists to take politically correct stances vis-à-vis the PLO leadership situated outside the OT meant that social mobilization responded to PLO bureaucratic imperatives rather than issues on the ground. This resulted in a crisis in the direction of social mobilization which has only been exacerbated with autonomy. According to Moustafa Barghouti, 'many leaders haven't faced this crisis. They are stuck in the past with unrealistic solutions to the current crisis, and many people are just tired.'[103] Today, the PA is preoccupied with security issues (largely its own security) and still has no real coherent program for reconstruction and development.[104] Hilal asserts that

> ... the PLO could not, given its oversized bureaucracy, adjust itself easily and quickly to the shift in the OT. Its bureaucratic elite, as well as the leaderships of its constituent organizations, saw in the emerging political reality a threat to their command and their privileges.[105]

Seven years earlier, Cossali and Robson had noted that:

> Much of the dissatisfaction and occasional disillusionment expressed (toward) the leadership outside Palestine [i.e. the PLO, which is usually referred to in the interviews as the 'outside leadership'] centres on the widespread belief that money is being sent into Gaza in an irresponsible way.[106]

Lindholm Schulz (citing Tamari) notes that: '*Sumud* [i.e. steadfastness, a word denoting the Palestinian goal of standing fast against the pressures of Israeli occupation rule] degenerated after the establishment of the *sumud* fund in the late 1970s when the Arab states decided to support Palestinian steadfastness. *Sumud* money largely fed into the pockets of the already wealthy and *sumud* as a concept decreased in legitimacy.'[107] Frustration with the status quo has been left to smoulder in the face of the limited scope within which opposition might articulate alternatives, find meaningful directions, or produce tangible results.

At the outset, most of the grassroots movements were cross factional and represented specific sectors or interests such as women's rights and student's organizations. Within a few years, however, these broader affiliations broke into factionally controlled groupings. Fatah, with its leadership in control of the PLO patronage purse strings, played a leading role in this factionalization. While the factionally-based popular organizations did perform valuable functions, the leadership locally and in Tunis ultimately 'saw these activities and services as a means to a political end ... in retrospect, (it is clear that) many of the mass-based NGOs were predominantly used as a means of recruitment for a particular faction.'[108] The result was a competition between organizations that undercut their expressed aims of general grassroots development in favour of factional maintenance. The responsiveness of a professional staff to an external bureaucracy rather than indigenous community support further undermined the community efficacy potentially manifested by these organizations. As Israeli repression increasingly restricted the effective spheres of operation for these groups in the late 1980s, the nominally active NGOs and popular social groupings became even further detached from the local community. 'By 1991, many of these formerly popularly-based grass roots initiatives had become professionally based, foreign funded development centres which targeted clients as opposed to working with a constituency.'[109]

Known on the street as *dakakin,* (little shops), many (but by no means all or even most) NGOs issue reports almost exclusively in English and thus cannot be described as targeted for local consumption.[110] Israel's closure of universities in the OT exacerbated this tendency by pushing academics into the restricted job market.[111] The large number of unemployed law graduates may have played a role in swelling the ranks of the NGO community in Gaza as well.[112]

Fischer et al. note a high degree of duplication and waste among NGOs in the OT during the later stages of full-fledged Israeli occupation. There are many grant-dependent organizations, each struggling to find its own niche in the local society. They compete for limited external resources, and face a limited scope for community mobilization. The result has been the factionalization of aid organizations and even other structures such as chambers of commerce.[113] The proliferation of NGOs which seemed to have little real purpose or effect in the community encouraged the public to take a sceptical stance toward the effectiveness of these organizations.

At the same time, foreign donors were demanding that funded projects have a cross factional base and be tied to activities with measurable outcomes – i.e. not political mobilization. As local NGOs responded to the changing and often narrow priorities of donors, the effect was inconsistency and a distancing between organizations and specific constituencies within the community. With Oslo, many local NGOs in Gaza were existentially threatened as the funding priorities of donors shifted from the local NGOs to the PA. According to Sara Roy:

> The result has been a strong tendency among donors to fund mainstream Fatah institutions over institutional bodies affiliated with the political opposition and the nonaligned movement, these last categories including a large percentage of indigenous NGOs.

Roy argues that this raises a number of issues:

> First, if political affiliation is a key criteria of assistance, then development per se is subordinated to using such assistance as a means of promoting a specific kind of political order; development is not necessarily precluded but democratic practice is. Second, the funding of a party's political, economic and social infrastructure *prior* to elections could predetermine future events in a way that not only favours the chosen party, but the political and economic interests of the donor governments themselves. Thus, the donors, intentionally or otherwise, are playing on the contradictions between political parties in the Gaza Strip, fanning existing tensions and fuelling the fragmentation process. Third, if opposition groups are excluded from the funding calculus, then a significant segment of the Palestinian population will be cut off from the development process.[114]

In fact, it appears that Arafat is struggling to control the funding process not to promote development, but to micro-manage the process of PA consolidation.

The privileged 'inside space' of local elites and activists was thus threatened by the transition.[115] The NGOs responded collectively, asserting themselves as working on behalf of civil society to check any possible undemocratic tendencies within the PA.[116] As Hammami points out:

> … despite the fact that the Palestinians in the OT had always asserted the unity of the 'inside' and 'outside' and had actively thwarted all attempts by Israel and the US to nurture an alternative local leadership, the NGOs had a long experience of the Tunis leadership's authoritarian nature and its fear of independent initiatives. The impending arrival of the PNA and the seeming scramble of donors to support and strengthen it was, then, viewed in by many NGOs with outright suspicion … [The PNA] seemed to assume that most NGOs were its former clients, or were, at least, former loyalists who, now that the revolution had come home, would either join the PNA or simply whither away. What is clear is that the leadership from Tunis had little grasp of, or loyalty to, a group of institutions whose history was completely foreign to its own … [117]

Hammami argues, furthermore, that the inability of the NGOs to mobilize broad-based constituencies to collectively address crucial social and economic issues highlights the failure of the Palestinian left to stand up realistically to the challenges and potential dangers posed by the Oslo agreement. The external nature of almost all material support for such groups encouraged would-be civil society groupings in search of funding to take politically correct stances rather committing themselves to the needs of the communities in which they operated. With the notable exception of Hamas later on, civic organizations became institutions more engaged in the fight over limited external funds rather than seeking legitimacy within the population.

The aid dependency of Palestinian autonomy may force groups in society to respond to changing themes and slogans in the international aid establishment as opposed to dealing directly with problems on the ground. This tendency has led informed observers to comment that donors seem to be distributing aid without recognizing many of the complexities in Palestinian society.[118] Rather than organize to respond to pressures felt in the streets, aid-dependent 'grassroots' organizations may arise articulating needs so as to appeal to external sources of funding. Aid-based affiliations could contribute to the isolation of various groups in society and deflect pressures for accountability from the new Palestinian regime. If such a pattern emerges, it could condition civil society in such a way that it does not systematically engage authority in a constructive and defining dialogue within which national reconstitution might be understood. On the other hand, Arafat has been lobbying to control virtually all of the donor funding coming into the autonomous areas. The result is that he is able to manipulate the incentives for compliance this funding provides within particular social configurations. Many observers have noted the shortcomings of Arafat's management style in this regard,[119] and the NGO community in Gaza has vehemently protested against new legal restrictions on NGO activity put in place by the PA.[120]

However, the organizational culture of Gaza should itself share the blame for its vulnerable position. Most organizations in Gaza are, according to Roy, 'one person operations that work in relative isolation. They depend on one individual and, as is often the case, on that individual's political party.'[121] In many cases, this has meant that organizations are 'legitimized' – i.e. recognized as political players – through the dependency of a constituency rather than on through the provision of specific services. Even while some of these organizations and their chair-people have combined considerable success with political independence, weakness at the lower levels of the organizational structure make them more vulnerable to factional exploitation or PA co-optation if these strong personalities were to be, for whatever reason, unable to perform their duties. In general, the Gaza Strip is deprived of experienced and educated people to fill mid-level administrative functions. The entrenchment of these tendencies has left Gaza prone to dependent factional penetration at the expense of structural change and integration in Gaza political society

Conclusion

Some of the conditions conducive to factionalism have been described in this chapter and it has been suggested that factionalism represents a strategy of political control that seeks to bypass issues of development and social welfare. We have also seen how Gaza's historical social fragmentation greatly complicates the task of national reconstruction. Gazan society has been conditioned to respond to factional incentives as part of broader coping strategies in an environment which lacked political accountability. A social retreat into 'primary solidarity structures' was reinforced by the absence of effective state services, protection and mediation, as well as by a lack of employment opportunities.

From Arafat's perspective, perhaps the fragile balance of national unity which legitimated the PLO's transformation into the PA does not seem strong enough to withstand the potentially divisive impact of a concrete social agenda. As Arafat noted in an interview in 1970: 'We do not debate the structure of the new state in detail because what we need now is the greatest possible national unity.'[122] As we shall see in later chapters, it is questionable whether the powers transferred to the PA would allow Arafat to transcend this model and to initiate changes in ways that encourage a base for self sustained and integrated mobilization from below as well as from above. While Arafat has skilfully used the factional framework to sustain national identification against strong forces that were working actively against it, it remains to be seen whether it effectively represents the limit of his vision of political organization and mobilization.

From the perspective of the Palestinian street in Gaza, the structures of factionalism made sense as a refuge from the material uncertainties and the vagaries of power under an unaccountable occupation regime. These structures also offered clues as to the accepted boundaries for expressing frustration and rage. The danger today, however, is that the reinforcement of factionally-based coping structures under PA patronage only deflects attention away from the PA's inability to 'deliver the goods' of self-rule. Factional incentives in the new order are also ominous in that they preserve the status quo and personalize the intermediary linkages between the street and the state/authority. This means that PA elites are not held accountable to any broad-based civil or economic agenda. One can assume that these mediators – 'the tips of the factional icebergs' as it were – are in a position which inherently encourages them to take conservative responses, thus protecting their own relatively secure position in the status quo. Indeed, it might be argued that, like their traditional predecessors before 1948, today's Palestinian elites would feel more threatened than anything else by the rapid social mobilizations implied by structural change, economic development and national reconstitution.

The traditional clan-based social formations seem to be informing the new bases of factionalism in Gaza, as does a restructuring of some of the old PLO factional configurations around the patronage networks, tools and incentives established under current agreements. The security forces have been singled out as an example where this phenomenon seemed especially recognizable. However, more research is needed to understand exactly how these relationships are working; i.e. how the social structures are connected to the quasi-institutions of autonomy and exactly how patronage flows are (re)-shaping social structures.

It does seem clear, though, that Gaza society's inability to respond to these factional bases of control with more productive alternatives is rooted in the ability of elites to manipulate access to basic needs in order to encourage political compliance. Economic dependence has locked Gazans into reproducing and responding to structures which, while they meet short term needs, undermine the possibilities for change at the grassroots level. Elites manipulate these structures to ensure a hold on institutions of limited power, but they are of little use for initiating operative and integrated policy. By encouraging people to take sides based on notions other than interpretations of the law, elites can more easily pursue personal agendas without reference to the legally defined content and boundaries of state institutions.

In a situation of acute economic hardship and uncertainty, the ability to meet basic needs becomes dependent on political connections to those which have control over the apparatus of governing and thus of patronage. The same is true of personal security, which becomes contingent on support for the regime. The PA, with its control of the administrative apparatus of autonomy, has the ability to selectively empower individuals or groups in society, and through these linkages, cultivate dependent relations with those who are in a position to mediate further down the vertical structure of a fragmented society.[123] The effects might become particularly pronounced in a political unit such as Gaza, where so few alternatives exist.

The political conditionality of basic needs represents a strategy akin to 'divide and rule.' Its presence in Gaza is alarming because its success depends on undermining the kinds of structural change and developmental demands which if met, might enhance the position of Gazans in the long term. But in the short term, such change would threaten the position and the base of the regime itself, and call the results of the peace process into question. Accordingly, the regime has little incentive or ability to transcend what have been described here as neopatriarchal and neopatrimonial tactics of rule.

Making survival conditional upon political compliance offers a way for political elites to consolidate their position above society without reference to developmental concerns or a social agenda which they are either unable or unwilling to implement. A danger is that by pushing opposition outside of the framework of functioning institutions, a precondition of social superfluousness and potentially violent opposition to the new order manifests itself. There is no economic base upon which a political opposition could sustain itself, i.e. those in opposition to the established regime risk losing jobs and access to things like aid largesse or the intervention of administrative authority on their behalf.

'The decline of armed struggle as a legitimizing source of authority for the PLO, originally an allure of resistance groups, has called for new forms of legitimacy.'[124] However, given that factionalism is operating in an unsustainable environment of economic hardship, it epitomizes relations of external dependency. Edward Said has said that 'To become a nation in the formal sense of the word, a people must make itself into something more than a collection of tribes or political organizations of the kind that, since the 1967 war, Palestinians have created and supported.'[125] His observation is worth bearing in mind.

The PA – has yet to figure out how to create social cohesion in support of its authority in conditions of economic hardship now that the strategic anchor of nationalist resistance is all but traded away. If the new bases of factionalism in Gaza are indeed to consolidate and offer sustainable solidarity bonds, economic security, and trust in the relationship between authority and society, then we could perhaps identify within this a political economy of meaning. However, resistance to and fragmentation within the autonomy indicate that this is not the case. Furthermore, the dependency of the PA on external funding and goodwill to sustain itself mean that the ultimate sources of the power that might hold such a socially fragmented autonomy together are located externally to the society itself. While no state–society relationship exists in a vacuum, the degree of dependency here, given the lack of PA power and the imbalance of power between the PLO and Israel, is extreme. The particular institutions and boundaries of autonomy are diplomatic creations rather than a local expressions of political will.

The PLO/PA is torn between the old imperatives of maintaining nationalist unity and the need to address the concerns of those they suddenly govern. The dimensions of the territorial and social bases of Fatah are in a state of transitional disequilibrium, and leaders lack the scope of power and patronage to service both concerns at once. The division has also been made apparent in elections within the organization. In many cases, Arafat has simply voided election results which were not to his liking and replaced local Fatah activists with his cronies or with individuals he felt were better placed to maintain the types of connections that would allow Fatah to keep its position as a nationalist front.[126] In spite of the populist rhetoric inherent to nationalist movements, this demonstrates Arafat's basically elitist conception of the current possibilities.

Many observers tend either to romanticize the structural character of

Palestinian unity and national identity or to deny it all together.[127] Just as an awareness of historical factors in one context encouraged identification with the broad national movement, the new conditions created by more clearly defined space and responsibilities tend to heighten awareness of contradictions in the PA's expression and use of authority in Gaza. Incongruity between the demands of a nationalist movement and those of practical governance have proven difficult to cover up in practice.

As memory of the initial flurry of activity that sparked rebellion fades, and commitment to the original principles is forgotten, activism has tended to turn to opportunistic efforts to manipulate a baser version of what the logic of resistance promised to all. By the last years of the intifada, the civil society structures that seemed to have such promise in the earlier stages of the uprising had turned to competition over the creation and capture of constituencies, many of which were responding to signals from above rather than reflecting social realities from below. This chapter has suggested that the fundamental conditions upon which neopatriarchy and factionalism have rested were not transcended by the intifada, as many optimistic analyses of 'a new, modern leadership' seemed to argue, but have persisted and been re-consolidated within the limited scope of self rule. Now, once again, people and power in Gaza are acquiescing within a context of factionalism, coping listlessly in a changing order. To provide what social competition there is, social formations have emerged to fight over the trickle of funds coming into the territory – thus fighting over 'what is left of society rather than trying to build it.'[128]

3

Defining Palestine: The Spatial and Demographic Contradictions of 'Self-Rule'

The signing of the Oslo Accord in September 1993 announced a framework for transition toward Palestinian 'self-rule' in the occupied territories. Still unclear, however, was exactly how self-rule would be institutionally, demographically and spatially defined. Subsequent agreements have not gone much further in resolving these issues. The result is that 'new contradictions have arisen over the shape and structure of Palestinian society – issues long delayed by a movement preoccupied by the confrontation with Israel.'[1] Going further, Mahmoud Darwish asserts that rather than establishing a framework for peace, the agreement represents 'a breakup of Palestinian society and its interests.' He also exhorts the opposition to 'demonstrate that the terms of the accords are not the limitations of the Palestinian cause, or of Palestinian rights.'[2] In the context of the provisional regime, such sentiments – while they do represent legitimate and pressing concerns – inevitably create confusion.

Certainly, defining Palestine depends on determining borders and defining the relationship between people, land and governing institutions; it also, by extension, depends on which of the rights and aspirations traditionally articulated through the nationalist ideology are incorporated by the new political entity. It seems increasingly unlikely, for example, that the claims of diaspora refugees will be satisfactorily resolved (at least not from the perspective of the refugees themselves) within the context of 'final status' negotiations.[3] The demographically exclusive political processes initiated with Oslo thus threaten the inclusiveness of the nationalist ideology. This could produce a disorienting crisis in the national movement itself, and upset the building of a consensus around the emerging status quo on the inside.

Simultaneously, Israeli authorities have used their ability to unilaterally determine internal and external security prerogatives to isolate Palestinian communities in the OT not only from Israel, but also from each other.[4] Fragmentation within the practical boundaries of the autonomy complicates the consistent execution of PA functions, and hinders the processes of social communication that are necessary precursors to integrated and coherent social mobilization. Such contradictions, while not inherently irreconcilable over the longer trajectory of mobilization and national institution building, will prove difficult to resolve within the trajectory of the peace process as it now stands. Contrary to expectations associated with self-rule, autonomy may heighten rather than transcend points of tension and frustration in Palestinian society.

This chapter focuses on the tensions generated in Palestinian politics and society as an uncertain process toward national reconstruction in parts of the OT which threatens to establish new norms of national inclusion and exclusion. In addressing the theoretical problematics of spatial coherence and demographic inclusion as they relate to a functional polity, the chapter also lays a foundation for analysing practical issues that are empirically addressed in subsequent chapters.

Self-rule Inside and Out

The experiences of occupation and exile, and the feeling of having been deprived of an 'authentic' destiny, encouraged Palestinians to reflect on the relationships between their national identities and social rights. The experience of having actively imagined a world of civil rights and power, while countering the absence of such phenomena under occupation perhaps makes the mundane powerlessness associated with interim self-rule more difficult to bear. Now, quite suddenly, in a move from above that society was in many important respects neither psychologically or practically prepared for, some of the socio-historical, political, and economic bases for Palestinian relationships with the national movement and for relationships with various NGOs have been pulled out from under many Palestinians. Together with Arafat, the centre of gravity in Palestinian politics has come to rest in Gaza, and the time has thus come when it is necessary to define what a Palestinian state might look like in practice. Palestinians are accordingly forced to deal with the differences in their experiences as they reflect different concerns and ideas about the exercise of power.

However, rather than resolving the relationship between Palestinianism as a mobilizing ideology and any legal or political regime, limited autonomy has rendered the situation more complex. The act of formally accepting the minimum aims of the movement – thus contracting its social and ideological meaning – has resulted in the alienation of many in the diaspora. At the same time, the PLO seems unable to procure through negotiations the powers which would enable the PA to make the current transition a meaningful experience for Palestinians on the 'inside' by consolidating national institutions and protecting basic economic and political rights. Hanan Ashrawi has argued that 'it is not who makes the agreement but what's in it' that determines its legitimacy.[5] Interestingly, this can refer to the human cartography of the agreement – the people who are 'in' the agreement and are most directly affected by it – as well as to the diplomatic and legal content of the agreement. The autonomy has certainly brought to the fore tensions which were traditionally apparent in 'inside/outside' cleavage in Palestinian politics.

As Abu-Amr has noted, Palestinian society on the inside has 'its own dynamics, norms and priorities' which might not coincide immediately and directly with those of diaspora nationalist leaders.[6] In general, 'insiders' have tended to be more willing to accept the minimal aims of national liberation – the end of Israeli occupation over the lands captured in the 1967 war. Still having interests to protect on the ground in Palestine, they were more likely to organize to do so. On the other hand, the politics of the diaspora was one of an appeal to militancy. 'For nearly two decades the PLO leadership has developed a style of work based on the logic of revolution and the diaspora, a logic that might be totally different than the logic of statebuilding and civil society. Reconciling the two logics represents a great challenge.'[7] While recognizing the PLO leadership, the agreement distracts the PLO from its foundational purpose – actively asserting and fighting on behalf of the historical claims of Palestinian refugees of 1948. It takes an essentially diaspora movement and grants it authority over the very portion of the Palestinian community least represented in its upper echelons, while at the same time threatening its claims to represent the interests of its traditional constituency.

'Insiders,' those who lived in the OT during occupation, resent the degree to which PA institutions have been staffed by a small clique of well positioned 'outsiders.' They see the PA being used to promote the interests of a largely 'outside' diaspora elite, often at the expense of addressing the needs of constituencies currently subject to its administration. Husam Khader, a member of the Palestinian Legislative

Council from Nablus, has given a blunt indictment of the PA elite: 'They cut up the pie among themselves. The Palestinian leaders thought that our economy was some sort of inheritance due to them and their children.'[8] The formulas brought to bear in holding together a national movement in exile – the quota system for example – are being challenged by leaders on the inside as they are applied to PA consolidation in the OT. These formula are challenged because insiders have been historically alienated from these structures and have no interest in seeing them dominate, and because 'demands are on the rise for democracy, accountability, and the rule of law within a parliamentary system that allows individuals to express their views with impunity.'[9] Interestingly, since the PA has cracked down on internal political opposition, many of the groupings who were performing civil functions during the intifada – particularly Hamas – have moved their political structure 'outside.'

'Insiders' have also complained about the style of those who have come back to assume power. Gazans speak of the conspicuous consumption amidst the general hardship. As one Palestinian in Gaza told the author, 'the outsiders are not happy here either, there is little for them to do compared to life in Paris, Cairo or Beirut, and their wives are upset about not being able to wear their new bathing suits on the beach.'[10] Lindholm Schulz has neatly summarized the several of the main points:

> 'Insiders' frequently use the term 'Tunis mentality,' referring to the PLO style of politics, and argued that the 'inside' experience was more democratic as opposed to the militarized outside. 'Outsiders were, [given] their experiences in the Arab world, perceived as less democratic. 'Inside-outside' also [reflected] another pair of perceived dichotomies, i.e. militarized/revolutionary-civil structures. The PLO in the 'outside' moved its militarized structure 'inside', whereas the 'inside' has had to rely more on civil structures, family influence, professionals, etc.[11]

The PA's detractors point out that current agreements represent a challenge to the social and spatial inclusiveness of the Palestinian nationalist ideology and structures. There is no longer any clear object of resistance – no authority with clear responsibility for economic and social hardships – and thus an important tool for social mobilization and carving out the awareness of unity has been blunted. On one level, the fragmentation in political mobilization and national solidarity can be expressed in terms of identity.[12] Palestinian sociologist Aziz Haydar argues that new ethnic cleavages have beeen brought to the fore in Palestinian society since Oslo. According to one Palestinian activist:

... we feel that our identity is threatened now, because you talk about Palestinians in Gaza, Palestinians in Jericho, Palestinians outside, Palestinians in the West Bank, whatever. So all these identities in the past [that were grounded in our resistance to] the Israelis [now face a 'settled' reality]. We have no enemy any more. And now when we try to talk about different issues, problems with identity emerge. Palestinians in Lebanon are different from those in Syria or Jordan, and we feel that our identity is in real danger.[13]

The effective space of the PLO – which could be said to extend in some material or symbolic way to almost every Palestinian constituency – has now been reduced to parts of the OT. The contraction of space implies a correspondingly greater specificity of political problems. The existence of the PA demands increased scrutiny from those who are asked to accept and identify with the new regime. By putting itself in the position of being accountable for the socio-economic situation in Gaza, the Fatah-based leadership of both the PLO and the PA has increasingly become a target of local discontent. Still, however, there is confusion on the ground as to who represents Palestinians and who bears responsibility for conditions on the ground. One poll suggests that 18.1 per cent of Palestinians in the OT feel that the PA is the legitimate representative of the Palestinian people, 25.3 per cent feel that the PLO holds this distinction exclusively, 38.2 per cent feel that the PLO and PA hold this distinction simultaneously, while 18.4 per cent either did not know or had no opinion.[14] Just as people on the ground also have conflicting opinions about which institution is responsible for the other,[15] the nationalist elite appear caught in the increasingly tangled organizational boundaries between the PA and the PLO, and are sometimes pulled in conflicting directions by the distinct organizational interests of these two bodies. But the PLO, which no longer able to effectively represent its traditional constituency, is still the official partner in negotiations, and not the PA, which is responsible for administering the accords in the self-rule areas. One potential consequence of this arrangement is that the PLO can still reject the agreement, thus ironically delegitimize the PA which will almost certainly be left in Gaza as Israel is unlikely to reoccupy militarily. This would, however, leave any remaining Palestinian political authority utterly ineffectual and dependent. The PA leadership operates under potentially contradictory conditions of accountability.

Given the lack of a clear social agenda and the present failure of the leftist factions to articulate an effective opposition strategy to the Fatah-based PLO and PA leaderships, 'the dangers confronting the Palestinian people (both in Palestine and in the diaspora) derive immediately from the rapid erosion of the PLO's mass-based legitimacy and its integrative and identity forming functions.'[16] The agreement recognized the PLO while simultaneously undermining its claim to represent the interests of its traditional constituency (at least in the short term) and giving it responsibility for a geographical constituency within the Palestinian human geography with which it had weak institutional and economic links. In one sense, it might be argued that the PA's most important new constituency is the international community. But, as Hanan Ashrawi has stated, 'what benefits a leader if he gains the whole world and loses credibility with his own people? Your own constituency is your source of legitimacy and strength.'[17] It is precisely this problem of finding a Palestinian constituency which is visibly served – or finding ways of servicing a particularly influential mass constituency – within the context of the provisional regime which has been the most pressing challenge facing the PA. The lack of a self-sustaining mass-based PA constituency within Gaza is symptomatic of a malaise underlying the current provisional regime.

The PLO has continued to try to resolve this contradiction by constructing a situation in which it rationalizes its own authority by becoming its own constituency. The PLO and the PA continue to keep up the distinction between themselves in order to confer upon each other mutual legitimacy. 'The PLO continues to say that it is the reference point, but at the same time it is the government. In other words, it is its own reference. This is a juridical ruse which fools no one.'[18] However, a new dynamic of inclusion and exclusion has emerged which is associated with concrete and territorially-based institutions of limited autonomy. 'With the agreement, factional hostilities have become more divisive: now there is something to fight about.'[19] Issues which were once easily assimilated into the politics of national unity and resistance now engender different responses to the conditions – the material and ideological implications – of a new order.

Since the signing of the agreement, the mediatory structure of Fatah has broken down and the movement seems to lack the organizational discipline, the incentives or the will to pursue the objectives of social order and economic development beyond what is needed to simply hold power. It has become a rather random collection of sub-factions lacking in any common socio-ideological commitments. Just as Fatah's control of PLO funds ensured that it became an arena for personal ambitions, Fatah's pre-eminent position in the PA ensures that it will continue to serve as a primary arena for petty politics and ambition. The signing of the accord has exacerbated a sub-factional tendency within Fatah that has been increasing in significance since the 1982 débâcle in Lebanon. Within the autonomy, three Fatah groupings have distinguished themselves; the patronage provided by Arafat seem to be all that maintains Fatah's nominal unity. Al-Jarbawi notes that:

> The first [group] includes Fatah returnees who preached and practised armed struggle during the years of exile. The second represents the new Fatah leadership inside Palestine, men who gained prominence during the intifada and who believed that, having faced imprisonment and expulsion, they should now have priority within the movement by virtue of their knowledge of the situation on the ground. The third group, on the fringes of the movement, comprises intellectuals and businessmen ... It should be noted that these groups are divided and weak, opening the door for possible cross alliances among elements of these three groups.[20]

Given that the PA is basically seen as a Fatah institution, and the peace process as a Fatah project, the disarray within the movement has a definite impact on self-rule institutions. The institutions that should regulate the transition are weak, inefficient or non-existent and there are real concerns about the readiness and ability of the PLO elites to build the kind of responsive governing institutions that are needed to develop a healthy economy and civil society. This may reflect that the fact that civil society structures which emerged during the intifada, and the PLO's linkages to them, were more tenuous than first thought. Chapter 2 suggested that, at the very least, they had started responding more to pressures and incentives from above rather than the organizational potential of constituencies facing common pressures from below. Haydar Abd al-Shafi argues that one of the worst underlying features of the agreement is that 'it was adopted before establishing unity, so it actually deepened the disarray among the Palestinians.'[21]

An indication of the serious nature of the Palestinian political crisis is the failure of an opposition to offer specific alternatives to the status quo. Fouad Moughrabi has indicted the opposition for its failure to articulate a 'politics of detail.'[22] Tts concern with grand gesture and statement may have visceral appeal, but does not really service the needs of any constituency or generate viable political projects. Its failure to articulate an alternative vision for governing and dealing directly with social issues reflects the lack of real options available to the Palestinian leadership. The left-wing factions also suffer from the lack of contestable powers and thus the inability to serve a constituency.

Khalil Shikaki has noted the effect that rituals of nation building on the 'inside' might have on the 'outside' Palestinian community:

> Although replacing the PLO [in line with Israel's historic attempts to create an 'inside' alternative to the PLO] is no longer an issue, elections [in the OT] serve a related Israeli goal: to focus Palestinian energies on the inside and its agendas, that is, independence, thus marginalizing the Palestinian diaspora and its agendas, such as the right of return.[23]

Zureik has reported on the post-Oslo disenchantment of diaspora refugees with the PLO, and reviewed the factors which fuel it. Primary among them are the breakdown of PLO sponsored services and benefits and, most importantly, a feeling that their right of return will not be implemented in the context of a 'final status.'[24]

Uncertainty surrounding the final status of national boundaries and rights is also a source of great Palestinian anxiety on the 'inside.' Shikaki again:

> ... the peace process has had a negative impact on national reconstruction by leaving unresolved major issues of the conflict, including the future of Arab Jerusalem, the Jewish settlements, and the Palestinian refugees, to say nothing of the question of sovereignty over the land and the nature of the Palestinian political entity. Deferral of these issues to future negotiations has created serious defects in the state building process and deepened Palestinian divisions regarding the Palestinian political order and the consensus on which it was built.[25]

Another Palestinian notes:

> The agreement is very clear ... it deals with part of the Palestinian people. It does not talk about the Palestinians as a nation, as *a* people. Fragmentation is the starting point. Nobody recognizes the existence of the Palestinian refugees. The agreement does not deal with territory, with the land; the land is separated from the people.[26]

One way in which disillusionment with the interim order has revealed itself is as a breakdown in the consensus over the content and symbols of Palestinian nationalism. Jamil Hilal notes that 'the historic irony entailed in the Oslo Accord is that, while it acknowledged the PLO as the legitimate representative of the Palestinian people ... it rejected the Palestinian's right to self determination as defined by hundreds of UN resolutions.'[27] It was, after all, this right which the traditional symbols of Palestinian nationalism represented. Political symbols gain their meaning from the way that they connect people, power, and institutions to suggest solutions to problems and represent consensus. The new order faces a very real challenge in sustaining these connections. According to one informant:

> Before Oslo, I identified myself strongly as a Palestinian. These days, I feel more Jordanian. I don't like the way our leadership handled our cause. I feel screwed ... sold out. In the place of dreams and values, we have this silly agreement. I do not feel much national pride.[28]

Salim Tamari, documenting the 'fluctuating state of Palestinian national identity' by analysing its symbolic manifestations in the street, reports that:

> aside from the PNA, no single party uses the [Palestinian] flag as its own banner ... the variety of articulations and uses that [national] symbols have gone through in the short period between the Oslo Accord of September 1993 and the establishment of a Palestinian authority in Gaza and Jericho in the summer of 1994 – less than a year – are baffling.[29]

At one end, the withdrawal from nationalist institutions is compensated by the turn to Islamism (discussed in greater detail in Chapter 6) – an ideology which denies or at least subordinates national liberation and unity to an appeal to Islamic liberation and unity. It offers an extreme outlet for frustration – martyrdom – a phenomenon which has become more rather than less prominent since the signing of the Oslo Accords and speaks of the desperation of many in the OT who feel disoriented and betrayed by the current regime. In practice, however, the nationalist and populist content of Palestinian Islamism has become more prominent since 1993.

Beyond the disintegrating impact of this inside–outside divide on the inclusive ideology of Palestinianism, spatial and affinal cleavages are also becoming more difficult to overlook within the OT, where a complex patchwork of varying jurisdictions and varying degrees of political autonomy mean that Palestinians are experiencing self rule differently, even within the 'autonomous areas.' Power relations and state building are indeed being initiated with an unclear relationship to territory. A United Nations official told the author in January 1996 that in his opinion the process was leading toward the creation of a Palestinian state, but added that, realistically, Palestinians should not expect sovereignty over any part of Jerusalem in the final status.[30] But can there be a Palestinian state that does not include sovereignty over East Jerusalem? Perhaps the international community could recognize the autonomy of such a Palestinian entity and perhaps even the PA, but would the Palestinians street? [31] A poll taken in December 1996 offers even further confirmation of this: 85 per cent of Palestinians in the OT rejected the idea of Jerusalem as the united capital of Israel entirely under Israeli sovereignty, even if the Palestinians were allowed to establish a capital at Abu Dis, on the outskirts of the city. Interestingly, Gazans were more adamant about this than West Bankers.[32]

In spite of assurances in the Declaration of Principles (DoP) that the integrity of the West Bank and Gaza Strip as a single territorial unit would be preserved, Israel continues to regularly restrict and prevent access between and within Gaza and the West Bank. More abstract factors reinforce this divide. For example, while Gazan schools focus on the teaching of Egyptian history, West Bank schools teach Jordanian history.

The overall effect of all this has been to give new-found meaning and urgency to the distinction between the 'inside' and 'outside' constituencies in Palestinian society and politics. The potential tension between 'outside' diaspora Palestinian forces and those who lived under Israeli occupation exposes the spatial contradictions between the nationalist movement and the goal of establishing a Palestinian state in part of mandate Palestine. As indicated above, the tension results at least in part from the fact that the PA and the PLO have yet to determine just who and what is represented from within the new territories. For example, even after the Palestinian national elections of 20 January 1996, it is still the PLO and not the PA who are officially in charge of the negotiations. It is the PLO and not the PA that is responsible for relations with other countries and international organizations. Furthermore, the Palestinian Legislative Council (PLC) which was elected at that time has been subsumed within the larger Palestinian National Council (PNC).

Thus Palestinians living within the OT could quickly find themselves hostage to diaspora interests, or, alternatively, the PLO could find itself irrelevant to the popular concerns of diaspora communities and gatherings while it is powerless to effect meaningful improvements in the quality of life in the OT using the framework of the Oslo Accords. Conflicting 'inside' and 'outside' perceptions of what the provisional regime's makeup should represent were noticeable within the framework of the elections. As Arafat sought to replicate the nationalist front – giving the most privileged positions to Fatah loyalists – resentment was created as many local leaders and prominent activists were forced out of the running.[33] Fatah's tight control over the campaign process, including the task of formally announcing the results, produced many irregularities. The people of Gaza were fully aware that the elections contested a limited array of symbols rather than substance (see Chapter 5).

A major question that remains is whether PA elites will be able to unite the Palestinian community around the provisional regime established by the Oslo Accords. To do this, they will have to transcend a basic political contradiction: they risk becoming an entrenched elite without a mass based political constituency. Indeed, the PA's most important constituency during the provisional period is external to Palestinian society. Put more bluntly, Israel is the constituency which grants the PA its immediate power. The international donors, who provide the patronage which sustains the passivity and withdrawal of the Palestinian population in the face of the new order's obvious economic inadequacies, craft loyalties based on dependence, which in turn are used to consolidate PA rule. By signing the Oslo Accords, the Fatah elite has weakened its claim to represent the rights and aspirations of diaspora Palestinians and has at the same time taken responsibility for a population without being granted the powers to address most of the immediate challenges facing the Palestinian community under occupation. It now has a constituency to which it is legally bound, and can less afford to bounce around various Palestinian communities to seek its alliances of the moment.

Palestinian economist George Abed, poignantly states that 'a Palestinian leadership that has unilaterally reduced its mission of national liberation to that of limited self rule has no right to fail in this more limited endeavour. Such failure would be catastrophic for the Palestinian people.'[34] He argues that there is a responsibility to succeed in the process as established so that success might provide the foundation for the next step and warns that it is perhaps better to make improvements in peoples lives than merely accept all the trappings of sovereignty in an environment and with effective situations which render them practically ineffectual or corrupt.[35]

Willy-nilly, regardless of any shortcomings in the current model of self-rule, there may prove to be no turning back from a trajectory founded on some kind of PA-based autonomy. Therefore it is within this framework that these contradictions must be resolved. This is especially true for Gaza as it is unlikely that Israel would choose to reoccupy the territory militarily regardless of future political developments. As Haydar Abd al-Shafi notes: 'As to some people's fears that a suspension could lead to Israel's return to Gaza, I think we can discount those. They were so eager to leave that I don't think they would come back even if invited.'[36] This means that most of the problems brought up by this study must be addressed with reference to some form and degree of Palestinian autonomy. As Birzeit philosopher Azmi Bishara has argued:

> The question now is not 'Oslo: yes or no?' The question is 'Oslo, now what?' This is the question people want addressed by their leaders. The PNA cannot answer it because the PNA is no longer the PLO. And the opposition can't answer it because they have yet to realize that the demise of the PLO is also their demise. They have to acknowledge this. They have to admit that they were complicit in a structure of politics that led to Oslo, no less than Arafat. But self-criticism that is not accompanied by constructive criticism as to what should now be done ceases to be self-criticism; it becomes self destruction.[37]

The future existence of the PLO/PA now largely depends on stabilizing and securing the interests of a specific community. If the objective remains some vision of absolute unity beneath the nationalist umbrella as represented by ideology and personalities rather than nation-state institutions, the PA must define its constituency in such a way that it does not simultaneously alienate others. It no longer seems to have the tools or the looseness of operation and responsibility that might allow it to perform this task, which requires the establishment of boundaries and effective institutions with consistent meanings throughout the Palestinian social space.

Spatial Variations of Authority and the Human Geography of Meaning

As Izhak Schnell has concluded, '(I)t is difficult for a social group to devise acceptable systems of identity and territoriality without a meaningful political base.'[38] This is so at least partly because political identities reflect the search for solutions to fundamental human problems. People must furthermore relate those solutions effectively to the places where they live, and also to sources and expressions of power capable of influencing the political and economic processes which most immediately affect their lives. The Palestinian case might demonstrate that when systems of identity and territoriality *have* been devised without reference to sovereign control over a specific territory and its inhabitants, the acquisition of rights (albeit limited rights) within a territory that includes only part of the previous constituency might induce processes of disintegration within the existing system of group cohesion. Furthermore, the current agreement has not adequately promoted consistency in the Palestinian relationship with political power, accountability and regulation within the autonomous areas. This complicates efforts at concerted and united political mobilization by Palestinians as they try to adapt to and affect the trajectories of the peace process and interim autonomy.

Ian Lustick has argued that 'variation in the shape of states is politically consequential.'[39] This insight is extremely valuable as we investigate the implications of the transition of the Palestinian nationalist movement from the vague conceptual and social spaces of national dispersal to a space which seems more specific, but remains far from conclusively defined. Lustick coins the phrase 'regime threshold' to describe situations in which a shift in the spatial identity or fundamental constituency of the state threatens not only specific governing administrations, but also the fundamental national institutions they inhabit. He also discusses the notion of ideological hegemony, referring to the problem of resolving one's commitments to a particular constituency without undermining the consensus upon which a state rests.

Inevitably, socio-political clarity requires some sort of criteria for establishing boundaries. This seems true for both tribe and state as well as for the notions of political autonomy or 'self-rule.' Democratic mobilization in particular requires clear boundaries and definitions: boundaries between individuals and institutional authority; boundaries of demographic inclusion and exclusion; ecological boundaries which make clear what is contestable in terms of regulation and allocation of the environment and its resources; and, finally, these boundaries must define who is permitted to contest power. If two people in different cities, for example, are to find ways of approaching these problems in common, they must share participation in institutions, and these institutions must be able to regulate, initiate and enforce in meaningful ways consistently across space.

The sudden shift 'from above' in the objective base – the human and territorial geography – of Palestinian politics creates new expectations and tensions. It suggests new interpretations of the structures and symbols which had determined awareness of a Palestinian politics. A state is defined by its inclusion and exclusion of ideas, spaces and peoples; and by the institutions, social dynamic and powers which shape, mediate and manipulate social phenomena within geographically defined boundaries.[40] The national movement, on the other hand, was inclusive and easy to identify with – one need only be Palestinian. It might be argued that the absence of a previous experience of a Palestinian state has contributed to conflicting qualitative and quantitative understandings among Palestinians of what their state should look like. Certainly such an experience would have made it easier to reach a consensus over the spatial dimensions of any eventual national state and provide a precedent for the linking of various social structures and institutions to a state authority. But every state once existed for the first time, and conflict in the process of consolidation should neither be seen as abnormal or even undesirable in and of itself. More disturbing is that the current process of national reconstitution tries to delegitimize such conflict within Palestinian society.

The Trajectory of Inside–Outside Tensions

Before the late 1960s, most Palestinians saw the liberation of Palestine as tied to the success of Arab nationalism. Such an orientation did not deny a distinct Palestinian awareness, it merely reflected the need to chose from available ideological currents and face the daily facts of power in whichever Arab state Palestinians found themselves after 1948. As for Palestinians who still lived on the 'inside,' that is within the 1948 borders of mandate Palestine, Jordan pursued policies in the West Bank aimed at integrating and diluting a politicized Palestinian identity and promoting a Jordanian identity in its place. Gazans, on the other hand, were recognized by the Egyptian regime as Palestinians.

As Gaza and the West Bank were under the administration of Arab states, the inside/outside dichotomy as such was not a real issue amongst politically active Palestinians. This was of course to change with Israel's occupation of these territories in 1967, which led elites to think in terms of protecting their interests by demanding greater local autonomy, while the indigenous masses could now more easily identify their situation within the broader context of national liberation. In any case, the military weakness and lack of resolve of the Arab states had been dramatically exposed in the 1967 war and forced Palestinians to reconsider their faith in liberation at the hands of other Arab states. One Palestinian group, however, had from the beginning argued that Palestinian liberation depended not on Arab unity or salvation by any of the Arab powers, but rather on Palestinian unity – namely Fatah, headed by Yasser Arafat.[41] Fatah's penchant for dramatizing its militant stand and keeping itself in the limelight gave led to broad recognition of its aims and sympathy for its positions. Although Fatah's ascension to the leading role in the PLO was to provide it with broad possibilities, the new focus on Palestinianism faced a very real problem of identifying a political base from which to direct meaningful mobilization.

The idea of a Palestinian mini-state in the OT began to gain some ground among intellectuals and local notables in the years following Israeli occupation, yet the PLO 'devoted little of its time to gathering support in the OT and had no desire to see locals challenge [its] right to represent the Palestinian people.'[42] Interestingly, Arafat had previously been critical of the old Palestinian elite for not standing firmer in 1948 and establishing a mini-state in the West Bank and Gaza Strip that could be used as a base for mobilization against the Zionist state. However, Arafat's realization that his organization had no real linkages to or support within the OT during the late 1960s and early 1970s encouraged him to work against the initiatives of local elites within the OT who proposed reaching any kind of autonomy accord with the Israelis. Thus, a major reason for Fatah's failure to press for a mini-state in the OT during the initial years of Israeli occupation was the recognition that it had no base there.[43] The conflicting context within which these two groupings saw their immediate interests, and the need for people within the OT to protect immediate interests while not undermining their commitment to national unity, informed much of the dynamic of the inside/outside divide. After 1970, the combination of high visibility activism and a growing potential to distribute patronage in the OT encouraged 'inside' identification with the PLO, which increasingly became an ultimate reference point coordinating activities and interests associated with the Palestinian experience.

Leaders on the 'inside' became increasingly concerned about how the concentration of power in the hands of a small diaspora clique might affect the course of events in the OT. Several young leaders in the West Bank, for example, formed the Palestinian National Front which had as its aim to collectivize the leadership of the movement. Mainly composed of members of the communist party, they called for a greater emphasis on institution building in the OT. As Migdal and Kimmerling note:

> It gradually became more apparent that the Front more closely reflected the shape of events on the West Bank and in the Gaza Strip than it did the desires of the PNC or the PLO leadership. All of its local leaders publicly accepted the authority of the PLO, while quietly positioning themselves to influence its decision making and taking on increased autonomy. Their chief concern was reducing

the West Bank's utter dependence on the Israeli economy.[44]

In Gaza, Israeli authorities appointed the pro-Hashemite Rashad Shawa, a Palestinian citrus grower from a local notable family, to be mayor and form a municipal council in Gaza City in September of 1971. The council organized by Shawa consisted entirely of members of the local upper class, and represented an attempt by Israel to work through traditional structures to stabilize what up until that time had been a turbulent occupation of the Strip. Not surprisingly, nationalists condemned his acceptance, and the appointment found little popular support. As Roy notes, though, the de facto existence of a local municipal structure and the effective defeat of the resistance struggle (Israel had largely neutralized the PLA elements which had resisted Israeli occupation during the first three or four years after the 1967 war) marked the start of an age where 'political struggle began to challenge armed struggle as a tactical approach for confronting the occupation.'[45]

Soon, however, Arafat's fears that elements within the OT might bypass the PLO and negotiate a deal for autonomy – together with the brutal crackdown on PLO institutions in Jordan by Jordanian forces in 1970 ('Black September') – led him to reconsider the organization's opposition to the idea of an autonomous Palestinian entity in the OT. An official shift in PLO strategy came at the PNC (Palestinian National Council) session of 9 June 1974. Reflecting new found confidence in its ability to penetrate life in the OT – (a confidence due in no small measure to the influx of funds from the Gulf states after 1974)[46] – the organization called for a 'transitional' solution based on recognition of UN resolutions 242 and 338. This seemed to signal to the inhabitants of the OT that their interests were becoming more central to the aims of the Palestinian movement and represented a shift from just a year earlier when 100 local notables from the West Bank and Gaza Strip had petitioned the UN for local sovereignty over the heads of PLO leaders. The PLO leadership had responded negatively to this local initiative and undermined any local negotiations oriented toward an alignment of OT notables with the Hashemite monarchy in Jordan.[47] The new funding afforded an increased feeling of efficacy all around, but structures normally associated with a strong civic base for eventual self rule were not established.

In some ways, however, the new approach after 1974 signalled the beginnings of a possible contradiction in the movement: were the occupied territories to be seen as playing a supportive role in the broader context of a national struggle, or were they to be the central focus of struggle in a new strategy? If the latter, how would the interests of the diaspora Palestinians be represented in this new conception? Given i) the widespread popularity of the PLO throughout the 1970s; ii) the pragmatic realization that the current imbalance of power between the PLO and Israel made immediate resolution of problems unlikely, and iii) the PLO's geographical distance from accountability for conditions on the ground, such dilemmas were relatively easily dismissed at the time. In any case, although PLO politics generally did not respond to trends in the OT and did not develop a strategy to face them, the PLO's diplomatic and financial successes of the 1970s encouraged broad social identification with the nationalist leadership and its vaguely articulated strategy.

Exiled to Tunis after Israel's 1982 invasion of Lebanon, the PLO was increasingly distanced from its constituencies inside and out. Its ability to engage in the struggle against Israel in immediate ways was weakening. Even more ominously from the perspective of the institution and its bureaucracy, it was losing its grip on the claim to be the sole representative of Palestinian rights and claims. Concurrently, Palestinians in the OT were increasingly aware that any hopes for a just solution that depended on the military or diplomatic intervention of the PLO were at best unlikely. The inside/outside dichotomy in Palestinian politics was widening. The absence of representatives from the OT in the PLO's national institutions, (which in any case increasingly played only a partial and ineffectual role in the decision making process), suggested that 'inside' interests were systematically marginalized within national institutions:

> ... while true decision-making within the PLO does not take place within the national institutions, neither are these institutions as now constituted properly representative ... [when the Oslo Accords were signed] there [were] still no representatives from the occupied territories after nearly six years of the intifada and two years of Palestinian–Israeli negotiations.[48]

The intifada introduced a threat of transforming listeners into positive actors. It also brought home to the PLO leadership just how divorced they had become from events on the ground and the realities of life in the occupied territories. Long preoccupied with their position in Lebanon and with intra-Arab politics, the organization had ignored the possibilities for mass organization in the territories.[49] Resistance in the OT gained its special character from countering the structures and the limitations imposed under occupation with the creation of alternative networks and possibilities.[50] It thus represented the kind of autonomous civic initiative vis-à-vis state power that is perhaps crucial to the development of vibrant and effective civil society. Reacting to, and eventually co-opting, developments on the 'inside', the 'outside' leadership now sought to invest the sympathy gathered for Palestinian autonomy in world opinion by the events of the intifada into pressure for a negotiated settlement recognizing the PLO as a basis for self rule in the territories. The intifada seemed to offer a chance to revitalize the PLO and give it a new and more meaningful territorial base from which to influence the course of the Palestinian movement.

Although the uprising signalled that the inside had taken initiative in reformulating the nationalist discourse, the PLO leadership quickly manoeuvred to enforce its 'monological,' factionalized and top down control over Palestinian political activity using the carrot and stick combination of patronage and threats. Arafat charged one of the most widely respected Fatah leaders, Abu Jihad, with the task of organizing a Fatah base of participation and leadership within the intifada. The Unified National Command of the Uprising (UNCU) was soon established. Composed of the four main factions of the PLO together with the Islamic Jihad, it used communiqués to direct the daily activities of the intifada through a network of popular committees, strike committees, neighbourhood committees, and merchant committees.[51] According to Gowers and Walker, 'Wazir's [Abu Jihad's] word [was] law in the 400 towns, villages and hamlets in the OT. The people of the OT ... quickly transformed into a flexible mass movement with popular committees which could withstand arrests, pressure, etc.' The PLO patronized student organizations and openly encouraged people under their umbrella, seeking to 'provide infrastructure for the Palestinian movement at all levels.'[52]

The PLO declared Palestinian independence in November of 1988 (as King Hussein of Jordan gave up his long-standing claim on the West Bank). This move created considerable controversy within the territories about how to proceed with the uprising. Muslim Brotherhood sources in the OT, arguing that it would distract attention from confronting the Israelis and perhaps also worried that it would eventually lead to an erosion of their newly won prominence in the political life of the OT, described the 1988 PLO (PNC) declaration of a Palestinian state with itself as a kind of government in exile as a stab in the back of the intifada.[53] Certainly, the co-optation of inside activities by a leadership unaccountable to, or subject to, pressures on the ground distracted the focus of a nascent civil society in the OT that was mobilizing in response to specific concerns. Contact between Fatah and its activists in the OT was basically unidirectional – money went in, but little input or information came out. Loyalty was increasingly conditioned on payment. The PLO increasingly became, if not a one man show, at least the stage of the Fatah elite. According to one observer:

> The intifada [had] a paradoxical impact on the PLO. On the one hand, it strengthened its standing and influence, and as such, was an essential factor in persuading Israel to come to terms with the PLO. On the other hand, the intifada exposed the inflexibility of the PLO's organizational structure and bureaucratic style of leadership, thereby encouraging the rise of new political formations outside it, in direct challenge to its leadership in the OT.[54]

These developments had decisive impact on the relationship between the PLO and its diaspora constituencies. As Zureik points out:

> Official and non-official Palestinian approaches to the refugee issue in general and the right of return in particular have evolved from a rejection of anything short of full implementation of Resolution 194[[55]] to an adoption of an accommodating stance toward Israel. The crucial turning point in Palestinian thinking on this matter came in 1988 during the nineteenth session of the Palestinian National Council in Algiers … .this accommodating stance remains unacceptable to a segment of the Palestinian constituency and is far from being shared by the refugees themselves … .the Palestinians entered the multilateral discussions on refugees without any clear notion of how to reconcile their political objectives with the mandate [implied by participation in the peace process].[56]

The PLO and many of the Palestinian national institutions at the time of the signing of the Oslo Accords were self interested factional bureaucracies resistant to reform and democratic initiatives,[57] and were in obvious need of reform if they were to face the socio-economic contingencies of the OT. With the intifada came the realization that the OT might represent an increasingly dense, united and immobile demographic core of Palestinianism. But while the PLO seems to have recognized the political potential of this, especially as it related to its own institutional revitalization, the leadership may have failed to recognize the degree to which its own ongoing legitimacy would be related to its ability to ameliorate the conditions which had deteriorated dramatically during the last ten years of occupation. As Roy notes, the nationalist leaders

> ... have not [during any time of the occupation] addressed the importance of development and its critical relationship to political change, let alone [articulated] development strategies ... the Palestinians do not have a coherent development strategy for the occupied territories.[58]

In the diaspora, the PLO had a history of initiating national institutions that collapsed as the organization was forced from areas in which it had previously operated freely (Lebanon after 1982, Jordan after 1970, 1971, the Gulf after the second Gulf War). By the early 1990s, thoughtful commentators expressed open concern about the weak and increasingly irrelevant role of the PLO on Palestinian life. Hilal notes PLO ineffectiveness and mentions the overall decline of support for the PLO in the period leading up to the Oslo Agreement.[59] The fall out of the Gulf War had further exposed the PLO's dependence on external funding to keep its political front united. The loss of funds from the Gulf states 'undermined (the PLO's) ability to function effectively ... its position to defend Palestinian interests and perform 'government tasks' was considerably weakened.'[60] Furthermore, Andoni argues that the assassinations of Abu Jihad and Abu Iyad proved 'the extent to which the PLO in its present form depends on 'historic symbols' rather than institutions' to project identification and legitimacy with the PLO in the OT.[61] Largely through its patronage and its control over the recent mythology of nationalist legitimacy, Fatah made ostensible gains in Gaza during the uprising, recruiting in particular economically and socially frustrated young men and encouraging a militancy that was to prove counterproductive over the longer term (see Chapter 6). As Faisal Husseini noted, the Israelis were more afraid of peaceful demonstrations than they were of violent acts.[62] As of June 1991, approximately 60 per cent of the population of the West Bank favoured a confederation with Jordan, perhaps reflecting doubts over the real governing potential of PLO institutions.[63] This situation might be connected with issues raised by leaflets and memoranda circulated in July and August of 1991 which accused the PLO of 'corruption and inefficiency and personal aggrandizement at the expense of institutions.'[64]

At the same time, however, centralizing tendencies within Fatah could be discerned as it sought ways of entrenching itself further in the OT. By using the alternate 'Oslo channel,' for example, Fatah assumed a preeminent role in the peace negotiations at the expense of many local leaders. Factional violence in June of 1992 may have been in response to the increasingly urgent scramble for influence.

Members of the Palestinian People's Party [formerly the communists] led calls for the concentration of power in the OT. Concerns that this would lead to an alternative leadership were dismissed out of hand on the grounds that the alternative leadership slogan is an Israeli invention that had been seized upon as an excuse for not giving the occupied territories leadership its appropriate weight in Palestinian decision making.[65]

Kuttab documents the high-handedness of PLO leaders in their relationships with the non-PLO negotiators (mostly local leaders and activists).[66] At one point in the tenth round of the Madrid negotiations, the PLO insisted that the 'inside' leaders who represented it by proxy at the negotiations respond to an American proposal which insisted that any interim self-governing authority's jurisdiction cover 'functional areas' rather than territory.[67] The 'insiders' were outraged:

[Palestinian People's Party representative] Ghassan al-Khatib refused to attend the meeting with the US official, noting that the PLO statement had been sprung on the delegation at the last minute and not even discussed .... In an open letter to the Jerusalem daily *al-Quds* on 10 July (1992), Haydar Abd al-Shafi noted that, while he was not opposed to Chairman Arafat as the head of the collective leadership, he strongly believed that decisions should be made in a more collective and democratic fashion. And Hanan Ashrawi, generally supportive of the PLO position, stated that members of the delegation had a right to participate in the decision-making process.

Little information has been available to the Palestinians in the occupied territories as to the reasons for the PLO leadership's about turns, as when Tunis strongly denounces certain positions only to accept later the very positions it had publicly opposed. A number of explanatory hypothesis have been offered by analysts and even members of the delegation, including: U.S. pressure on the PLO via Arab countries, especially Egypt; the continuing delay in the Gulf countries' release of funds to the PLO; fear of Israeli assassination attempts on top PLO leaders if they refuse to soften their positions; and promises of PLO-Israeli meetings.[68]

PLO concerns that the track of negotiations sponsored by the United States might lead to an alternative leadership in the OT encouraged it to accept many concessions in secret talks under Norwegian auspices. According to Hanan Ashrawi, who like her fellow negotiators was unaware of the secret talks in Oslo, the Palestinian delegates to the Washington and Madrid negotiations advised Arafat to keep the same delegation once the PLO had achieved recognition at the talks in order to utilize their expertise and experience at dealing with the Israelis. 'But that was not to be. With recognition later came a whole overhaul of the 'inside' Palestinians and an attempt at reinventing the negotiations wheel.'[69] The underlying suggestion is that Arafat loyalists in Tunis were getting increasingly afraid that they would be bypassed if the Washington negotiations led to anything substantial. Rather than wait for eventual recognition under the formal process, they went underground and sought a deal that would recognize the PLO with its diaspora structure as the basis for a provisional authority in a new relationship between Israel and Palestinians.

The intifada widened the popular base of participation and decision making at the grassroots level in the OT; but the concurrent shrinkage of the PLO base in the diaspora had transformed the PLO structures into political fronts with little independence or popular organizational base. Between 1991 and 1996, there have been few convenings of the consultative national councils and committees as called for by the PLO charter, and Arafat has increasingly monopolized his control over the purse-strings of the movement and alienated many factions and prominent individuals within the PLO. Although the PLO had changed its strategy, its institutions and structures were not reformed. The factionalism and bureaucratic structure of the PLO institutions had a very negative effect on the popular resistance councils of the intifada, onto which the PLO tried to graft its own structure and agenda.[70] In 1991 the PLO was as visible in the OT as it had ever been, but the local rank and file of the various factions held only tenuous links to their respective leaderships.[71] The massive defection of these young activists and militants from the Fatah ranks since the autonomy suggests that while Fatah was able to mobilize through its patronage and mystique, it was not able to or willing to create self-sustainable grassroots structures. In fact, many of these younger activists were stricken from Fatah preliminary lists before the January 1996 elections in favour of Arafat cronies, in spite of overwhelming local support.[72] According to one local candidate, 'The Fatah independents yearn for democracy more than the official Fatah candidates. If we win, it is a sign that we are the real Fatah representatives.'[73]

Indeed, Ashrawi states that when she first saw the Declaration of Principles that were at the heart of the Oslo Accord, her 'first reaction was one of shock. 'Its clear that the ones who signed this agreement have not lived under occupation."[74] The conclusion reached by many inside leaders was that the diaspora PLO elites had been naive, hasty and perhaps self interested in seeking to get something for themselves at the expense of the stated goals of negotiations. Many of the responsibilities turned over to Palestinians had already been administered by Palestinians under the Civil Administration. Now, the functions might simply go from Palestinians on the inside to those from outside. The tactical imperative of forcing Israeli recognition of the PLO as the legitimate representative of the Palestinian people seems to have been taken to the level of final strategy. PLO interests and the interests of Palestinian communities living in the OT were conflated in the abstract upper echelons of nationalist and, eventually, diplomatic thinking.

Observations on developments within the Palestinian Trade Union movement in recent years provide an interesting case study of the 'inside/outside' dynamic in practice. Labour union activity had increased dramatically after the 1967 war, but 'more as a vehicle for national unity than of class struggle.' Still, 'the trade unions, with their highly democratic settings and generally fair elections – at least until Fatah's effort to control their activities – were models for a common effort transcending family and other ties. They also served as excellent schools for local and regional leadership.' As union rolls grew, internal conflict, particularly between Fatah and the Communists, increased. 'At stake was not only who would have his hands on the levers of power in society but also the distribution of funds provided by Arab states as a result of the 1979 Baghdad conference.'[75]

The labour union movement in the OT – the Palestinian General Trade Union Federation (GTUF) – was organized according to faction rather than sector or district. This reflected its general attachment to outside sources of patronage rather than any specific internal contingency. Furthermore, 'the GTUF has no definition of a member, no membership records, and no occupational base'[76] – hardly conditions conducive to internal accountability. According to Moustafa Barghouti, 'the union movement regressed because none of its leaders were even interested in their own union's constituency.'[77] In fact, Roy reports that Gaza's seven trade unions claimed only 500 members, or less than 1 per cent of domestic labour.[78] Such an observation would seem to justify a re-evaluation of the indigenous civil society structures that were supposed to inform the transition and guard against repressivene new institutions.

In spite of the effective irrelevance of the trade unions as a representative of civil society in Gaza, their history since the signing of the Oslo Accords illustrates the problematic nature of superimposing the PLO bureaucratic institutions on the structures which supposedly represented labour interests in the OT. According to Usher,

... there was the problem of amalgamating the GTUF with its counterpart in Tunis, the PLO's General Union of Palestinian workers (GUPW). For the GUPW's general secretary Haidar Ibrahim, Oslo necessitated the fusion of the two wings of Palestinian trade unionism. His notion of fusion, however, looks like a takeover. Of the GUPW's 19-seat executive, he allocated only two places for representatives from the occupied territories: one for Gaza's GTUF General Secretary Rasem Bayari and the other for West Bank General Secretary Shaher Said. Palestinian unions 'inside' flatly refused the deal. The International Labour Organization (ILO) insisted that it could only deal with 'elected' representatives from the territories, not appointees from Tunis. The result is an ongoing turf war between the 'outside' and the 'inside.'[79]

The withdrawal of financial assistance from the Gulf States in the summer of 1990 perhaps increased pressure on the bureaucratic survival instincts of the PLO, and the leadership sought to find itself a new framework within which to secure its external funding and its pre-eminence in defining the boundaries of the national struggle – hence its participation in the peace-process. Throughout the Madrid round of negotiations, and after an accord was reached through the back-door Oslo channel, most people in the OT were willing to take the position that the PLO – rotten though it might be – was still the political leadership and the only party capable of representing collective Palestinian interests in negotiations. From other perspectives, however, it seemed that it was the PLO's willingness to 'sell out' that encouraged Israel's sudden acceptance of it as a negotiating partner.[80] In spite of the limitations of the agreement signed in Washington, the promises made by Fatah elites upon their arrival in Gaza show that they realized that their legitimacy was on their ability to deliver economic improvements and strike a balance between compromise and historic national claims. However, evidence was now mounting that in the OT, and particularly in Gaza, identification with the broad PLO cause, as well as some of its 'heroic' figures, was and is stronger than faith in its institutions. This lack of faith may be proving justified. At the time of the signing of the Oslo Accords, the PLO was in the worst position financially and politically that it had ever been. One observer concludes that:

Israel rescued the PLO, gave it a *raison d'être.* After the Gulf War, the destiny of the PLO had appeared clear. It was a disintegrating bureaucracy in Tunis without money. Its only aim was survival, and its only claim was that it represented Palestinians ... Israel's recognition re-conferred on the PLO the international status it had steadily lost since 1982 and particularly after the Gulf war.[81]

The Inside-Outside Divide and the Peace Process: Three Scenarios

In spite of the creation of an internationally-sponsored Refugee Working Group (RWG) during the Madrid round of peace negotiations, current Palestinian–Israeli agreements make no operative mention of the status of the refugees.[82] According to evidence presented by Zureik, involvement of the refugees in the current negotiations was not only blocked by Israel, but by the refugees themselves. The latter felt that by signing the DoP, the PLO was marginalizing their interests within the peace process.[83] A failure of the 'final-status' negotiations to resolve the status of the four million or so Palestinian refugees would risk entrenching two distinct Palestinian constituencies – an 'inside' grouping and an 'outside' grouping.[84] The 'final-status' of the refugees not only holds implications for Palestinian socio-political development – what would be the impact of a massive influx of refugees to the OT or, if refugees claims are ignored, how would the formation of an alternative PLO impact ideology and politics in the OT? – but also for the viability of any 'final-status' as well as the stability of the region as a whole.

The prospect of Israel allowing a significant number of 1948 refugees to return within it borders is, to say the least, highly unlikely. Accordingly, regardless of the outcome of final-status talks, dissatisfaction within this community might remain a potential source of instability. This is especially so as the rights and freedoms of the refugees in many Arab states, and particularly in Lebanon, can only be described as limited and vulnerable. Indeed, if there is one issue uniting the various factions of confessional politics in Lebanon, it is resistance to the notion of integrating the Palestinian refugees. There are many possible scenarios for how this dilemma might play itself out. Three are offered below. These are not intended as definitive, but rather as starting points for thought and discussion, and as ways of illustrating how this problem relates to the issues raised generally in this study.

Refugees in the case of full implementation of a 242/338 based final-status:[85] self determination v. right of return

The ostensible aim of the PLO decision to recognize the state of Israel and call for the creation of a Palestinian homeland in the West Bank and Gaza Strip was to achieve 'self-determination' and formal recognition for the Palestinian people. While not necessarily prejudicing issues of compensation for properties lost in 1948, the creation of such a homeland would demand a compromise on the issue of whether refugees could be allowed to exercise their right to return to areas within Israel proper. If seen in terms of the right of self-determination, this 'right of return' could be reduced to a right of all Palestinians to return to a newly established Palestinian homeland in the OT.

At present, however, a scenario based on operative Palestinian sovereignty in the West Bank and Gaza Strip appears unlikely. Moreover, such a compromise could even undermine the PA's position within the OT. Polls conducted in December 1996 show that 85.6 per cent of Gazans feel that a final-status should guarantee the right of refugees to return to homes they were forced to leave in 1948, while only 11.1 per cent agreed that the right of return might be limited to a return to an eventual Palestinian state in the OT. Israel's proposals for the Palestinian entity (the Labour leadership did not object to using the word 'state' to describe something less than full sovereignty, while Likud objects to the term on ideological and strategic grounds) do not generally include Palestinian sovereignty over the entity's borders, nor, by extension, over Palestinian re-migration. The Israeli Labour Party's most general proposals involved allowing a limited and phased re-migration of Palestinian refugees into the new entity.[86]

While compensation and right of return to a rump Palestine might deflect some of the ideological explosiveness of the issue, there would still be problems. First, many refugees are likely to feel that such an accommodation is an unacceptable compensation for what they have lost. Refugees in Lebanon, for example, generally came from Galilee and have little desire to settle in the West Bank or Gaza Strip.[87] A limited survey suggesting that negative attitudes toward the PLO and Arafat are above 75 per cent among refugees in southern Lebanon (indeed, Munir Makdeh, a Fatah leader in Ain Helwa refugee camp in Lebanon threatened to kill Arafat following the signing of the accord).[88] These factors imply that these refugees would not feel inclined to migrate to the Palestinian entity. Furthermore, many Palestinians who have 'returned' since 1993 have expressed disillusionment and difficulty in adjusting to their new surroundings.[89] Their negative reports might further prejudice the attitudes of potential returnees against relocating to the OT. Other problems with the prospect of return to the OT include the obvious environmental and economic constraints to absorbing a massive influx of refugees. In Gaza, businessmen spoken to by the author already talk of transferring a considerable proportion of Gaza's population to the West Bank.[90]

When considering this scenario, it should be remembered that nowhere in the over 500 pages of agreements signed by Israel and the PLO is self-determination mentioned, and is only hinted at via the references to UN resolutions. Israel continues to insist on its right to control any flow of people across borders into the OT, and has offered to allow no more than up to 2,000 refugees to return annually to the territories on the basis of family reunification.[91] Anyway, with regard to the invocation of 'self-determination,' it is striking that this concept seems to have been more the slogan of dictators than of democrats in recent years.

The refugees in a status quo model of Palestinian containment

In the event of a stalemate in the peace process, or in the event that 'final-status' negotiations yield an only slightly more palatable version of the current levels of self-rule, the chances that the concerns of refugees will be addressed in a viable manner are slight. Interestingly, the perpetuation of the current model of PA rule might also have the effect of pushing 'domestic' political opposition to establish a base on the outside. This would have serious implications for the development of a viable Palestinian polity in the OT. An alliance of 'outside' rejectionist forces and 'inside' opposition to the PA might offer an excuse for the PA to consolidate an authoritarian base of rule, and would offer Israel with excuses to interfere in the development of Palestinian institutions and interests. Competing bases of loyalty and a probable perceived need to continue resistance against Israel would distract from the building of national institutions aimed at addressing purely 'domestic' issues.

A central irony in the continuing story of inside–outside tensions is that the opposition which once had its base on the 'inside' has been pushed 'outside.' In 1994, a coalition of Palestinian opposition groups met in Damascus to form what was then called the 'Alliance of Palestinian Forces,' also known as 'the seven' since the alliance that emerged from these first Damascus talks was comprised of seven alienated PLO factions and Islamist groupings. In mid-October 1996, ten opposition groups with offices in Damascus issued a statement rejecting Arafat's call for national dialogue. After a meeting in Damascus on Saturday 2 November 1996, Hamas announced a more formal association between eight opposition groupings which would now be known as Palestinian Independence

Front. The proposed umbrella group would be organized along lines similar to those of the PLO. It would include a national congress of 100 members who would meet every two years (implying a long term strategy), a central committee of 30–32 members who would set policy every six months, and an executive committee responsible for implementation. According to the new Front's official spokesperson, 'the PLO ceased to exist when it renounced the Palestinian charter.'[92]

Interestingly, this alliance is comprised of the leftist movements – which had their heyday in Gaza in the late 1970s and early 1980s – and the Islamist groupings – which were of course prominent in the intifada. Both (at least their branches in Gaza) tended to be more concerned with on the ground civil initiatives in Gaza than Fatah was during the same time periods. However, it is an alliance that might have a hard time seeing eye to eye on issues other than opposition to the current peace accords. Therefore, inasmuch as this alliance claims to be an alternative to the old PLO, the fact that its members are unlikely to sit down to articulate a common social agenda may mean that it becomes prone to some of the same kinds of problems and tendencies which make the old PLO bureaucratic culture so inappropriate to ruling in the Gaza Strip.

The dissolution of the peace process: a precondition of bi-nationalism?

The collapse of the peace process is a frightening prospect for both sides. If Israel were to attempt to simply freeze the status quo, Palestinian self-rule areas (areas 'A') would find themselves more isolated and choked off from their ecological milieu than ever before. The collapse of the peace process might also lead to the abdication of the PA in these areas, which in Gaza might force the Israeli government to assume direct control over a population it had long been attempting to rid itself of. It is also not unthinkable that Israel would attempt to resume direct military occupation and circumstances might compel it to.

Such a scenario suggests the possibility of intense and sustained violence from both sides. Still, as of spring 1997, the Israeli government seems arrogantly confident of its ability to unilaterally implement its ideological and strategic objectives in contravention of the spirit and letter of current agreements while containing Palestinian reaction and deflecting international criticism. Palestinians, on the other hand, increasingly feel they have less and less to lose by responding in ways that threaten a peace process exposed as an inadequate framework within which to defend their rights and interests. The utter irreconcilability of Israel's imposition of its objectives through force and any meaningful conception of Palestinian rights to security and property suggests that defining Palestine depends in no small measure on defining Israel.

However, a more idealistic scenario might also be drawn. If a collapse of the peace process were to have the effect of removing the PA as a mediator between the Palestinian street and Israeli power, Palestinians in the OT would be forced to reconsider their positions as subjects of Israeli power and authority. Civil society in the OT would once again have to align to protect itself against and challenge the ethno-exclusivity of Israeli authority. In turn, Israel would be forced to confront the contradiction between its claim to be democratic state grounded in an even application of law and enforcement of equal rights and obligations amongst all its citizens, and its actual ethnocratic and exclusivist character. Such a situation has ironic implications for the fulfilment of Palestinian national aims. According to current demographic trends, demographic parity between Jews and Palestinians in the area that was mandate Palestine will be reached by the year 2010. In a democratic environment, such circumstances imply the possibility of achieving national aims by working within the framework of Israeli national institutions.

This last scenario is admittedly extremely unlikely and would certainly be actively opposed not only by Israelis (as it would threaten the Jewish character and demographic base of the state), but also many Palestinians (who have long rejected the prospect of an Israeli identity).[93] However, whether intended as a tactic or final strategy, the dismal performance of the PA and the shortcomings of the peace process in general have encouraged several Palestinian intellectuals to advocate just such a solution. Specifically, in something of a mirror image of the old PLO call for a binational secular (i.e. non-Judeocentric) state in all of mandate Palestine, many Palestinian intellectuals are more openly considering calling on Palestinians to claim full Israeli citizenship rights. This has been brought up by independent Palestinian intellectuals (not necessarily to imply 'accommodationist' or even centrist) including Daoud Kuttab and Azmi Bishara,[94] as well as by elements in the rejectionist factions. As one PFLP sympathizer argues:

> I think the option will be ... one democratic state in all of Palestine. I think this is the only good solution, not only for the Palestinians, but also for the Jews. The name is not important to me. If its name is Israel or Palestine, it is not important [nor for that matter] if it is Israpalestine or Palisrael. I think the solution of

having two states for two peoples is not solution because [the populations are already so spread across both territories].[95]

PFLP spokesman Riad Malki has replied to all those who call such an idea a dream: '[if the current peace plans represent a realistic policy], then I prefer to be a dreamer.'[96] Significantly, this perspective seems to recognize that ultimately Palestinian rights will have to be asserted against Israel, which remains the force most significantly influencing Palestinian life in the OT. Throughout the interim phase of the agreement, the rights of Palestinians remain in Israeli hands; they have not been achieved merely with political recognition and 'national' administration.[97]

Conclusion: Exchanging Fire Over the Dividing-lines of Transition

Ironically, now that the nationalist elites have found their way to a reduced Palestine, they seem more remote and smug than they had appeared to many Gazans from a distance. The contrast between the world of occupation and the world of self rule has not proven as great as had been imagined or promised, and this is inevitably raising questions about the inherent ability of the new elites to make political decisions informed by the interests and values of the local population. At the outset, people seemed willing to give Arafat the benefit of the doubt; but he paid for support with heavy promises on which he has so far been unable to deliver. The failure of the bearers of nationalism causes questioning as to the viability of the ideology itself.

Concurrently, the failure of the final status negotiations to effectively deal with the concerns of diaspora Palestinian refugees leaves a base for Palestinian activism that is not incorporated within any polity. PA repression of opposition groups within Gaza has the effect of pushing these groups into the 'outside' communities, where they might find a ready base for mobilization within a group left rudderless by the demise of the PLO. The establishment of such linkages between inside and out may have an undermining impact on the development of strong attachments of society to the institutions of a Palestinian polity in the OT. One response in Gaza has been to embrace ideologies which transcend nationalism in scope – specifically, to embrace Islam as a framework and rational for political activism.

The repressive and patrimonial character of PA authority at present is therefore measured against the ideals of self rule: accountability, sovereignty together with strong efficient and recognizable institutions. The high-handedness of the PA elites has also been measured against their seeming lack of understanding for local values and lack of moral restraint from the street level perspective in Gaza. There is no small amount of resentment from Gazans towards the PA elites who are seen as having come in to reap the limited fruits sown in years street level resistance by Gazans against Israeli occupation.[98]

As the PA superimposes its diaspora bureaucratic structures on society in Gaza and the West Bank, it is ill prepared to deal with the circumstances which informed a crucial part of the national awareness of the inhabitants of these territories. At an abstract level, two trends can be identified: the first is engaged in the attempt to remould Palestinian national identity in the OT based on structures and strategies similar to that of classical PLO politics of national maintenance; the second attempts to define the tasks of civil society in relation to the provisional/transitional order. The complaint against the former is that it fails to account for the socio-economic basis of legitimacy. The attack against the latter is that civil society institutions in Gaza might not be strong enough to stand up to an authoritarian PA regime or Israeli intervention in an institutionalized, peaceful way. The failure of the outside leadership to integrate itself fully into the life of Gazans both institutionally and viscerally – to become part of a solution rather than the new force responsible for containing the problems – has transformed the cleavage between inside and outside into a profound gap between elite and mass. This divide imperils the foundations of Palestinian nationalism as represented by existing institutions, while the peace process has been set up so as to depend upon these institutions.

The fragmented spaces of autonomy are not held together by the integration of social and economic activity, but by their linkages with and dependency upon the PA. The cantonization of the autonomy space thus reinforces the factional tendency in Palestinian politics. The following chapters build on this theme. The de facto restrictions placed by Israel on trade and movement between the Palestinian areas (discussed in Chapter 4) undermine economic planning and the establishment of economic linkages between Gaza and the West Bank which might be an important step in national integration generally. The inability of the PA to overcome the debilitating impact of the isolation between Gaza and other parts of the autonomy, and its inability to press Israel to make substantial progress in negotiations on these issues highlights the degree to which PA power is dependent on Israeli power (discussed in Chapter 5). In precluding integrated political mobilization on an 'autonomy-wide' scale, the isolated bailiwicks of limited autonomy might become pockets of frustration. The lack of productive channels for such frustration, and the resulting feelings of isolation and hopelessness, might increase the likelihood that opposition, while isolated, expresses itself violently and unpredictably (see Chapter 6). Such developments would not only challenge the relevance of Palestinian autonomy, but could derail the peace process itself.

4

The Economic Quicksand of Autonomy

It has become a journalistic cliché to refer to the Gaza Strip as 'squalid' and 'one of the most densely populated areas on Earth.'[1] Crucial to understanding the significance of these descriptions, however, is an awareness of the Gazan economy's political determination. The density of population constitutes a more decisive variable if constraints on the development of a territory's human and natural resources preclude indigenous investment and planning in agricultural inputs, variegated trade or sustainable industrial and service sectors. More important than the pressures that dense population places on Gaza's ecology and living conditions, Palestinians in Gaza have not in recent history had a political authority whose economic decisions were accountable to their interests, or that regulated the territory in such a way as to encourage any form of development or economic growth.[2] While current Palestinian–Israeli agreements would seem to have changed this latter obstacle, they have done so only very superficially. As is shown below, the PA remains unable to challenge the character of the OT's economic relationship with Israel, or restructure its 'domestic' economic incentives in ways that might encourage investment, growth and thus sustainable local employment opportunities.

Israeli economic policies in the OT were an integral part of a larger strategy of disenfranchisement and control of the Palestinian population. Menachem Begin is reported to have said, 'we'll make the Arab workers work for 100 shekels a day and we'll make sure that they need to spend 150.'[3] Israeli policy effectively made it more expensive for many farmers to attempt to cultivate their land than it was to leave it fallow; the consequence of not putting land to use was possible Israeli confiscation.[4] Gazans were forced to get permits in order to reclaim their own land or replace an aging citrus tree with a new one.[5] Furthermore, as Sara Roy has noted in her important work on the 'de-development' of the Gaza Strip, 'to preclude the establishment of a Palestinian state, the [Israeli] government had to eliminate any foundation on which it could be built.'[6] Local economic investment, integration and mobilization were therefore actively subverted in the Gaza Strip during the Israeli occupation of the territory.[7]

Declarations of autonomy and the promises of international aid do not in themselves reverse this situation.[8] That would require a fundamental restructuring of economic relations locally and generally, and the prospect that this might be accomplished within the framework of current agreements appears unlikely. While the agreements do grant the PA more control of trade for selected items relevant to ensuring that basic needs may be met, and while they have powers related to the import of Mercedes Benzes,[9] the broad range of economic powers used by sovereign states to encourage economic development and shape the attachment of the local national economy to the global economy are well beyond the scope of autonomy as accepted by the PLO on behalf of the PA. Current PA policies reveal an inability or unwillingness to counter Israeli policies with the construction of viable Palestinian alternatives.[10] Furthermore, trends in donor funding reveal that aid to the 'Palestinian areas' has been redirected from long-term initiatives and human development toward short-term high visibility projects and immediate income generating activities.[11] This threatens not only to produce distortions in the economic development of the OT, it also – by disguising accountability and changing the focus of the Palestinian side – removes pressure on Israel to alter its policies.

A poll conducted in December 1996 found that 59 per cent of Gazans felt their economic situation to have worsened since the signing of the agreement, with only 9.6 per cent reporting improvement.[12] This must be seen against the already dire economic situation prevailing in Gaza as of 1993. What are the possible social and political consequences of this trend? What are the features of the current political environment which reinforce it? What might the PA do to address the current economic malaise?

This chapter characterizes the pieces of Gaza's shattered political economy and evaluates the capacity of the PA to pick up those pieces and assemble them into a meaningful configuration of economic autonomy. The dependence resulting from the inability of the PA to articulate long-term policies designed to transform Gaza's de-developed economic base is described and its impacts emphasized. A brief historical overview of economic trends in Gaza is also provided and the recent economic trajectory of Gaza is documented. The role of PA corruption in undermining both long-term economic planning and undermining public confidence is also addressed. The significance of economic factors in social integration and meaningful autonomy are stressed throughout in order to suggest the crucial correlation between economic development and the future of Gaza's political development.

The Agreements and the Economic Challenges in Context

In their rush to ensure that they were granted political recognition, it can be argued that the Fatah-based PLO elites ignored the imperative of securing the powers necessary to restructure economic relations between Israel and Palestinians. Article 6, paragraph 2 of the Declaration of Principles (DoP) states that: 'With the view to promoting economic development in the West Bank and Gaza Strip, authority will be transferred to the Palestinians in the following spheres – education and culture, health, social welfare, direct taxation and tourism.'

These hardly represent the tools most commonly associated with economic sovereignty and in fact represent domains which traditionally result from development rather than precede it. Article 7, paragraph 4 states that in order to promote economic growth, the Council will establish: 'a Palestinian electricity authority, a Gaza sea port authority, a Palestinian export promotion board, a Palestinian environmental authority, a Palestinian land authority, a Palestinian water administration authority, and any other authorities agreed upon.'

However: Gazans remain dependent on the Israeli electricity grid;[13] they have no port;[14] they inherit a severely degraded environment;[15] the most productive land in the strip is still under Israeli control and no new authority or administrative function was transferred to Palestinian hands by the 4 May 1994 Accord;[16] Palestinian access to water resources is still subject to commercial agreements with the Israeli water company Mekoroth and administered under the auspices of a Palestinian–Israeli joint committee where the Israeli side enjoys veto rights;[17] and not many other 'authorities' have been granted.

But perhaps by creating new jobs, these 'authorities' might promote growth by stimulating flagging consumption.

Direct employment in the PA continues to grow significantly. Some 30,000 to 50,000 people are currently employed in the police, security forces and budding bureaucracy (the annual costs of a security force of 27,000 are estimated by the World Bank to cost $180 million, a heavy burden on an, as yet, unproductive economy). This issue, however, is political, and money seems to be forthcoming for the tremendous costs involved: 'The PA does not need a 30,000 strong police force to facilitate the economic, social and political development of its 2.3 million people. A police force of that size is required only to keep the lid on the people in the absence of such development.'[18]

The PLO/PA failed to negotiate to itself the ability to influence fundamental economic policy – that is to create incentives and construct an empowering environment through powers to regulate the use of natural resources, set taxes and tariffs without reference to Israeli rates in many of the areas that might encourage investment and trade, or influence monetary policy. Everything about the new situation seems to reinforce the fact, apparently overlooked by those who place the blame for continued instability and resistance on the PA's shortcomings in the area of repression, that people do not live on slogans and expectations alone.

According to one source:

> Terms such as autonomy and self government have no precise definition in international law with respect to either the political or economic responsibilities of a governing authority. Historically, 'autonomy' has referred to a wide variety of arrangements ... among these, economic rights have always been the most precisely defined.[19]

The authors go on to emphasize the primacy of control over natural resources, trade, taxes and finances as paramount to the recognition of the autonomy of a particular spatial or human geography.

The economic features of the limited and supposedly transitional Palestinian autonomy are regulated according to the terms of Annex IV (Protocol on Economic Relations between the Government of the State of Israel and the PLO representing the Palestinian people) of the Gaza-Jericho Agreement. This annex, signed in Paris on 9 April 1994, is also known as the 'Paris Protocol' or 'Protocol on Economic Relations.' According to the agreement's preamble: 'The two parties view the economic domain as one of the cornerstones in their mutual relations. This protocol lays the groundwork for strengthening the economic base of the Palestinian side and for exercising its right of economic decision making in accordance with its own development plan and priorities.'

The actual powers granted at this stage of negotiation fall far short of this goal. From the Israeli point of view, the agreement is circumspect. The Palestinian economy, and the PA powers over economic decision making, remain limited and highly regulated. The agreements effectively perpetuate Israeli controls on Palestinian water use, which obviously plays a very important role in the development of an area whose indigenous economy is still premised on agriculture. Infrastructure standards for both private and public concerns are set at the 'highest international standards,' a conditionality that might increase start-up capital requirements for small businesses.[20] Fishing, a once important sector in the local economy that was severely restricted under occupation, is not mentioned in the protocol.[21] Since the signing of the Paris Protocol, Israel has – according to the US State Department – imposed new standards on Palestinian agricultural products which are higher than those required of Israeli producers.[22] Items which can be imported into the Palestinian self-rule 'areas' are limited to those on a detailed list, and a quota based on past consumption patterns – as determined by a 'panel of experts'[23] – regulates the quantities of even those listed items allowed into the Palestinian administered areas.[24] The Palestinian economy has furthermore been devastated by varying degrees of closure of the OT's borders that have been in force since 1993.[25]

Autonomy in areas of environmental and zoning regulation also constitutes a power relevant to economic planning. Israel's right to participate in joint regulation of environmental issues (and indeed their effective veto right in many strategic areas related to development) and their monopoly of relevant information have been used to undermine PA planning in vital areas. Dr Mohammed Ajjour, director of environmental planning in the PA's Ministry of Planning and International Cooperation has pointed out some of the difficulties:

> We requested that the Israelis give us some help to finish an environmental impact study for the Gaza airport, and pass on some information needed by the Canadian team contracted to make this study. The Israelis were not very cooperative. Many permissions are also needed [in general]. We need Israeli permission for some small environmental improvement projects and they have been giving us trouble.
>
> Big projects have many complications which must be tackled. If you build a joint treatment plant you have to agree on who will pay for it, how you share costs, what standards and guidelines will be followed, and environmental considerations. All of this requires much coordination and it will take some time for us to come to these agreements.
>
> We are also subject to movement restrictions which affect us. For example, if I want to meet with the West Bank staff, I have a problem. We have not been able to get together over the last five months due to restrictions on movement.

The political environment of the last five months has limited the ability of the Palestinians to meet among themselves or with the Israelis. The security restrictions and the political troubles cannot all just be forgotten.[26]

The restrictions mentioned by Dr Ajjour also undermine the Palestinian position in negotiations generally by interfering in the PA's ability to coordinate information and prepare negotiating positions. Indeed, the World Bank reports that the agreements have effectively 'split the West Bank and Gaza into a number of largely separate economic units with little economic inter-relationship among them, breaking up an already small domestic market into even smaller ones.'[27]

Agreements also make the building of roads and Palestinian public buildings subject to such environmental and security review by Israel.[28] The PA must consult Israel on issues such as where to build strategic infrastructure including an eventual port complex. And the PA must even inform Israel of road repairs that are being made within the autonomous areas.[29] While Israel continues to confiscate Palestinian land and destroy Palestinian property invoking its general security jurisdiction, Palestinians are not allowed to build in any way that might threaten the existing infrastructure related to settlements and/or military installations in the OT.[30] According to Annex III, Appendix 1, Article 27, paragraph 3b of the *Interim Agreement*, 'A sub-committee established by the CAC [Civil Affairs Co-ordination and Co-operation Committee] shall, upon request by the Israeli side, discuss [any proposed PA 'Planning Scheme']. Pending the decision of the committee, planning procedures shall not be concluded and no building activity shall be carried out pursuant to the said Planning Scheme.'

Article II paragraph 26 sets out regulations for what the Palestinians may put on postage stamps (postal services are still dependent on the Israeli postal system, a situation which has on occasion caused problems as Israeli postal workers refused to handle mail with Palestinian Authority stamps). The 'Erez Agreement' annex IV shows how the administrative functions give the right to issue the licenses regulating the tourist trade, but as is noted in greater detail below, they lack the powers that would be needed to promote a comprehensive tourist industry, providing instead the peripheral service rather than controlling the fundamental elements of infrastructure. Annex V of the same agreement notes that property taxes are still the domain of the Israeli government. According to Gaza-Jericho Agreement Annex II, Article II, paragraph B28b, custodial absentee land rights do not fall to the PA. Furthermore, the PA has no real foreign policy mandate.[31]

The PA can also issue import licenses, but these licenses (in spite of Arafat's unilateral declaration of reinstating Egyptian contract law in Gaza and Jordanian law in the West Bank – a move which would facilitate a patronage and *baksheesh* based economy) are technically subject to standards and requirements in Israeli law.[32] This right grants the PA means to control a source of bureaucratic selective empowerment, but affords no real power to determine import priorities or quality standards associated with the granting of such licenses. As discussed in greater detail below, the issuing of licenses and the granting of monopolies is one of the major mechanisms of neopatrimonial corruption within the PA.

The pricing of key items and taxes, tolls and duties are rigorously pegged in relation to existing prices and taxes inside Israel, and clauses concerning environmental degradation, disease prevention, and security give Israel broad veto powers over autonomous Palestinian economic planning.[33] While the potential for slightly lower prices on items such as gasoline and a 1–2 per cent lower VAT might offer some marginal relief to a small number of consumers in Gaza, they certainly don't offer the kind of price and tax incentives that might encourage outside investment in Gaza considering the other challenges facing the strip. Importantly, the imbalance of power between the two sides in the enforcement of this and other agreements means that the Israeli government's interpretation of various clauses tends to win the day. Israel has consistently delayed shipment of goods out of Gaza.[34] No one who seriously wants to produce for foreign markets would reasonably invest in Gaza at this time. According to Odin Knudsen, World Bank representative in the OT, 'private companies do not invest in countries that are under an economic embargo. Effectively, there is an economic embargo in place (over the West Bank and Gaza Strip). Its very difficult for private investors to come in and make investments [when people] cannot move their commodities or move themselves.'[35]

While quotas concerning trade in traditional agricultural products between Israel and the PA-controlled areas are set to be lifted in 1999, this delay will almost surely encourage farmers away from the production of foodstuffs and toward the production of ornamental plants. This is in line with pre-agreement Israeli plans to forcibly restructure the Gazan economy (discussed below). Whilst not necessarily impeding sectoral growth, the situation does illustrate the ways in which the agreement protects the interest of Israeli producers – ostensibly over the short-term – but de facto over the long-term as well.

The PA also has no ability to influence monetary policy, which has far reaching consequences in terms of its ability to set trade policy and encourage investment and employment. Moreover, its ability to determine its import and export needs are restricted by Israel's powers to protect its own interests at the expense of the Palestinians.[36] In fact, the general lack of reliable statistics, together with the ability to use the institutions set up by the agreement to determine import policy in certain key areas (particularly those related to infrastructure development) opens the door for corruption; in particular collusion between wholesale importers and PA officials. While the PA has no powers in the area of foreign relations, it can seek foreign donor funding and economic agreements.[37] All in all, the PA has few powers through which to counter Israeli policies with viable Palestinian alternatives.

To understand the meaning of these restrictions on the civil exercise of autonomy, the relationship between Gaza's economic trajectory and the economic expectations associated with the acceptance of self-rule must be reviewed. In Gaza, the PA has inherited conditions of severe economic distress. Its strategies for consolidating its political control in such conditions will in no small measure be determined by the scope of regulatory, monetary and legislative powers it is able to negotiate for itself in the context of the Oslo process. Israel's continued control over 44 per cent of the Gaza Strip (including the most productive land area which houses about 1,200 settlers) and 80 per cent of the available water resources offers a strong indication that those features of the occupation relationship relevant to a liberalizing and restructuring the Israeli economy are still being enforced.[38]

Some commentators claim to have observed in the PA's economic strategy an increased tendency to *seek* dependency on Israel. Aisling Byrne, for example, argues that:

> Encapsulated in its response to the closure and to its emerging industrial and development policies, the impression one gets is that not only do current PA policies do nothing to lessen dependence on Israel, but, the direction they are headed is down a road taken by so many developing countries: a road of increased dependence (as if this was not the intention of Oslo); of debt (of the $2.6 billion promised to the Palestinians over the next five years, 2/3 is in the form of loans – currently $760 million assuming no additional loans are taken – which with an interest rate of say 8 per cent (the rate is reported to be less than 10 per cent) means a doubling of debt within a ten-year period); of unsustainability (with near term complete reliance on 'donor funds' for short-term, emergency assistance projects) and of a developmental strategy with clear

political underpinnings ... far from being the cornerstone in the mutual relations between 'the Palestinian side' and Israel in the context of Oslo, the economic sector has not responded as expected, (private because they won't, and public because they can't).[39]

From Occupation to Autonomy: Economic Meanings of the Transition

Nationalist movements have often sustained themselves by defining economic rights in line with the aspirations and grievances of their potential constituency(ies). Although often submerged within the more romantic rhetoric of historic national rights, loyalties to particular ideologies and expressions of religious and ideological unity, it may be argued that contemporary Palestinian national awareness grew out of a unique experience of sudden and overwhelming economic alienation. At a psychological level, the sudden break with traditional modes of economic existence represented the destruction of an order which seemed to have been more humane and comfortingly authentic in comparison with new realities. At the material level, it represented the sudden loss of land, shops, trade links and resources upon which people drew to survive.

Thus Palestinian nationalism grew as a united effort to confront an injustice which led to economic hardship, and more subtly, it grew into a complex web of linkages and patronage which could be accessed through expressions of loyalty to the various organs of the nationalist movement. The nationalist movement promised a long-term strategy to redress economic grievance and injustice, and offered short-term possibilities of economic survival – the possibility of sustaining *sumud* – if not economic efficacy. While fragmented, tenuous and often ineffectual, a political economy of resistance and survival emerged in Gaza and elsewhere in the Palestinian community which gave a certain degree of meaning and security in an environment where people had very little control over or say in the way political power and economic forces were shaping their lives. The appearance of self-rule has brought with it new realities which in turn create new interpretations of the relationships between economic circumstances and the exercise of power and authority.

In the wake of Oslo, the labour force in Gaza remains unusually dependent on outside political and economic contingencies. There is little internal accountability for the political generation and determination of economic alternatives. Furthermore, the historic isolation imposed on

Gaza's economy has desensitized local producers to meeting the demands and standards of competitive international markets.[40] Many commentators, noting the pernicious influence of external force in perpetuating local conditions of unaccountable authority and in necessitating large migrations of local labourers to work in the politically dominant economy, have referred to the situation as 'bantustanization.'[41] Bantustanization refers to the capturing of a labour force and market through the manipulation of a monopoly on coercive force while 'internal' mechanisms of administration are set up and recognized by the dominant state to lend an appearance of local accountability and legitimacy to a regime dependent on the dominant state. The South African apartheid policy of tribal homelands offers the prototype of Bantustanization. In Gaza, however, the dramatic increase in border closings after 1987 (the beginning of the intifada) seems to indicate that the desire for pacification rather than exploitation has informed Israel's attitude toward the Palestinian population.

Noting these trends, Sarah Roy refers to the economic relationships that obtained in Gaza under occupation as 'de-development.' De-development is defined by Roy as:

> the deliberate, systematic destruction of an indigenous economy by a dominant power. It is qualitatively different from underdevelopment, which by contrast allows for some form, albeit distorted, of economic development. De-development is an economic policy designed to ensure that there will be no economic base, even one that is malformed, to support an indigenous economic existence.[42]

The policies enforcing this phenomenon are intended not merely, or even mostly, toward the exploitation of a population, but rather to ensure that the dominant political power has unrestricted access to resources, especially land and water, as well labour surpluses at the expense of even the most uni-dimensional development in the colonized space.

As we try to identify a departure point for the economy of Palestinian 'self-rule,' and try to interpret the meanings of continued Israeli control over crucial components of the almost non-existent economic autonomy in the self-rule areas, Roy's model offers some useful insights. De-development is characterized by the systematic dismantling of an indigenous economy by external, militarily backed political force. Political domination aims at the exploitation of land and resources rather than exploitation of the population, the latter being considered an inconvenient but for the short-term unavoidable obstacle to securing the first objective. In order to maximize the benefits of the land and its resources (water being crucial), the population is alienated from the land both by physical force and by policies designed to minimize the benefits of indigenous production. The population is then left with no option but to work and produce for low wages in the occupier's economy (assisting the cause of direct control of the population) or to immigrate. The policy is designed to encourage attrition, the economic limitations encouraging indigenous inhabitants to seek opportunities elsewhere, but not promoting conditions so bad as to provoke unmanageable unrest. Furthermore, those who leave by apparent choice can be more easily be made to seem to have voluntarily given up their right to return or claim land and other property left behind.

The lack of an integrated economic base in the territory, and the political restrictions inhibiting the growth of one, allow the dominant political economy to cultivate separate relations with different economic sectors – i.e. each sector is dependent on Israel for inputs and the distribution and sale of outputs. Political policies imposed by Israel preclude alternatives to this dependency. These isolated and vertical relationships in turn facilitate political control by ensuring that short-term economic interests of each group are dependent on compliance to the terms stipulated by the occupying power. The isolation of economic interests facilitates political fragmentation and vice-versa. Likud's current intransigence on issues of greater Palestinian economic sovereignty suggest that this model might be useful in understanding Israel's attitude toward the negotiations which continue to define the boundaries of Palestinian autonomy.

In the OT – and particularly in Gaza – the intifada upset this balance of the occupation's costs and benefits from the Israeli perspective. Many Israelis began to realize that suppressing a rebellious population had social and psychological costs as well as economic costs. For a brief period in the late 1980s and early 1990s, active and broad based resistance to Israeli occupation seemed poised to transcend Gaza's economic and social fragmentation. The forging of economic linkages in Gaza society – in particular by encouraging home production and other strategies of self-sufficiency – was seen as crucial to breaking Israel's comprehensive and divisive political and economic grip on Gaza. An ideology of economic nationalism was introduced to counter actual fragmentation and (as in the Ghandian model) to undermine the benefits of occupation for the occupier. While these initiatives generated enthusiasm in the early stages of the uprising, they ultimately failed to accomplish the desired political or economic objectives. The structural gaps in the Gaza economy were too great to be bridged by such a strategy.

This lack of an economic base capable of encouraging some kind of coherent economic-social agenda from the PLO or PA must be considered especially troubling given evidence of the economic rationale behind the initial support of the agreement by Gazans. Ali al-Jarbawi provides a statistic which suggests a relationship between acceptance of the declaration of principles and anticipated improvements in the overall economic situation: a 65 per cent majority of the Palestinian population supported the declaration of whom 74 per cent indicated that they thought the new order would bring about improvements in their economic situation.[43]

In many respects, the economic situation under self-rule might be described as the transition from de-development to traditional neo-colonial underdevelopment. However, even in underdeveloped states political leaders and institutions enjoy the internationally recognized rights associated with state sovereignty – the ability to distribute and protect the sovereign use of the natural resources of the state territory, to make laws, issue currency, to set trade policy and make laws without other states having a direct or absolute right of veto.

Whether these powers of economic arbitration and redistribution are exercised within the scope of a governing agenda that works through institutions to address the economic concerns of a broad national social base, or whether the state is run simply on behalf of a small power elite, is another question. The answer to that question depends in part on the political and social groupings upon which the state leaders have based their power. With Palestinian autonomy at present, the political relationship at the formal level in many ways reflects 'standard' tendencies in relations between the developed and underdeveloped states in terms of the imbalance in power. The real economic relationship, however, is still characterized by a regime of resource exploitation and the use of relative political advantages to impose restrictions on the development of a viable Palestinian economic base capable of generating indigenous economic opportunities. Not even much pretence exists to suggest any PA economic sovereignty in the self-rule areas. The Gaza economy may in fact be on a course toward increased marginalization and eventual obliteration in the context of self-rule.

Thus the entire basis of economic relations which underlie the agreement – relations which given the imbalance of power between the negotiating sides may ultimately define the limits of autonomy as willingly granted by Israel – is being questioned. Many observers warn that the new arrangement merely represents a contracting out of the occupation in line with the liberalization of the Israeli economy in general; i.e., it represents a restructuring of dependent relations.[44] From this perspective, rather than being an agreement between sovereign entities, the new track represents a process of decolonization with a quasi captive neocolonial relationship being institutionalized in its place.[45] The donor-funded basis of the new economy has also fuelled competition for external producing fragmentation which channels energy and attention away from economic competition and longer term developmental imperatives.[46]

Noam Chomsky argues that the transition implied at this stage of the peace process reflected a 'standard colonial pattern' in which the former colonial powers look to a set of indigenous elites willing to carry out the administrative front of authority while economic exploitation continues.

> It is like the British when they held India. They didn't use British troops. They used 90 per cent Indian soldiers. In Rhodesia, the worst atrocities were carried out by Black mercenaries. And that's exactly Rabin's reason. Then you don't have to worry about all sorts of bleeding hearts and all sorts of vengeful fathers. With the PLO willing to take on this task, the Israelis are perfectly happy to deal with the PLO. Now their job is to protect Arafat and make sure the forces he brings in, (mostly PLA forces from the diaspora), will be able to carry out this task.[47]

From a dependency theory perspective, the PA elite might indeed be identified as a *compradore* class. But even in the post occupation era, Gaza's dependency on Israeli political imperatives seems much more dramatic and comprehensive than the traditional core/periphery relationships described by classical dependency theorists. The PA has few of the tools normally associated with economic sovereignty which might be used to affect and influence the character and social impact of dependent international economic relations. The resources most fundamental to human survival (water and productive land) continue to be extracted not on the basis of trade, but on the brutal facts of uneven military force. A situation of socio-political dependency based not on unequal exchange relations, but on very little exchange whatsoever, describes the current condition of so-called Palestinian autonomy.

The Economic Trajectory of Gaza

The scope of economic dislocation in Gaza cannot be understood without a brief summary of the territory's erratic economic trajectory. Gaza's economy has been overwhelmingly politically determined, and while global economic trends have had a major impact on local economic trajectories, Gaza as a coherent political and economic entity has not confronted the international economy through directly accountable institutions, but rather through the mediation of occupiers: Ottomans, British, Egyptians, and, after 1967, Israelis. In effect, the result has been a process of peripheralization that reached an extreme with Israeli occupation.[48] In varying degrees and forms, the political powers used to shape resource flows, generate incentives and encourage specific modes of economic production were accountable not to the interests of the local population, but to the interests and ideologies of occupying powers. This has inhibited the construction of a local response to the challenges of economic internationalization. Gaza's economic fate has largely been shaped by events and political initiatives designed to serve ideological and economic interests external to the Strip itself.

Before 1948, the Gaza province included the districts of Gaza and Beer Sheba. Already the poorest administrative district during the mandate period (with citrus exports being a lone bright spot), in 1948, all but 2.5 per cent of the province fell under Israeli control. After the *nakba* 'Of the 5,000 acres of citrus plantations, barely 1,000 remained; of the 250,000 acres of grain growing land in the Negev, less than 10 per cent was still accessible.'[49] Not only was the area that became the Gaza Strip cut apart from its traditional ecological milieu and forced to bear a burdensome influx of refugees, but the development of a productive and integrated economy was stifled by militarily enforced occupation policies – first under the Egyptians, and then the Israelis. The population of the remaining strip of land under Arab control was 280,000 with 190,000 of those being refugees.[50] A survey of 20,000 refugees in 1949 found that 18 per cent were skilled and semiskilled workers, 17 per cent professionals, merchants and landowners, and the other 65 per cent were farmers or unskilled workers.[51] Between 1948 and 1967, Gaza was administered by Egypt. Gaza's major trading partners during the period, besides Egypt, were in Eastern Europe, a situation which reflected political imperatives in Cairo.[52]

The results of the 1948 Arab–Jewish war had severed traditional trading links and created a large refugee population in Gaza which had been alienated from its traditional economic base.[53] After 1948, trade between the West Bank and Gaza was all but nonexistent. Besides market restrictions, the lack of natural resources or sources of energy discouraged the development of industry. The Clapp Commission toured all the Middle Eastern countries where there were Palestinian refugees and found economic opportunities everywhere except the Gaza Strip. Roy goes on to cite a Quaker representative working in Gaza at the time:

> The prospects for the early removal from the deadening hardships are dim. Members of the Clapp Commission, who visited the strip, completed their work in less than two hours. No other act has recorded so powerfully the impossibility of increasing the productivity of the land so that the local population will be able to maintain itself.[54]

The establishment of a duty-free zone in the Strip in the middle 1950s and the tendency to look the other way when it came to smuggling activities encouraged tourism from Egypt.[55] Low customs duties and a free trade zone in Gaza encouraged trade.[56] Commercial life in Gaza experienced an upswing with the opening of Eastern European markets. Gaza's citrus production, in particular, enjoyed benefits.[57] However, there was little productive investment and Gaza was in fact merely a stopping off point for goods to Egypt with no value added locally. By 1960, 83 per cent of the working age refugee population was officially unemployed, as compared with 35 per cent of the working age 'native' population of Gaza.[58] This reflected not only the lack of productive investment and the scarcity of land in a traditionally agricultural/pastoral society but also the hope of many refugees that they would soon return to their homes which were now in Israel proper. Such hopes encouraged a refusal among many refugees to settle and become economically active in their new environment. Some sources put the pre-1967 per capita income at around $80 per month,[59] and many refugees were establishing a dependence on a growing UNRWA bureaucracy.[60] As the population grew, so did the imbalance between already plentiful and under-utilized human resources and scarce, over-utilized natural resources. By 1966, citrus products accounted for 89.4 per cent of the Gaza Strip's exports, 'a clear indicator of Gaza's economic vulnerability and structural underdevelopment.'[61]

By cutting off trade links, ending Egyptian tourism and implementing policies aimed at further undercutting already limited local productive potential, the Israeli occupation led to the erosion of the few opportunities for enrichment and mobility that had been gained by traditional and professional middle classes after years of Egyptian control.[62] Once again, the inhabitants of Gaza would have to start facing another direction to see how they would make ends meet – trade was redirected toward Israel. The economy of Gaza was integrated into the Israeli economy in line with Israeli interests.

The system of integration was two tiered and severely unbalanced; it was 'based on a protectionist system of military orders and taxation procedures which effectively prevented Palestinian business from competing with Israeli producers for Israeli as well as foreign markets.'[63] Many educated Gazans were forced to migrate in order to use their acquired skills, and others found themselves deported. Gaza suffered a severe 'brain drain' that further undermined economic and organizational potential even as it rather ironically propped up local income through remittances. Although Palestinians were systematically excluded from high-paying and traditionally prestigious professions, family income did rise as access to low wage jobs expanded and the larger family group had access to multiple sources of income. Besides low wage labour in Israel, three other factors boosted the local economy through the early 1980s: PLO distribution of resources originating in the oil-rich Gulf; the increased demand for both skilled and unskilled labour in the Gulf; and agricultural buildup in Jordan. By the early 1980s, however, all of these areas were experiencing prolonged recession, and this had a severe impact on family income in Gaza.

The occupation also placed severe restraints on the traditional economy. Water sources were capped and severe restrictions placed on fishing, which had previously been an important sector in the economy of the Gaza Strip.[64] Palestinians were not only restricted in their access to water, but were also forced to pay four times the price paid by the Israelis per unit of water.[65] The long-term impact of this stifling of local economic potential included: (i) heightened dependency on external sources of employment (leading to migration and immigration and stress on the traditional family structures); (ii) an undermining of the independent economic base of peasants through the commercialization of agriculture; an eclipsing of the traditional crafts industries and (iii) the replacement of traditional economic relations with those determined by more immediate market imperatives.

Roy argues that the intent of Israeli policies throughout this period of occupation was to allow for a basis of individual Palestinian economic sustainability which was alienated from local land, resources and productive potential. Not only did this strategy seek to increase de facto

Zionist control over land and resources, it also sought to undermine any economic base for Palestinian political integration and social mobilization, and thus undercut and immobilize any effective institutional expression of national will.[66] Meron Benvinisti has pointed out that these policies allowed for individual prosperity while they at the same time led to communal stagnation.

A huge trade deficit between Israel and Gaza emerged which was financed by the export of Palestinian labour to work in the Israeli economy. One immediate impact of occupation on the Gaza Strip following the 1967 Arab–Israeli war was that per capita income increased rapidly as labourers from Gaza migrated to work in the Israeli economy.[67] Accordingly, household consumption also increased.[68] The result was a proletarianization of a considerable portion of the local labour potential and the introduction of new consumer attitudes and expectations. By the mid-1980s, the value of wages was declining rapidly for a labour force not allowed to organize and which had no political influence in the country in which they worked. Also, workers were exposed daily to the vast gap between the level and quality of services and infrastructure in Gaza and that in Israel.

Israeli regulations created distortions in the Palestinian economy. For example, while Palestinians were allowed to accumulate capital, they were denied investment opportunities in a local economy, and investment by Arabs in the Israeli economy was strictly prohibited.[69] Israeli Journalist Asher Davidi notes that:

> A whole generation of Israeli manufacturers tried to crush every possibility of capitalist industrial development in the territories. The Israeli occupation authorities operated as an arm of the Israeli bourgeoisie, making it impossible for a Palestinian capitalist to obtain the thousand and one approvals required for establishing any large business without producing a document stating that he would not be competing with an Israeli company. In this way, the authorities prevented the establishment of dairies, cement factories, food factories, and textile plants.[70]

Fischer et al. report that:

> Among the military policies that have been reported as blocking the opportunities for development of the industrial sector in the West Bank and Gaza are:
>
> :A licensing policy that discouraged the establishment of large industrial enterprises (abandoned as of the beginning of 1991, according to Israel);

:Military restraints on the movement of materials into and out of the territories;
:Limited local banking for the financing of local industry;
:Restraints on the development of free trade zones, other industrial zones, and related infrastructure;
:Restraints on the development of supporting public institutions.[71]

While economic growth was initially rapid under the occupation regime, serious structural imbalances characterized the relationship between the Israeli and Palestinian economies – economies that, while increasingly integrated, remained subject to different levels of political restriction and regulation. These structural imbalances included: '(i) the heavy dependence on outside sources of employment for the OT labour force; (ii) an unusually low degree of industrialization; (iii) a trade structure heavily dominated by trading links with Israel and a large trade deficit; (iv) inadequacies in the provision of public infrastructure and services.'[72]

Quality of life indicators showed improvement during the twenty-six years of occupation. However, these reflect trends in the region in general and should not be attributed to any benign effect of the occupation itself. While per capita income was higher in Gaza than in the region as a whole, real buying power was eventually less. In the context of the customs union, funds were extracted from the occupied territories and reinvested elsewhere within Israel's economy and social and service infrastructure. The World Bank described this policy as 'fiscal compression.'[73] These and other political restrictions imposed by Israel impeded the development of economies of scale.[74] As Roy poignantly notes, 'these measures were designed not only to appease and then fragment Palestinian society, but to render it unviable, and to do so quietly and without notice.'[75]

In the aftermath of the 1967 war, some 300,000 Palestinians migrated out of the OT and emigration continued at 1 per cent per annum afterwards; 'nevertheless, the Palestinian labour force in the OT grew by 100 per cent in the 25 years between 67 and 93 while employment opportunities grew only 25 per cent in the same period.'[76] The high demand for skilled labour in the Gulf encouraged the migration of 40,000 people from the OT to the Gulf in the 1973–82 period.[77] Of those migrating to work in Israel, by the early 1990s 68 per cent were employed in construction and 12 per cent in the agricultural sector.[78] After a period of growth in household income during the 1970s and into the very early 1980s and stagnation in the mid-1980s, Øvensen noted as of 1994 that 'the economy of the occupied territories [was] in the process of adapting to a new situation of reduced household income.'[79]

While products in Gaza's shops were overwhelmingly made in or shipped via Israel, the gap in the real buying power of Israelis and Palestinians was growing. A 1988 study by Shadid and Seltzer documents that Palestinians saw their economic conditions deteriorate during the first half of the 1980s.[80] At the same time, increases in the working age population were creating greater unemployment pressures. Severe restrictions on water use and infrastructure investment were exacerbating dependence on outside sources.[81] The pumping of water from Gaza into Israel proper placed severe strains on the supplies, leaving water resources too salinated for human consumption and agricultural purposes.[82] Population pressures, inadequate services and external exploitation of resources were leading to a situation of general environmental degradation and placing extreme constraints on the growth of agricultural production and employment.

Thus, the intifada broke out in a climate of job market shrinkage which frustrated newer entrants into the labour market. The economic instability and social uncertainty of the intifada period reached its climax during the crisis which developed over Iraq's invasion of Kuwait. Border closures became more extended and restrictions were targeted against specific segments of the population deemed as security threats (for example, closing the border for all males under thirty). During the height of the Gulf War, Gaza's Palestinian residents were subject to over one and a half months of twenty-four hour curfew, a curfew enforced by the IDF's shoot on sight policy which aimed at ensuring compliance.[83] Although Israel quickly overcame the effects of the war, the OT:

> continued to suffer. The entire economy of the OT was brought to a halt as businesses ceased to open and farmers had been unable to water, harvest or market their crops. By the time the war ended and the curfew was lifted, the OT was working at 25 per cent. The estimated cost of the curfew to the OT was between $150 and $200 million, and total losses throughout the year were projected to be in excess of $600 million from a national income that had reached $2.4 billion in 1988' but which had been in decline as the intifada dragged on.[84]

This situation was exacerbated by the return of 30,000 refugees to the OT in the wake of the Gulf War.[85] This occurred while Israel was in the process of absorbing hundreds of thousands of new immigrants from the former Soviet bloc. Concurrently, Israeli authorities were looking the other way with respect to growing illegal use of labour imported from East Asia. The position of Palestinian labour was weakening dramatically. Gradually, an increasing portion of the population was threatened with economic redundancy.

On the eve of the protocol, the Palestinian economy could be described as service and agriculture-based, with agriculture contributing around one-third of GDP.[86]Small, underdeveloped enterprises continued to dominate Gaza's private productive sector. Industrial establishments accounted for 14 per cent of the labour force working in Gaza, but the typical industry was 'cottage' – i.e. family owned and employing few people. At the same time, Israeli restrictions on the movement of goods and services out of Gaza place further severe restraints on any possibility of export led growth in the Gaza economy. The ideal of a new Singapore in Gaza, promoted by many diaspora politicians on returning to Gaza, is therefore unrealistic under the current provisional conditions. While there is potential in regional markets, Gaza is at present poorly positioned to take advantage of them. Goods continue to flow in from Israel and increasingly from Egypt, both these countries place severe restrictions on the import of Gazan goods and services. Trade deficits are therefore accruing rapidly. In the future, if there is no productive investment in Gaza, the PA will lose an important potential source of tax revenue that could be placed into infrastructure and service projects which would in turn perhaps encourage further investment.

The Gaza economy has long been largely determined by political events, political interference and hostile manipulation. The result is an almost total lack of viable and sustainable internal employment opportunities, severe ecological restrictions on agricultural production, and a dependency on various external sources of income (workers' remittances from the Gulf states, international NGOs – most notably UNRWA, and daily migrations to work in the Israeli economy, usually for one third less wage than Israeli counterparts in the same job).

In the middle and the late 1980s, many factors in Gaza promoted increased awareness of the need to unite across social classes and backgrounds to confront an untenable situation. These included: un- and underemployment across all social classes; an agricultural sector being subjected to hostile policies undermining the ability to access inputs and market goods (affecting both large and small landholders); the restrictions on the entry of day wage labourers into Israel; and the closing off of 'borders' by the Israelis to restrict the import of what little goods and produce were available for export from Gaza. Survival was at stake. During the intifada, social unity was in part inspired by shared experiences of a deteriorating economic situation across cleavages of class and social grouping. Awareness of the external political factors that were enforcing and even encouraging this decline brought the society together in political opposition. In many ways, ironically perhaps, some degree of unity was temporarily forged around an awareness of the lack of an indigenous economic base which was accountable to local market demands and skills, and an awareness of the need to come together to create one. A boycott of Israeli products was encouraged to stimulate local production and strikes were called on a regular basis to alter the balance of costs and benefits of occupation for the Israelis.

This period saw further attempts at institutionalizing networks of home production and other strategies of self reliance that were intended to create internal economic linkages and to break the grip of the occupier's economy. The initial phase of the intifada wrought some advances in this area, introducing the notion of 'resistance development' (*sumud muqawwim*) which emphasized mobilization around local developmental potential to replace the externally funded resistance – (*sumud*) – that was increasingly criticized as inducing economic passivity and thus facilitating the Israeli drive to claim control over natural resources in the strip.[87] According to Roy:

> The political changes wrought by the Palestinian uprising in its first two years were accompanied by a fundamental attitude change that produced a new development paradigm. This paradigm was characterized by a new emphasis on self reliance. Two key alterations in economic activity took place: (1) a shift in emphasis from consumption to production; and (2) a reorientation in economic strategy from external competition with and employment in Israel to internal, local production for local markets. Although economic activity in Gaza was geared to addressing the immediate needs and burdens imposed by the intifada, it also aimed to redefine development according to local needs and criteria.[88]

Cossali and Robson's work indicates that these ideas, recognizing the correlation between political and economic dependence, had their roots in strategy debates of the early 1980s. One of Cossali's and Robson's informants, advocating the need for a structural economic basis of national mobilization rather than one based on rhetoric, describes the intent of this strategy:

> We've got labour and we've got a big internal market, so our economy has to

exploit this – producing labour intensive products that can be consumed locally and that are produced on a small enough scale to avoid posing a threat to Israeli monopolies, initially at least. I'm proposing that we create a whole range of cottage industries – things that can be made at home and which use our few local natural resources.[89]

The goals included a lessening of economic dependence on Israel. Through a grassroots boycott on Israeli products, and a willingness to endure short-term deprivation to achieve political goals, progress was made in this area.[90] However, there are problems in applying this 'small is beautiful' approach to grassroots development in Gaza. Consumption patterns have changed, there are difficulties associated with getting rid of surpluses when, with so few alternatives, everyone else is producing similar products rendering the sale of most home-produced goods outside Gaza impossible, the strategy has imposed hardship upon and Israeli retaliation against the petit bourgeoisie and made it feel that it has borne a disproportionate part of its negative consequences.[91] In the context of the dramatic decline in personal income and savings in the late 1980s, and the overall economic disruption during the intifada, the strategy simply represented 'too little, too late.' By the end of the intifada, unemployment in Gaza could be characterized as structural – i.e. entrenched within ecological and political constraints. Much of the unemployment must therefore be described as chronic and systemic, and not the temporary consequence of a periodic downward cycle.

Under occupation, the separate integration of Gaza's principle economic sectors in the Israeli economy, combined with the extremely atrophied condition of Gaza's productive base, forestalled the integration of economic sectors within the Gaza Strip. The overwhelming majority of productive enterprises tended to depend on subcontracts from Israeli producers and employed fewer than ten people.[92] Enforced by military occupation policies, the fundamental economic exchange and linkages in the stages of production that might have encouraged economic integration took place between Israelis and isolated Palestinian producers rather than between Palestinians. Thus, conscious Israeli policies fragmented the manoeuvring space for class and sectoral based political mobilization. While individuals and small groups in Gaza were responding to changing economic conditions and possibilities throughout the course of the occupation, they did so largely independently of the coordinated efforts of a political or social leadership. Economic change was therefore not accompanied by structural social and political change.

Thus, the overall trend during the intifada was toward ever increasing economic hardship. The initial phase of the intifada saw a 30 per cent drop in gross national product, a decline in per capita income from $1,700 to $1,200 per year (with some families losing considerably more), a 75 per cent drop in remittances from outside, and, with increasing closures and entry restrictions, the loss of income from work in Israel. The use of child labour increased, requests for UNRWA food supplements increased by 200 per cent and there was a sharp rise in the numbers of people needing emergency food aid.[93]

Economic Realities of Self-Rule: The View from Below

The impact of the changes wrought by Oslo on Palestinian society in general and in Gaza in particular has been necessarily complex – the new order applied to Gaza at once covered up and exposed social and developmental contradictions. The Palestinian leaders who had placed themselves at the centre of the national consciousness after the *fedayeen* ascendancy within the PLO in 1969 now found themselves under siege in the realm of local politics, powerless to affect improvements in the fundamental economic issues which had been a prime condition of the local enthusiasm over the return of the PLO to Gaza. To be sure, the economic situation in Gaza has continued to decline in Gaza since the signing of the Oslo Accords. Elmusa and El-Jafaari observed in 1994 that: 'Approximately 12 per cent of Gaza's population, or at least 102,000 people, are now dependent on some form of cash or food assistance. Of this number, it appears that approximately 40,000 were impoverished since the signing of the agreement.'[94]

The situation has worsened since then. Accordingly, whoever controls the influx of assistance and donor funds has considerable resources with which to cultivate factionalized and dependent relationships. Add to this the dependency on the PA and external labour markets (Israel) for jobs and the scope of economic dependence on the PA becomes clear. Roy identifies the economic crisis as the driving factor behind instability in Gaza. Immediately prior to the Gulf crisis, there were between 45 and 50,000 Gazans working in Israel – a figure which was already down from a height of 70,000 before the intifada. These workers were supporting close to 250,000 people.[95] Since the signing of the accords, the number of Gazans working in Israel has shrunken resulting in the dramatic exhaustion of savings (once a bright spot in the local economic indicators[96]) and unemployment. The situation reached a point of extreme crisis in the wake of Israel's response of collective punishment and increased separation following the spate of four suicide bombings in late February/early March 1996. Yasser Arafat warned of impending hunger in Gaza.[97] Father Manuel Mussallem, director of the Latin Patriarch school in Gaza, noted that: 'There is no economic situation here. There is only a struggle for life.'[98]

Within a couple months of its election, the Likud government had issued 22,500 permits for Gazan Palestinians to work in Israel (up from 8,500 or so issued by the previous Labour Government). However, closure and the increasing difficulty of finding work mean that far fewer are able to find regular employment in Israel. As of early 1997, UNRWA was supporting 90,000 hardship cases in Gaza alone. The World Food Programme was forced to increase its distribution by 70 per cent in 1996. Even as the number of hardship cases increase faster than these agencies can cope, there is worry on the street that these welfare organizations will be transferred to what is perceived as a corrupt and incompetent PA.[99]

Today, 'so many families have reached such a low level of subsistence that the most minimal job assistance – (the promise of) a few days of work each month serves to calm unrest.'[100] Dependency on the PA for jobs means that few will risk family employment by criticizing the PA. Meanwhile, there is little basis within the structures and tools of limited autonomy upon which an opposition might articulate an alternative socio-economic vision to guide. Thus any talk of a challenge to the PA's economic policy chokes on its own lack of alternatives. Two EU contractors charged with the building of a hospital in Khan Younis, frustrated at the slow progress of their project, related an anecdote which highlights the current predicament. The Palestinian workers building the hospital were intentionally sabotaging work deadlines. The workers know, the contractors said, that if the work progresses quickly, they will be unemployed again sooner. The repackaging of Gaza's difficulties under autonomy has not disguised fundamental realities as they are seen from the ground in Gaza.

The Gazan labour force in mid-1996 was around 185,000-strong and was poised to increase dramatically.[101] While the official PA statistics put unemployment in Gaza at 39.1 per cent, it should be noted that 'employed' was defined as anyone who worked at least one hour in the week that preceded the survey. Frequent closures and high rates of underemployment have led most observers to estimate actual rates of unemployment at around 60 per cent, and as high as 71 per cent.[102] Assuming a figure of 60 per cent, this means that thirteen Gazans are dependent upon each regular wage earner (74,000 employed in a population of 963,055). Per capita income has dropped to as low as $700 per annum in an economy with price levels roughly equivalent to those in Israel. Gazans are in situation where, with approximately 5 per cent of Israel's per-capita income, they have to pay Israeli prices. According to USAID statistics, approximately 33 per cent of all families in Gaza are living below the poverty line of $470 per year.[103]

Amira Hass, the Gaza correspondent for the Israeli daily *Ha'aretz,* has offered a revealing anecdote:

> In the early days of April 1994, when the first Palestinian policemen began to arrive and (base themselves in) an ex-Israeli police building, a group of Palestinian refugees, mostly from Beach Camp, gathered curiously around Israeli soldiers and policemen preparing to evacuate ... They were waiting for Arafat. 'And what do you expect him to achieve?' they were asked. 'To convince Rabin to open the borders and let us return to our jobs in Israel,' they replied.[104]

This expectation had its basis in Article 7 of the Cairo Agreement which calls for the free movement of labour over the borders subject to the possibility of occasional and temporary restrictions with proper notification. The current circumstances reflect the inability of the Oslo framework to meet even this short-term goal. While it was always the case that Palestinians, for the most part, took jobs that most Israelis were not inclined to accept, rising levels of unemployment in Israel make the import of Palestinian labour less rational to Israeli politicians. Unemployment in Israel increased from 4.8 per cent in the mid-1980s to 11 per cent in 1992.[105] This of course creates a tremendous disincentive for Israeli politicians to uphold article 7 of the Cairo Agreement. Hass also notes that 'as fewer Gazans are allowed to enter Israel, the more, it seems, they forget the physical and emotional strain involved in working there. Some complain that before peace "broke out", the procedures were less harsh and humiliating.'[106]

Given the depressed state of the Gazan economy and the continued dependence on goods produced in Israel, wage levels simply do not meet cost of living. Since day labour in Israel, although offering on average one third less for Palestinians than Israelis, more closely reflects the Israeli pegged cost of living than wages available in Gaza, workers are discouraged from taking more prestigious but lower paying jobs in Gaza. Besides placing tremendous stress on poorer families, this distortion in the local economy has the effect of creating a kind of 'brain drain' of Gaza's more educated and creative productive base, who are forced to accept menial jobs in Israel.

Given the rapid expansion of the Palestinian labour force, Salah Abd al-Shafi predicts that at least 100,000 workers from Gaza will have to cross at Erez daily if basic needs are to be satisfactorily met in the Strip. However, Abd al-Shafi also argues that as of the end of 1994, the Israeli economy will only require about 40,000 workers from Gaza suggesting a shortage of 60 000. Less pessimistically, operating on the assumption that demographic trends from the early 1980s remain constant, Fischer et al. report that the Palestinian economy would have to create 29,000 jobs a year between 1994 and 1999 if it were to be able to make up for the loss of jobs in Israel over that time.[107] Recent trends, including Israeli importation of cheap labour from East Asia and the political pressure to crack down hard on Palestinians as a collective punishment for suicide attacks by Islamic militants in Israel, make it even less likely that anywhere near that number of workers will be able to return to jobs inside Israel. It is also often overlooked that even now after the agreement, the Israeli state still controls about 44 per cent of the Gaza Strip. This 44 per cent includes some of the territory's most fertile and productive land and produces considerable Israeli exports to Europe.[108]

Envy and anger toward the wealthy is prevalent, especially toward the newly arrived diaspora elite. Aid workers told the author that this was having a very detrimental impact on social solidarity, and the success of several local development schemes; e.g. small loans programmes. Attempts at introducing small loan programs for individuals in Gaza have been hindered by very low repayment. When confronted by a programme assistant, delinquent borrowers often showed little concern, arguing that since all the returning PA bigwigs were benefiting from the donor largesse, they felt entitled to their share. When assistants pointed out that failure to repay simply meant that the funds would not be available for their neighbours to borrow at a later date, most just shrugged their shoulders. This was in contrast to the West Bank where there were fewer problems with repayment, and delinquent borrowers were reported to have consistently displayed an uneasy conscience when the social implications of not repaying were laid out.

Compounding this cynicism is public awareness of widespread corruption within the PA itself. Indeed, there is a legitimate fear that the few productive opportunities that exist within the peace process may be lost in corruption and patronage. Aisling Byrne describes the process:

> The lack of clear development and industrial strategies of the PA has created a vacuum which is rather rapidly being filled by 'private' entrepreneurs [with close links to the PA] and their families. The trade structure that is emerging, especially in Gaza, is of suppliers with exclusive rights, making deals with Israeli companies and sometimes dubious individuals, to be single suppliers to the captive Gazan market. Small and middle level [actors] and businesses cannot compete.[109]

A class basing its political and economic clout on contacts within both Israel and the PA is being entrenched within the autonomy.

The possibilities for corruption increase in the context of unreliable information, and PLC members and donors alike have complained about the lack of economic transparency within the PA. Elmusa and El-Jafaari – pointing to incidents in which contracts were given without public auction in cement, communications and petroleum, and in which particular merchants were favoured – note situations in which the agreement might incur costs on the already burdened consumer, who is in a weak position in the majority of Gaza's households.[110] According to economic researcher Aisling Byrne, the process works like this:

> Several key deal brokers – Israelis and Palestinians – have made a speciality of [making] arrangements under which a single Israeli firm is awarded a lucrative contract to supply a certain product throughout the Palestinian autonomous areas. Competing firms are frozen out. In return, the single supplying firm usually pays a handsome commission to the deal brokers ... a person responsible for making sure that only approved monopolies import products (is) Mohammed Dahlan, head of the preventative security forces in Gaza.
>
> Such deals already cover fuel (supplied by the Israeli company Dor Energy for a reported $100 million per year), cement (supplied by the Israeli company Nesher), and there are similar reports of deals (sometimes with two or three suppliers) for steel, frozen meat, paint, flour, gas, cigarettes, communications and computer hardware/software. Many raw materials are now supplied exclusively by Shirkat al-Bahar (an 'independent' holding company with reported close and direct links with Arafat and the PA) which is buying shares in a wide range of companies – described by one economist as 'branches of al-Bahar with direct links to the PA.' As for the money, according to the *Jerusalem Report*, 'part of the commission ... is channelled into an unaudited fund controlled by Arafat

himself. Arafat does not use the fund for personal purposes, but rather to boost his popularity.[111]

American State Department reports suggest that 27 monopolies are currently operating in the territories. According to Husam Khader, 'every honcho got himself a fat slice of the imports into the Authority. One got the fuel, another (the son of the Palestinian trade minister) the cigarettes, yet another the lottery, and his crony the flour.' The security forces control the monopoly on gravel, Muhammed Rashid (Arafat's chief economic advisor and head of Shirkat al-Bahar) controls the cement monopoly, Interior Minister Nabil Shaath's Egyptian-based company imports computers into the territory.[112] According to economist Saleh Abd al-Shafi:

> Like a cancer, these monopolies are slowly penetrating every sector ... the centralization is even worse than in the former Soviet Union. In the former Soviet Union, benefits were for the state bureaucracy, the emerging picture in Palestine, however, is for the benefit of pseudo-official 'economic gangs.'[113]

Word on the street has it that prominent members of the Palestinian security forces essentially force local businessmen to accept them as 'partners.' Other reports suggest that Palestinian police regularly confiscate goods from merchants (such as expired food products) or stolen items only to resell them for personal profit. As in transitions elsewhere on the globe, new and often reinvented elites are using the resources of the state to allow for the primitive accumulation of capital and distributing these 'privileges' tactically in ways that allow the regime to hold its power – i.e. the neopatrimonial strategies discussed in Chapter 2. On a more promising note, the PLC has taken an active role in criticizing such developments, but is sadly powerless to do anything about it. Husam Khader has expressed the frustrations of the Council in this regard:

> I could yell in parliament and set up commissions of inquiry, but nothing would come of it. We do not get the information from the Authority that we ask for. We do not know how much the monopolies earn, or where the money goes. The senior economists and monopoly owners, especially Muhammad Rashid, are not willing to appear before the parliament; and when they do appear, they just leave unanswered questions behind them – and all this under the guise of state security, its all classified.[114]

The absence of an environment in which specific alternatives can be presented and the lack of any real broad social base to inform either the ruling or opposition ideology, means that resentment, in the place of abject cynicism, often takes on an 'Islamist' character. The want of economic sectoral bases of opposition leaves Islam as one of the few possible orienting poles of social integration and opposition in Gaza (see Chapter 6 below). If any opposition is going to be strong enough to challenge the PA's relative local monopoly over coercive force with viable alternatives for popularly based government, some sort of economic or social formation that cuts across the cleavages of Gaza's fragmented civil society must inform the proposed alternatives. This would seem to apply to any viable opposition, or, for that matter, to any regime hoping to sustain authority into the future.

The PA has proven unable to ensure that funds intended for public services actually result in the provision of required basic services. As the direction of external funding shifts from NGOs to the PA, social services are contracting as the organizations which met many daily needs under occupation run out of funds.[115] PA funding finds is accountable to the pressures of keeping an elite coalition together and at the same time meeting external demands upon its limited powers and resources for security and stability. This change in the direction of funding with few tangible benefits to the local population has buttressed claims of corruption, incompetence and cronyism within the PA.

Thus the provisional regime also threatens several economic coping strategies without providing immediately satisfying or promising alternatives. Previous public to private transfers – UNRWA support to '1948' refugees, a limited amount of need based social benefits from the Israeli civil administration, the redistribution of *zakat* by religious institutions, and support to families of martyrs distributed by the PLO from outside – all created special interests serviced by institutions scheduled to be taken over by PA authorities.[116] Extended family solidarity informed the direction of private to private transfers of wealth and patterns of investment in material and human resources. Remittances from workers abroad, especially the Gulf states, constituted an important source of income which was lost after the Gulf War.[117]

Such factionalized coping strategies promoted little economic solidarity within civil society institutions and continues to reflect the developmental disorientation which seems to be at the base of much of the factionalism in Palestinian society – disorientation which has been driven by Israeli policies as well PLO strategies. It also facilitates factionalized responses to PA authority. This in turn allows the PA to take an approach to co-optation which does not include the articulation of a social agenda or the defining of a developmental basis for the legitimacy of its rule. Arafat himself has, however, noted the link between economic conditions and political stability in the OT on several occasions. It would certainly be one of the central contradictions of 'self-rule' if autonomy for the provisional regime did not include the ability to shape the political economic environment, or at least formulate effective responses to economic concerns using the kind of means available to other governments, including diplomatic initiatives and control over taxation, customs, and the determination of economic imperatives and linkages to shape market forces to some internal advantage, comparative and otherwise.

PA employment policy seems to be centred around direct employment in PA bureaucratic and security organs, and around short-term job creation schemes. Byrne points out that the World Bank puts the cost at a 27,000 man security force alone at $180 million while total employment in the PA as of Summer 1996 might be much higher. Furthermore, $73 million (much of it in loans taken out by the PA) has been spent by the Palestinian Economic Council for Development and Reconstruction (PEDCAR) on creating 21,000 to 50,000 short-term jobs of three to twelve weeks duration with the stated aim of 'alleviating hardship pending the normalization of the bilateral climate.' To cite examples in Gaza, $20 million was spent on the 'clean up Gaza' and 'Gaza Sites, Parks and Neighbourhood Retransformation' campaigns in 1994. Such funding priorities for projects which involved 'sweeping the dust from one side of the street to another' was, not surprisingly, highly contentious. Byrne points out that such spending puts a heavy burden on an unproductive economy. Palestinian economist Adel Samara argues: 'what productive resources do Palestinians have to repay these loans? We will be forced to pay with our political position.'[118] Also, the absorption capacity within the Palestinian economy has been exhausted for this type of unproductive and unsustainable employment. Some municipalities have approached NGOs for assistance in implementing more useful projects, but the current emphasis on projects with little if any developmental component is a cause for concern over the long-term.[119] Current policy only enhances the dependent, patrimonial basis of the emerging Palestinian political economy.

According to the 1993 Declaration of Principles, 'the PA would assume direct responsibility for education, culture, social welfare, direct taxation and tourism.'[120] However, many of these functions, education for example, were already administered by Palestinians, and the Israeli authorities retained power over 'other spheres not transferred,' and could thus continue to close schools after the signing of the agreement of 29 August 1994.[121] While the Israelis gave the PLO the right to administer spheres already under Israeli control, 'Israeli control or veto remained in the more strategic areas of water, energy, financial development, transport and communications, trade, industry, environment, labour, media and international aid.' In other words, 'Israel would divest itself of the expensive functions of government but retain control of matters directly related to economic development. (Direct taxation can be considered an expense, since a climate of widespread politically rationalized tax evasion had made revenues increasingly marginal to Israel's costs of occupation.)'[122] 'Total control over water resources remains in Israeli hands, and all military orders – such as those requiring permission to plant tomatoes and eggplants – continue intact.'[123] The various agreements have only abrogated 70 of the nearly 1,000 military occupation order which were used to govern Gaza.[124] Furthermore, 'there is little likelihood that the PA will succeed in developing tourism, one of the transferred sectors, when it cannot grant licenses for entrepreneurs to build hotels or tourist centres outside municipalities, and lacks access to adequate sources of water or control over border crossings.'[125]

'One area in which the Palestinians did not achieve improvement was in that of labour, and Israel continues to control the flow of Palestinian workers into Israel.'[126] While Abed argues that it is ridiculous to base Palestinian development over the long-term on dependence on the Israeli labour market, in the short-term it is a necessity. Indeed, the Israeli policy of closure of the OT – enforced in varying degrees since the 1993 signing of the agreement but never entirely lifted – has had a profoundly negative impact on economic wellbeing in Gaza.[127] Statistics released by the Palestine Ministry of Information pertaining to the period between January 1996 and 10 November 1996 put the days of closure of the OT at 99. In addition, a maritime siege was imposed on the sea off Gaza for a total of 36 straight days, during which time fishing vessels were not allowed to sail.[128] Even the right of safe passage explicitly referred to in the agreement has not been fulfilled in practice, isolating Gaza's exports not only from Jordanian and Egyptian markets, but from those of the West Bank as well.[129] One large landholder in Gaza complained to the author that closure had forced him to dump his tomatoes in Gaza at 3 shekels per 20 kilos as he was not allowed to transport them to the West Bank where the market price for the same 20 kilos was 55 shekels. The inability of the Gaza's farmers to reach this market meant that it was Israeli producers who were enjoying these prices in the West Bank markets.

Not surprisingly, these restrictions have provoked reaction in Gaza. In mid-September 1996, Gaza workshop and factory owners blocked a main Gaza thoroughfare passing in front of the PA ministry of interior with machinery laden trucks to protest the restrictions on the movement of goods between Gaza and the West Bank.[130] In late October 1996, Palestinian authorities banned the entry of Israel food products to protest the sealing of borders.[131] According to Palestinian Agricultural Minister Abdel Jawad Salih, 'Every day, we lose $500,000 as a result of the closure.'[132] On Sunday 23 November, 'hundreds of Palestinian motorists jammed a one-mile strip in front of the settlement of Netzarim for most of the day to protest Israeli travel restrictions that have been in force since February.'[133] Said al-Mudallal of the Labour and Employment Department warned of a 'social explosion' if the blockade were not lifted.[134]

Current proposals for the restructuring of dependent relations in line with Israeli wishes and American support largely follows the model proposed by Israeli economist Edra Sadan.[135] The economic restructuring from above is in many respects determined by outside appraisals of the efficiency of certain models designed to bring employment in Gaza up to a livable status quo without exceeding the limits of what is politically acceptable for any particular Israeli government. The imbalance of power seems to have led to a redeployment of direct occupation without any real concessions on the part of the Israelis in terms of their ultimate economic control.

Sadan has argued that the traditional agricultural base of the Gaza Strip should be allowed to deteriorate and be replaced with industrial agriculture emphasizing the production of non-food plants (flowers). Ornamental plant production is labour intensive and costs in Israel are high. Before 1991, there were no cash crops of flowers at all in Gaza. Production was introduced by the Israeli military authority in the wake of the Gulf War.[136] As of 1994, there were 140 greenhouses in the Strip dedicated to the cultivation of ornamentals.[137] Since the markets were in the hands of Israeli importers, very little would be lost to the Israeli economy by way of low cost competition.

In practice, however, the dependence of Gaza flower growers on the Israeli marketing board (Agrexco) for both seedlings and sale has proven problematic. Flowers are an extremely perishable commodity, and producers are dependent upon a timely arrival in markets. However, the marketing board has consistently marketed flowers produced in Israel before those produced in Gaza, which means that by the time the Gaza flowers reach the front of the line, many have deteriorated. They are then declared unsalable by the marketing board and the Palestinian producer must accept the loss.[138] Unlike food crops, damaged ornamentals cannot even be used or sold as animal fodder. Furthermore, flower production 'is a very water intensive activity and therefore highly inappropriate for Gaza given its serious water problem.'[139]

The Sadan plan also called for the building of industrial parks (pockets of infrastructure) on the Gaza-Israeli border (Israel recently confiscated the land of the proposed sites, even though the basic issues of land and location have not been resolved after years of negotiation[140]). The World Bank's prescriptions fit Sadan's exactly. Since infrastructure for the whole strip would cost too much, the Israelis could aid in building up certain areas. Rather than migrate over the border into Israel, Gazan workers would commute to pockets of infrastructure which would allow Israeli and Palestinian capital to utilize low-cost labour in Gaza while removing the costs of occupation to the Israeli state. Instead of labour migration, it called for developing a system of subcontracting between Palestinian capitalists, who would be allowed more opportunities for investment inside Gaza than before (liberalizing of licensing agreements), and sectors of Israeli capital (of course, the nature of these investments would be controlled to suit the needs of specific sectors of the Israeli economy).

The problem with such a plan is that it gives a basis for denying economic sovereignty to the PA. It also excludes the PA from a role in labour relations and confuses the ability of workers to organize and protect and promote their rights and interests vis-à-vis any regulating and arbitrating authority. Given the differences in scale between the two economies to begin with, Sadan concedes that concern in some Israeli sectors over competition from Palestinian producers was nonsense.[141]

Similar industrial parks already exist in Israel; e.g. the Ramat Hov Industrial Park which operates as a free port zone. According to Israel Shahak, the businesses located in this zone are 'freed not only from paying any taxes, but also from the restrictions of labour and ecological laws.' It is thus a 'legal' way of neglecting Palestinian labour rights.[142] Another is the Erez Industrial District, a site which operates like a military district with soldiers and police overseeing all entry and exit into the site. Work permits are issued by the 'Israeli-Palestinian Liaison Committee,' and Israel inspects all trucks and goods without PA officials present.[143] In more recent developments, the Israeli government held up the authorization of the PA's Karni Industrial Park by the Nahal Oz checkpoint in Gaza protesting its location directly on the border with Israel. According to PA plans, the Karni park would provide 20,000 jobs, but the PA remains dependent on the Israeli government to provide infrastructure for the project.[144] Countering the idea that Palestinian development should base itself on isolated enclaves of investment, Elmusa and El-Jafaari call for greater economic integration of the West Bank and Gaza Strip.[145] Certainly, assuming that national identity and solidarity in the state building context has an economic foundation, such an integration would encourage a sense of sharing a material basis for future common action.

In a somewhat superficial sense, the current economic transition represents a shift from a colonial to a neocolonial relationship.

> Instead of blocking all development in the territories and bringing the Palestinians into Israel for cheap labour, it makes a lot more sense to keep workers in the territories and move the assembly plants over there, and then exploit people unnoticed. Israelis wouldn't have to worry walking around their cities, and they could keep control of the resources and thus create a semi-colonial area … this was openly discussed in the Israeli media.[146]

In few other cases, however, is such a blatantly militarily imposed relationship given such international political support or heralded as the model for peace and stability. The relationship is still based on politically imposed conditions of dependency. The opportunities for productive development outside of these industrial zones would still be subject to Israel's political control over borders and trade, Gazans would still be largely dependent on Israeli goods (although Egyptian goods are increasingly available in Gaza) and indeed, Israel would be inclined to protect advantages it gained by these zones – economic interest might make it more difficult for Israeli politicians to make the concessions that would allow the Gaza economy to become less dependent on such zones. In this model, self-rule becomes a device blunting the accountability of Israeli capital in relations with Palestinian labour.

As has been noted, the occupation's civil and military bureaucracy was used to stifle competition with Israeli economic interests. The result today is that Israel enjoys comparative advantages in all the crucial sectors of Gaza's economy, primarily citrus fruits. Subsidies to Israeli producers and strict border controls reinforce these relative disadvantages. Given the high costs of living in Gaza, one must wonder whether wages could ever sink low enough in Gaza to offset these financial and political subsidies to Israeli production, especially since the Palestinian economy is subject to Israeli monetary restrictions, making expansion on public spending dependent on outside aid.

For many Palestinians, the success or failure of the current track of the peace process, and with it the legitimacy of the current provisional regime, will be measured in terms of its impact on their own pocket books. In this context, the fact that living conditions have deteriorated since the signing of the Oslo Accords bodes ill for the ability of the forces empowered by the agreement to secure the stability and economic growth and development that would prove conducive to peace in the region over the long-term. 'Despite the subsequent agreements reached in Paris and Cairo, and the $2.4 billion fund offered by international donors, by the beginning of 1995 hopes of economic development had floundered, living standards were still falling and the donors themselves were declaring their strategy a failure.'[147]

Rather than granting any basis for the meaningful policy manoeuvrability which constitutes a relative degree of economic sovereignty, the agreements basically pass responsibility onto the PLO for the administration of Palestinian welfare as Israel restructures its economic relationship with the territories. As only a fraction of the promised aid money has trickled into the PA administered areas, few new jobs have been created in Gaza and people have not been allowed to return to their jobs in Israel, the result has been a loss of faith in the opportunities supposedly been presented by the agreement.

The initial agreements suggest that Israel has reduced the costs of occupation without really giving up the most notable benefits. Meanwhile, the PA acceptance of the stipulation in Article XI(8) of the August 1994 agreement – which states that the PA is responsible for 'any shortfall in tax collection that is not covered by the donor countries' and all expenditures beyond the six months agreed upon budget – effectively creates 'a budget deficit before there is even the prospect of a Palestinian state.'[148] The Israeli demands that Palestinians 'harmonize their tax and customs regime with the high levels in force in Israel,' and limit direct trade between Gaza the outside (re: Egypt and Jordan only), to the servicing of 'market needs' place severe restrictions on the ability of the PA to attract investment. These problems are exacerbated by the fact that shipments of goods and services are still subject to politically motivated border closings, subsidized Israeli competition, and discriminatory enforcement of quality inspection standards. The Cairo Agreement added insult to injury by adding two conditions protecting Israel from competition and the payment of reparations for damages incurred during the occupation. '(A)rticle VII accepted that all laws and military orders imposed by Israel should remain in force unless amended or abridged in accordance with the agreement. The PLO thus accepted the legitimacy of a vast number of military orders used to constrain the economic activity of the OT.'[149] Under the current terms, the PA must assume all fiscal responsibility for those spheres omitted by the agreement.[150]

Abed has argued that the Fatah-based administration was neither technically, administratively nor institutionally prepared to manage its economic responsibilities during the transition. A situation of near-anarchy has been the result. The role of institutions are the cornerstone of any discussion of the effectiveness of the transition in the self-rule areas. This requires legal and bureaucratic reform which the Arafat administration seems thus far unwilling or unable to implement. In spite of the talk of private enterprise being the engine of Palestinian development, the role of the fiscal and legal administration in facilitating economic activity, coordinating tax systems and managing aid and other sectors of development is unavoidable. Effective administration must be executed in the context of efficient institutions and in line with a strategy developed in accordance with an accountable understanding of the general interests of the community, rather than a specific faction maintaining a relationship with power.[151] In the absence of institutional capability, this is not apt to be the case. In the light of the Israeli policy of 'separation,' Palestinian options may have even been reduced by the signing of the agreement, and in spite of the donor-sponsored face-lift of some parks and roads and a relative boom in construction, productive long-term employment prospects remain grim for many if not most Gazans.

Conclusion

The only power possessed by the PA in the area of what might be described as foreign policy is that its representatives are allowed to go abroad and seek economic aid and investment. However, instability, talk of corruption, and a peace process which seems stalled create a climate not conducive to attracting foreign investment. It is a tragic irony that economic isolation and the political instability associated with current economic hardships produce conditions which make amelioration even less likely, thus encouraging a downward spiral. Salama A. Salama reports that:

> When Yasser Arafat, President of the Palestinian National Authority, visited Germany recently to ask German industrialists and investors to invest in the Palestinian territories, he was told by the president of the German Chamber of Commerce and Industry that in light of the present political situation in the region, it would be illogical for German private sector companies to make any long-term investments in Palestinian territory.[152]

It seems unlikely that the PA will be able to emphasize the growth of the local economy or developmental issues as a basis for its legitimation in the near term. The chances of Gazans presenting a united front to encourage the articulation of a PA social and economic agenda are slim. Instead, political compliance may be rewarded with the patronage largesse of autonomous institutions. Furthermore, the extreme dependence of the autonomous structures on outside funding must be noted – a situation made more stultifying by the fact that these structures offer the primary source of employment within the strip. The costs of the Palestinian police forces might quickly run as high as '$500 million a year, not to mention the cost of a PA civil bureaucracy of 27,000 employees.'[153]

> The idea that the PA can financially cover such non-productive sectors from locally generated revenue while running much needed services is wholly imaginary … What such an inflated public sector (in which nearly 70 per cent of all jobs are security related) actually portends is an interim period every bit as economically and politically conditioned by donor money as was its Gaza-Jericho preamble.[154]

On Wednesday 20 November 1996, World Bank chief James D. Wolfensohn announced that the PA would receive 945 million dollars in support from donor institutions. Given the current environment, this money can be invested in to little else but patronage dependency that sustains the political process without addressing the fundamental structural concerns which undermine the economic sustainability of Palestinian autonomy.

There is a danger that anti-developmental incentives and modes of economic behaviour based around short-term adaptation and survival strategies will be ingrained into any future independent Palestinian political entity. This would make it less likely that Gaza will be able to transcend dependency on and determination by Israeli political policy and economic realities in the future. Conditions of economic fragmentation are unlikely to be resolved and the productive economy will remain largely outside the regulatory scope of Palestinian politicians. The use of industrial zones may mean that relations between labour and employers will not be arbitrated by Palestinian authorities or subject to internal laws and procedure. In any case, such issues have not been addressed and the author is unaware of any models upon which resolution of such issues might be based. The inability or unwillingness of either the patrons of the Oslo process or the partners to the agreement to address the continued structural inadequacies of Palestinian economy (many if not most of them politically imposed or reinforced, others having to do with the short-term imperatives of the PA itself) may contribute decisively to political instability in Gaza in the future. At any rate, economic integration will not serve as a basis encouraging a broad base supporting integrated social identification with the PA regime.

The legitimacy of PA structures, such as they are, will in no small measure be decided by their ability to effect economic improvements. More significant over the long term, however, is the relevance of these structures to procuring and protecting a degree of economic independence that might underpin political independence, and sustain the meaningful participation of individuals and groups in civic development. The flow and distribution of economic resources in a society – together with the relationship between economic activity and the ability of political authority to regulate in response to structural shortcomings and to account for (or compensate for) ideological concerns – are crucial signifiers of actual and potential trends in civic development. An examination of these phenomena in the context of interim autonomy suggests that crucial structural preconditions for the development of a fully democratic and associative civil society are lacking. (The implications of this for PA strategies of consolidation, and the ability of the Palestinian street to identify with the new order, are the subjects of the next two chapters.)

Finally, Netanyahu's call for the expansion of settlement activity on the most productive land of the Gaza Strip indicates an intention to hold on to the resources of the Gaza Strip, and perhaps use the settler presence as a base from which to intrude in the eventual autonomous function of Palestinian planning in infrastructural and developmental affairs.[155] If this is so, the outlook for the peace process to lead to the kind of structural transformations that might contribute to corresponding political integration and social stability cannot be described as promising.

5

Institutions, Rituals and Power: PA Consolidation 'from Above'

Many critics have chastized the Palestinian Authority (PA) for being too repressive. Others have criticized it for not being repressive enough. Yet few observers suggest how the stances of PA elites toward Palestinian society in the 'self-rule' areas have been determined by the limited options contained within the framework of current PLO–Israeli agreements. Article II, paragraph 2 of the 'Agreement on Transfer of Powers and Responsibilities' signed at Erez on 29 August 1994 defines the PA as 'the authorized Palestinians.' Such a formulation begs the question of who authorized them and serves as a reminder that autonomy refers to a specific scope of authorization – an administrative and disciplinary mandate – as opposed to abstract authority or sovereignty.[1] Palestinian citizenship remains a promise suggested rather than ensured on paper, and 'self-rule' has yet to trickle down to the Palestinian street.

In essence the PA project, as outlined by Oslo and subsequent agreements, is one of social mobilization (or in this case demobilization) 'from above': Rather than building on structures already existing in the grassroots, autonomy is premised on re-organizing and 'stabilizing' Palestinian society using mechanisms and incentives that reflect and protect the immediate interests of the PLO elite and its negotiating partners. This chapter examines the agreements and trends in the early phases of PA consolidation, to see how the law and rituals associated with self-rule are shaping the process. It also suggests how the PA elite's understanding of power and its uses is shaping identification with the institutions of the new regime, and discuss the potential implications of the PA's limited ability to effectively govern. The central questions are: how, in the classic sense of elite based political mobilizations, is the PA elite trying to reshape the interests of Palestinian society to more closely correspond with its own? and how are the subjects of PA administrative coercion identifying their rights and obligations within the new order?

In the interim context the greatest portion of PA power is circumscribed not by accountability to the society in which it operates, but rather by the demands and constraints placed upon it by external actors and international agreements. The balance of power within the context of the peace process means that the PA must hold itself accountable to external demands which often seem to contradict the hopes associated with self-rule on the street. Azmi Bishara bluntly argues that Oslo:

> inaugurates a process which sustains Israel's historic position of no withdrawal from and no annexation of the OT; (but the process also) addresses the problem (of the unacceptable status quo ante which had emerged with the intifada) by bringing in the PLO to solve it on Israel's behalf. This is the essence of autonomy.[2]

The present contours of Palestinian power and quasi-citizenship are regulated through agreements with Israel, with whom the PA shares the responsibilities of government by joint committee.[3] Rights and obligations are bounded by accountability to the superior economic and coercive potential of the Israeli state, and in no way does the 'inevitable' trajectory of the peace process ensure change. As of January 1997, internal Israeli debates concerning the aim of eventual 'final status negotiations' remained centred around whether Palestinians will have 'a limited state' or 'expanded autonomy.'[4]

The major donors (particularly the United States) seem to have decided – their stated commitment to promoting a 'culture of democracy' notwithstanding – that the peace process demands an authoritarian PA to 'deliver' the peace. This has been suggested by a senior USAID official who reports that Dennis Ross (the senior American negotiator) has ordered that USAID not promote activities that might strengthen municipal and local administrations and encourage bases of power and mobilization that might 'diminish the power of Mr Arafat and the PA to carry out the tasks of the day.'[5] Issues such as those mentioned here have a profound effect on how the PA uses self-rule institutions to promote stability and consolidate their political position. In the overall context of the 'peace process', the correlation between 'autonomous' institutions and their effective functions and meanings has become convoluted. In order to protect the peace process, nascent, quasi-democratic institutions are invoked to fulfil functions other than those of transparency and accountability. The institutionalized bases of power relations that might characterize citizenship are accordingly undermined. The PA's circumscribed ability to govern effectively during the transitional period limits its potential to inspire confidence in the new order.

The Israeli prime minister Benjamin Netanyahu has argued that Palestinian autonomy as currently constituted would not be allowed to lead to 'a state in the classic sense, but [would represent] a completely new sort of political unit.'[6] Netanyahu has openly likened the future of this Palestinian entity to the US protectorate of Puerto Rico.[7] Netanyahu's groping to justify continued Israeli control over land and resources with an apparently benign reference suggests continued Israeli-imposed conditionality on the future scope of obligations, rights and sovereignty between authority and subjects in the space of what has been optimistically described as Palestinian 'self-rule.'

Imbalances, Arbitration and the Conditionality of Palestinian Power

The Israeli historian Ilan Pappé has noted that the Oslo Accord 'embodies the immense imbalance of power between the two sides: Israel can do what it wants, Arafat cannot even say what he wants.'[8] According to Ghassan al-Khatib, the peace process represents 'a sort of dictation rather than negotiations. It starts with Israeli proposals and ends with agreements that are extremely similar to the initial Israeli proposals. Israel makes use of the weakness of the PLO [as well as] the lack of democratic decision-making process within the PLO.'[9] Shimon Peres himself noted during the discussions on the transition to greater Palestinian autonomy that 'in some ways we are negotiating with ourselves.'[10] Pappé continues:

> Arafat in Gaza and Jericho has established a mechanism over which he has control. It is a limited control, but he has the powers of patronage, of salaries, of prestige, the rudiments, if you like, of a bureaucratic mini-state. This may bear little resemblance to the aspirations of the Palestinian people, but it is a form of power ... [albeit] a wholly unstable form of power ... should the Oslo process remain stuck, will Arafat remain content as head of a bureaucracy oiled by five or six secret security services? Maybe he will, but then again, maybe he won't. If he does, then he is confirming [Edward] Said's vision of perpetuating the occupation on Israel's behalf.[11]

On the one hand, it might seem that Arafat has simply fallen to the temptation of organizing along lines similar to Egypt or Syria, which have proven resilient models of milito-bureaucratic elite consolidation (i.e. corporatism). Indeed, in both cases, the state itself seems quite stable as long as the configurations of power are themselves sustained. However, regime change or structural transition in such a framework brings with it vulnerability and uncertainty. The PA lacks many crucial components associated with legal sovereignty which do provide resources other than simple patronage to the regime. Some observers, have argued that the PA's 'legitimate use of force' constitutes a foundation of the PA's emerging 'stateness.' However, the distinction between 'legitimate use of force' and the classical Weberian definition – 'monopoly on the use of coercive force' – is crucial here. Interestingly, this lack of a monopoly creates inconsistencies and dubious lines of accountability of the manifestation of force in society thus undermining its accountability. It must be remembered that the PA coercive functions are first and foremost legitimized by and held accountable to the peace process, and therefore do not represent legitimacy in ways denoting popular accountability.

The argument that instability is inherent in such a limited degree of government seems especially pertinent given the intentional vagueness and ambiguity over the end result of the negotiations over power.[12] The agreements proposed continued negotiations while at the same time ensuring the PLO that the final status was a foregone conclusion.[13] The agreements – and the framework for arbitration and negotiation they established – were perhaps seen as making up for the effective powerlessness the PLO took to the negotiating table.[14] In fact, however, this imbalance of power leaves the PA dependent on international arbitration to push forward Israeli concessions that might lead to a permanent status agreement. The resulting predicament has been mocked in the Islamist press: 'Arafat will resort to "arbitration" should his peace goal prove far from reality. Arafat has said: "Arbitration. We have the United Nations, we have the Hague, we have the Security Council, we have the Europeans. We'll go to arbitration."'[15]

The results of the Washington Summit in early October 1996, and the effective exclusion of Europe from any role other than to pay PA bills, highlight the weakness of Arafat's position in this respect.

The limitations of power also indicate the limitations on the constituency of that power. The powerlessness of Palestinian politicians to articulate and execute positive policy on the one hand, and the pressures of state building and social competition on underdeveloped and underempowered institutions on the other hand, contradict the expectations and promise of 'self-rule.' As Sara Roy has trenchantly noted, 'with regard to autonomous decision making, the difference between the past and the present regimes is that there are now more Palestinians in positions of no authority.'[16] The emerging contradictions – i.e. relative powerlessness under the title of self-rule, and a new context for internal Palestinian socio-economic competition without corresponding accountable economic government institutions – combine with a dismal economic situation to threaten the stability of the Palestinian space as well as that of the region as a whole.

The need to press ahead with international obligations taken precedence over Palestinian civil rights under autonomy. At present, the failure to contain abuses of administrative privilege and coercive force within the self-rule areas suggests a lack of real institutional accountability. Internally, this lack of accountability manifests itself in the apparent arbitrariness of 'self-rule's' coercive face. According to Usher:

> The most ominous feature of the security forces is their proliferation, amorphousness, and their lack of terms of reference, which makes it impossible to define their different responsibilities. The difficulty of definition is clearly shared by the representatives of the various services.[17]

It has become difficult for Palestinians to distinguish between the unaccountable situation of occupation and the supposedly more accountable condition of autonomy. The imbalance of power has occasionally pressed the Palestinian Security Forces into tasks which made them appear more answerable to external interests than the security of the society in which they operate.

Why does the provisional regime seem unable to encourage the social and economic reconstitution of Gaza's civil society? The ability of Israel to win concessions on so many issues of substantive authority has left the PA with few tools with which to win broad recognition of its provisional authority. Current agreements limit the PA's ability to inject its power and will into society in meaningful ways. In accepting the symbolic elements of autonomy (the public display of the Palestinian flag, the Palestine postage stamp and telephone calling code separate from that of Israel) and assuming that this would inevitably lead to more substantive authorities – perhaps even a state – the PLO elites seem to have assumed that their historical status would carry legitimacy within Gaza throughout a new phase in the nationalist movement. But in this they may have erred.

The inability of society to make demands of power leaves the Autonomy more prone to influence by external demands. Increasingly, individuals may turn to violence to force their demands to be taken into account when all other channels of communication between society and power seem to have failed.

The limitations on the PA's ability to shape consensus, (that is to produce the initiatives which mobilize society from above) encourages a strategy of rule characterized by an insecure stance toward civil society – weakening society in order to ensure success *over* society. The situation is encouraging short-term tactics for power consolidation which may ultimately exclude significant segments of the population of Gaza from strong feelings of identification with the new regime. Given the limited extent of resources and privileges to distribute as patronage, and given that crackdowns against opponents of the PA are seen by some as punishing legitimate resistance activities or affecting innocent as well as guilty parties, general mass alienation from the emerging political status quo may result.

Current limited PA powers might promote day-to-day stability by making Palestinian society socially and economically dependent upon it. But this arrangement could be inherently precarious as the PA is itself dependent on external funding, and is unable to promote the creation of an economic base capable of internally sustaining 'self-rule' institutions. PA elites do not seem to be shaping the interests and expectations of society to conform with their own over the short-term. Their ability to do so will not be facilitated by the probable intransigence of the current Israeli regime when it comes to making concessions in powers and territory to the PLO/PA. As an exchange between Sherif Elmusa and Haydar Abd al-Shafi indicates, the impact of a failure to move quickly forward could be profound.

Elmusa: 'Yet the PA officials insist that the process is heading towards a Palestinian state. What accounts for their optimism?'
Abd al-Shafi: 'Well, basically you are talking about Arafat. Because the rest of them, deep in their hearts, know that it is not going to be so. I sit with ministers who say frankly: "It's all over. We're finished." They actually say it.'[18]

Meanings of Power: Government and Social Mobilization from Above

National mobilization, state-building, and power

Both the national movement and the state-building project refer to specific contexts for social mobilization and suggest different scopes of power, constituency and possibility. These in turn shape a political dynamic which informs and orients individuals toward the institutions through which their interests are best articulated and satisfied. A national liberation movement is by its nature loose and inevitably presents an abstract ideal for government which clearly contrasts with existing inhibitions on rights and expression. The nationalist movement articulates general responses and mobilizes society in the face of perceived shared threats or challenges to a socially, politically, economically and psychologically 'self aware' community. State-building, however, requires the establishment of an order with social structures deep and dependable enough to mitigate internal social conflicts. The state must be capable of asserting coercive force within the bounds of totemic (symbolic, psychological and perceived historical) legitimacy. It does so by using power to enforce and reinforce institutions.

Ultimately, the sovereign political unit is recognizable through the exercise of power within identifiable social and geographic boundaries. Political power results from a variety of forces; *inter alia*, coercive technology, social mobilization, and the ability to regulate state-based economic privileges and incentives. These all contribute to the way in which a particular regime conceives of and uses power. The political unit becomes functional as such when power is situated within institutions capable of both instrumentality and will. Strict Hobbesian analysis suggests that institutionalization can only logically be manifested in the physical body of a single leader. Arafat's attitude toward national institutions often seems similarly premised. The agreements that establish the PA, on the other hand, call for adversarial democratic institutions to represent the foundation and character of the Palestinian body politic, both as it manifests itself currently in the autonomous areas, and within the framework of any final status. The problem with either scenario is that the elements of power which bind a society to its political institutions by uniting private and public interests and by creating an environment of security are lacking. The ability of the PA to repress its own subjects, evaluated beside its inability to protect Palestinians from continued settler violence, or prevent intrusions of Israeli Defence Forces into PA-controlled areas, highlights this skewed balance of power in practice.[19]

State-building represents a complex set of more or less recognizable political and socio-economic processes. In the broadest civic sense, it might be said to represent processes of inclusion and consensus within institutions – institutions which have both the power to enforce rights and obligations, and to address and adapt to new demands and contingencies. In the context of Palestinian autonomy, however, there is no certainty about where the process of autonomous institution building is leading; this in spite of the fact that the transition to a final status of Palestinian autonomy perhaps represents one of the most outlined, controlled and observed of such processes in history. Some of this has to do with imbalances of power between Israel and the PA. It also has to do with the powerlessness of Palestinian society in relation to the PA.

While the coercive potential of the Palestinian Authority raises a spectre which hangs over its lack of capacity in other domains, its weakness reflects and reinforces the inability of Palestinian society to address these shortcomings within the context established by the agreement. The powerlessness and political paralysis of Palestinian society ultimately reflects the powerlessness of its political elites. Citizenship, in the conception used here, suggests instrumental power accountable to citizens and not merely legal-technical recognition or cataloguing. Citizenship is certainly a condition which has certainly not been reflected in Palestinian institutions in the wake of the peace process; neither is it reflected in the consolidation strategies of the PA, nor the ability of individual Palestinians to respond to daily challenges by invoking the apparatus of the legal and socio-economic environment in which they live. In the current context of a withdrawal from politics in Gaza, it is too early to speak of a dynamic basis of Palestinian citizenship emerging from the context of autonomy.

Constituency, mobilization, and institutionalization

Hinting that some of the weaknesses in the agreement might be attributed to a scramble by PLO leaders to reassert the pre-eminence of the organization's institutions in Palestinian society at a time when it was threatened with relegation to the margins of Palestinian life, Hanan Ashrawi has pointed out that 'it's not who makes the agreement but what's in it ... after you have signed, what power do you have?'[20] Samuel Huntington has argued that it is not the kind of government, but rather the degree of government, that determines whether a society is prone to violence and fragmentation:

> The differences between democracy and dictatorship are less than the differences between those countries whose politics embodies consensus, community,

legitimacy, organization, effectiveness, stability, and those countries whose politics is deficient in these qualities.[21]

Huntington goes on to ask his central question and suggest an answer.

What was responsible for this violence and instability [in the developing world]? The primary thesis of this [Huntington's] book is that it was in large part the product of rapid social change and the rapid mobilization of new groups into politics coupled with the slow development of political institutions.[22]

The current constitutive transition in Gaza undoubtedly represents a 'rapid social change' which in turn encourages new patterns of social mobilization. The question is, however, whether the PA possesses the kind of power needed to legitimize and make effective the channelling of social, political and economic activity into the institutions of autonomy. The restrictions imposed by the agreement currently seem to impede the development of effective institutions. New institutions have sprung up overnight, but they lack institutionalization, they are shallow, weak, and have more symbolic than real power. Arafat is mobilizing society using some of the privileges of autonomy, but without incorporating social mobilization broadly within the institutions themselves.

We might argue accordingly that legitimacy is built through the exercise of government and not only in the mobilization of symbols and the awareness of shared social experiences. The ability of ruling state ideologies to penetrate society, and the willingness (or constructed need) of society to coalesce around governing institutions, ultimately determines whether or not society and ruling elites can accommodate each other and identify the ruling order as legitimate. In short, Huntington identifies institutionalization as a precondition to stability, development, and the ability of society and ruling authorities to condition each other in the identification of legitimate symbolic and physical manifestations of power. Power that lends its weight to institutions inspires confidence in those institutions.

A comparative context

Huntington does not reduce degree of government to the degree of coercive force. Rather, his examples of the Soviet bloc, or alternatively more recent examples of the emerging East Asian economies (to which Arafat likens the future of Palestine), or the success of the dual economy model in China (where an upwardly mobile bourgeoisie seem to be making no moves toward insisting on rights of democratic expression), say something about the ability of the government to use coercion and incentives based on institutions which extend broadly and deeply into society to ensure the success of its social mobilizations from above to produce meaningful stability.

By definition, institutionalization implies predictability in the manifestations of power and the institutions which mediate between power and the individual. The coercive element involves more than just the threat or use of physical force in the streets, it might also mean the arbitrary denial of an established right, procedure, or privilege. The degree of government can also be said to have an inverse correlation with the limitations placed on the ability of ruling institutions to make and enforce decisions. The neopatrimonial strategy of state consolidation, by personalizing power relations and moving effective decision making beyond the reach of open and transparent institutions, tends to undermine the features which Huntington identifies as conducive to stability. As Brynen notes, neopatrimony is 'generally corrosive of political institutionalization, since (it) suggest(s) the primacy of connections rather than the formal structures of law, constitutionalism and bureaucratic procedure.'[23]

The 'degree of government' currently accorded to the PA is extremely restricted, possibly inhibiting the formation of enabling social and political institutions, and certainly affecting the tactics used by ruling elites to consolidate and legitimate their authority. Rather than seeking legitimacy through the actions of governing – that is formulating and executing policy in the broad interests of society – the PA, without effective control of the tools by which states usually attempt to control and manipulate the political economies of the social and territorial space in which they rule, has been forced into legitimacy-building by: (i) manipulative sloganeering which raises public expectations; (ii) coercion (police functions being the one area where it almost enjoys an absolute power of state) and (iii) co-opting strategically located elites with the limited patronage available – i.e. a factionally-based divide and rule tactic that aims at breaking up possible broadly integrated opposition movements within Palestinian society. Ironically, it does not seem that self-rule has had the impact of strengthening and focusing the activity of civil society on the construction of socially legitimate and productive institutions of political economy. Under the terms of the agreement, the PA has very few of the powers usually invoked to co-opt the population to a state building project. In fact, it even lacks most of the powers over resources and territory of most post-colonial elites in Africa and elsewhere.

By Huntington's standards, therefore, the PA's condition is conducive neither to development nor the types of predictable and efficacious institutions which promote a high degree of legitimacy. Although it would certainly be wrong to assume that democracy is not a priority for the Palestinian people, the East Asian examples show that legitimacy can be built on aspirations other than the need to express choice over the names and faces of those who sit within ruling bodies. For example, in China today the dramatically successful free market experiments have not been accompanied by political liberalization, and the upwardly mobile bourgeoisie do not seem to be demanding it as long as the regime allows them to get on with business. However, the lack of democracy becomes more apparent to a population whose leadership seems unwilling or unable to ensure their more material needs, and on the other hand encourages aspirations.

The distinction between authority and administration

Tamari's definition of authority as a phenomenon encompassing 'issues of legitimacy and control,' is useful here. According to Tamari,

> ... the issues of legitimacy and control manifest themselves today as a crisis in Palestinian national identity. The crisis is reflected in the symbolic national icons on the one hand, and in the regulation of the relationship between civil society and the formative institutions of power – what can be called the institutionalization of authority – on the other.[24]

Even more interesting is the implication to be drawn from this definition, that national identity is subject to a meaningful relationship with authority.[25] Before elaborating on the issues of substantive authority versus administrative privileges below, a brief overview of the conceptual distinction between authority and administration should be made:

> **Au·thor′i·ty,** n., pl. **-ties. 1.** the power to control, command or determine. **2.** a power or right delegated or given. **3.** a person or body of persons in whom authority is vested. **4.** Usu., **-ties.** government. **5. a.** an accepted source of information, advice or substantiation. **b.** a quotation or citation from such a

source. **6.** an expert on a subject. **7.** persuasive force; conviction.[26]

Authority represents the coercive force in society. It is that body invested with the power to punish (definitions one and four), but it also refers to the sources which inform the decisions we make in every day life (especially definition five). The 'accepted' is crucial to note in definition five. In both a democracy or a client dictatorship, i.e. the extremes, it is important that we ask 'from whom' authority is delegated as implied in definition two. Observers should also be specific about the 'in whom' authority is vested as noted in definition three. Ultimately, if authority is to be effective, it must be convincing (see definition seven), and it must have the ability to arbitrate, which necessitates the generally recognized existence of a representative of definition six. As noted in the previous chapter, the positive 'power to control, command or determine' is largely missing in the current framework of 'transition' toward greater autonomy, leaving in its place the largely negative social function of coercion. From the beginning, we see that the PA lacked many of the tools and characteristics of authority. Functioning authority should contain a positive orienting impact which appeals to the well being of the individual beyond just the ability of the authority to physically discipline.

It is also important to distinguish between authority and administration. Whereas the former contains some notions of internalization and coercive potential, the latter seems to refer only to executive structure and certain procedural responsibilities within a given framework. The distinction is important because the administration of a particular order does not imply the powers to shape and determine the character of the given political condition to thus sustain legitimacy. The question of whether PA should stand for Palestinian Authority or merely Palestinian Administration becomes crucial to understanding Palestinian perceptions of the legitimacy of the new order. Just to be clear before moving on, the following definition is given:

ad·min´is·tra´tion, n. **1.** management, as of a government or a business. **2.** (often cap.) the executive branch of a government. **3.** the period during which an administrator or a body of administrator serves. **4.** *Law.* the management of an estate. **5.** the act of administering. — **ad·min´is·tra´tive,** *adj.*[27]

The important thing to note is that administration refers to the carrying out of pre-existing arrangements while authority denotes a positive creative relationship between agents and objects.

Coercion and Administration: the Powers of the Palestinian Authority

Developments as of 27 September 1996 make more pressing the need to understand just what kind of power structure is developing in Gaza.[28] If the peace process were to stall, and assuming that even a hostile Israeli government would not once again deploy the forces of direct occupation (at least not immediately), what would Gaza look like? Without the framework of negotiations promising a 'final status,' and an Israeli state at least willing to allow some workers inside the 'green line' so that basic needs might be met, the structures set up by the agreement until now would leave Gaza looking like little more than an overpopulated 'Fatah-land,' with many of the same faces in place who were responsible for the chaos in Southern Lebanon in the late 1970s and early 1980s. Netanyahu's stance is clear: 'I have tidings for [Labour opposition leader] Peres ... There really is a new Middle East, and in it there is not and never will be a Palestinian state.'[29] If the peace process were to fail, the population of the OT might be left isolated and suffocating, and the 'spectre of superfluous man' could pose a destabilizing prospect for the whole region.

Shikaki notes that throughout the early stages of the peace process, the PA seems to have held to the view that: ' ... the requirements of democracy may contradict those of national reconstruction, and that in the early stages of state building it is more important to assert the state's right to monopolize power and eliminate competitors for the people's loyalty.'[30] However, the personalization of and reliance upon central authority, or at the very least the reduction of authority to one faction (if not one man), has precluded the consolidation of state institutions. That is to say, Fatah has monopolized power and has not thus far transferred its powers into state-like institutionalization, at least not after the liberal model.[31]

Although Arafat has 'micro-managed' the structures of power, and kept his control over the emerging autonomous institutions he has as a result provoked scepticism from society. As of April 1996, only 39.4 per cent of Palestinians evaluated Yasser Arafat's performance as good.[32]

In fact, Arafat's power consists of the ability to wield coercive force and control over administrative privilege – that is to distribute aid money, jobs in the bureaucracy, and to regulate in civil matters through the granting of licenses and so on. Current agreements make clear this emphasis on 'security' functions as the cornerstone of Palestinian Authority. Article VIII of the original Gaza–Jericho First Agreement calls for a strong police force. The Interim Agreement signed in Washington on 28

September 1996 reaffirms this in several places, including Articles XII and XIV (but Article XIII, paragraph 2b(2) notes that 'the Palestinian police shall be responsible for handling public order incidents in which only Palestinians are involved').

Information on the various factions of the Palestinian security forces is sketchy, but the most important include the General Intelligence Service, the Preventative Security Force, the Presidential Guard or 'Force 17', the Special Security Force; and smaller forces such as the Coastal Police, the Military Police, the University Police and the Disciplinary Police. Usher sees the security forces engaged in three tasks: 1) police functions; 2) finishing the business of seeking out and punishing collaborators and 3) the surveillance of Palestinian opposition to Oslo.[33] They have been undermined in the first task by a lack of training, by placing organizational interests ahead of the unbiased enforcement of the law, and by the entrenched anti-authority attitudes amongst Gazans. The second two functions are as likely to provoke insecurity and violent responses as they are to promote the consolidation of PA rule. The agreements in theory limit the number of security personnel within PA to 9,000 under the Gaza–Jericho Agreement of 1994, and 12,000 under the Interim Agreement of 1995. However, as noted by Usher, limits on the numbers of personnel are simply not observed by the PA, Israel, or the various international sponsors. Usher reports that the police force of 30,000 for the interim period in the West Bank and Gaza is a figure 'not questioned by either PA or Israeli officials. But this too is likely to be fluid. In June 1995, the head of Civil Police in Gaza City, Ghazi Jabali, said that the PA would eventually require a police force of around 40,000 for the autonomy.'[34]

But while the numbers of police and their powers may seem frighteningly unlimited from the perspective of the inhabitants of Gaza,[35] the agreements in fact tightly regulate their accountability to the interests and powers behind the process and not to the people. Annex I of the Gaza–Jericho Agreement outlines the parameters of policing power down to the types of guns and ammunition allowed for the PA security forces, to the top speeds and tonnage of the few boats allowed to the PA coastal police.[36] However, the PA's strong policing and internal security mandate does not include jurisdiction over offences committed in the settlements or in the military installation area, nor may it arbitrate in offences committed in the self-rule areas by Israelis. PA powers are only to be used in arbitrating between and quelling unrest among Palestinians. In situations where Israelis are involved, the Israeli Defence Forces (IDF) have jurisdiction.[37] The high degree of integration between PA and Israeli security forces undermines the perception of the accountability of Palestinian police to the population.[38] Furthermore, 'nothing shall effect the continued authority of the military government and its civil administration to exercise their powers and responsibilities with regard to security and public order, as well as with regard to other spheres not transferred.'[39] This gives Israel broad scope for interference in Palestinian affairs.

Even administrative functions are strictly regulated. The PA is responsible for enforcing regulations, but it has only limited powers to amend existing regulations and, as noted in Chapter 4, most crucial regulations are fixed or pegged according to Israeli standards. These, together with the many examples noted in the previous chapter, illustrate the inability of the PA to administer the autonomy in ways accountable to the interests of Gazans.

This lack of effective PA power clearly poses a predicament for Arafat. In order to increase his authority in the Palestinian social space, he must first prove that he can provide stability; in order to produce stability and consensus around his rule, he first needs the authority and scope of political power to produce and enforce political and economic outcomes acceptable to the Palestinian population. In order to acquire the scope of power that might allow for the presentations of positive incentives for social mobilization, he must first demonstrate his ability to neutralize and repress that society. While it is tempting to attribute the failures of the PA to corruption and incompetence (especially considering the combination of cronyism and a new *wabenzi-ism*), it must at least be considered how the externally enforced dynamic of emerging autonomy is denying the PA the tools with which broad societal legitimation might be pursued.

Jurisdiction and Law: Establishing the Boundaries and Content of Power

The imbalance between the protective and the coercive functions of the security apparatus represents another problematic feature of the autonomy. Many point to the role of the law in taking the first steps toward creating a comprehensible base for self-rule. However, the legal context of the transition and the behaviour of the PA suggest that its role might be complicating matters as much as clarifying them in the short-term. First, the PA has only limited scope to distance the legal context of self-rule from that of occupation. Article XVIII of the Israeli–Palestinian Interim Agreement on the West Bank and the Gaza Strip states that:

4.a. Legislation, including legislation which amends or abrogates existing laws or military orders, which exceeds the jurisdiction of the council or which is otherwise inconsistent with the provisions of DoP, this agreement, or of any other agreement that may be reached between the two sides during the interim period, shall have no effect and shall be *void ab initio.*

b. The Ra'ees of the Executive Authority of the Council shall not promulgate legislation adopted by the council if such legislation falls under the provisions of this Paragraph.

5. All legislation shall be communicated to the Israeli side of the legal committee.

6. Without derogating from the provisions of paragraph 4 above, the Israeli side of the Legal Committee may refer for the attention of the Committee any legislation regarding which Israel considers the provisions of paragraph 4 apply, in order to discuss issues arising from such legislation. The legal committee will consider the legislation referred to it at the earliest opportunity.

This is basically the same as in the 'Agreement on Transfer of Powers and Responsibilities' (Erez, 29 August 1994) where PA legislative authority is limited to promulgating secondary legislation 'regarding powers and responsibilities transferred to it.' Article VII, paragraphs 2–5 of the same agreement list Israeli veto rights more specifically. A close reading shows that most of the powers to legislate cover the form of Palestinian administration, but do not threaten its content, which follows the pattern of the occupation's civil administration functions. Israel's military sovereignty throughout the West Bank and Gaza Strip and its veto rights are maintained.[40] Those laws which the PA does have the power to amend or replace are outlined in appendices to the agreement and include only a fraction of the laws and orders that were used to regulate the occupation.

Secondly, while the territorial integrity of the West Bank and Gaza Strip is repeatedly reconfirmed throughout the text of the agreements,[41] paragraphs subsequent to such reassurances usually reveal the actual patchwork of degrees and domains of jurisdiction. Article XVII of the Israeli–Palestinian Interim Agreement on the West Bank and the Gaza Strip notes the following exceptions to Palestinian jurisdiction: 'a. issues that will be negotiated in the permanent status negotiations: Jerusalem, settlements, specified military locations, Palestinian refugees, borders, foreign relations and Israelis; and b. powers and responsibilities not transferred to the council.'

The consistency of authority within given social and territorial spaces is also a factor that encourages individuals within a given community to identify common interests. In the OT today, however, one might refer to the Palestinians as one nation, divided under law. Questions of jurisdiction and legal precedent mean that Palestinians in different areas of the OT experience the rule of the PA through an inconsistent legal structure with uncertainty over who has the authority to arbitrate in many areas. This inconsistency is not as much a problem within Gaza, but it certainly does mean that Gazans will be experiencing self-rule through the lens of a different legal regime than inhabitants of the West Bank, just as the experience of occupation in Gaza was in many respects qualitatively different. The situation might not be conducive to creating the perception of equality in relation to institutions. The fact that people in different areas are experiencing the transition in different ways may be a factor undermining the future perception of the impartiality and independent character of self-rule institutions.

Thirdly, current confusion and instability is exacerbated by the various poles of legal authority existing in the OT. This is both in terms of personalities and in the hodge-podge of legal codes that prevail in the Palestinian areas. During occupation the Israelis variously employed British, Jordanian, Egyptian, Israeli, and military legal precedent as it suited them and under the terms of the agreements, these laws are the reference for the autonomy.[42] Many are draconian and designed to circumvent basic individual rights:

> In 1945, the mandate authorities issued a series of regulations called the emergency laws which were a compilation in one body of all the regulations and laws to deal with the special situation … three was provision for all kinds of collective punishments – house demolitions, curfews and so on as well as detention and exile for those individuals suspected of engaging in anti-British activities … these laws fell into disuse (under Egyptian administration) only to be resurrected by the Israelis when they occupied the West Bank and Gaza Strip in 1967.[43]

From 1967, over 1,000 military orders were issued by the Israeli military government in the Gaza Strip. Only seventy of these orders, which have the weight of law, are abrogated by the agreement.[44] Arafat has contributed to the confusion by his declaration, in direct contravention of the agreements, that all military and occupation laws were null and void. The contingencies of the situation have of course not allowed him to act meaningfully on this, and inasmuch as he has, it has been by ignoring the primacy of the rule of law in general. He has, though, not hesitated to invoke pre-existing laws when they increase his executive authority vis-à-vis the rights of Palestinians and the other institutions established with autonomy. The role of law in the attempted 'mobilization from above' has thus far been neither protective of subject rights nor institutionally constructive.

On top of this, 'Palestinian leaders from outside have brought with them a criminal code applicable in Lebanon.' Usama Halabi expands on these difficulties:

> Gaza and Jericho don't have the same laws. This complicates both the consolidation of the PA and people's ability to monitor the exercise of authority. For example, the head judge in Gaza issued a statement that courts in Gaza should make decisions based on Jordanian law, but Jordanian law does not apply in Gaza. How will the substance of legal matters be discussed and decided when there is not even a basic understanding about what laws apply ... It is a mess and no one has the authority to take any decisions to clarify matters.[45]

Finally on the question of powers and jurisdiction, not only are there problems with the nature and consistency of the laws themselves, but also over who is to administer them. In some municipal zones in the West Bank and in about 56 per cent of the Gaza Strip, it is the PA alone. In other areas, there is joint PA and Israeli jurisdiction. In still other areas only Israel is responsible for enforcement of the confusing legal situation. After the suicide bombings inside Israel in early March of 1996, the IDF made arrests inside the autonomous areas in the West Bank further obfuscating the character and boundaries of effective jurisdiction (as have school closings by the Israelis in spite of the fact that this was a function explicitly turned over to PA administration). The clarity of legal jurisdiction is further complicated by the lack of clear distinctions between the branches of Palestinian self 'government' and the vagueness of many job descriptions within the PA.[46] There are many different courts and the lack of effective powers means that there are institutions without immediate meaningful tasks.

In years past, the lack of faith in and the inefficiency of the military courts set up by the Israelis encouraged people to use the traditional system of *muhktars* (who were incidentally also appointed by the military authorities) to arbitrate disputes.[47] During the intifada and the general breakdown of the structures of military authority, Hamas played an increasingly important role in resolving disputes on the local level with even Christians resorting to and respecting its arbitration.[48] These trends have chipped away at faith in public institutions and increased the tendency to resort to local and traditional modes of social mediation, perhaps strengthening the foundation for the PA's factional control.

There are also cases which illustrate a dangerous trend toward the personalization and politicization of the justice system, and the limited ability of civil society to contain abuses of authority within the framework of current national institutions. Arafat has openly declared that he refused to be a 'puppet of the courts,'[49] a statement which reveals either ignorance or a lack of concern for due process in the content of 'self-rule.' He has insisted on being consulted personally before the court makes any decision, particularly in regard to his freedom to decide the content and course of 'internal security.'[50]

Journalist and analyst Graham Usher, for example, describes how Arafat:

> ... personally authorized the setting up of 'special state security courts.' These are independent of any civilian judiciary system, allow secret evidence, brook no appeal procedures, and are 'judged' by PLO military personnel appointed by the PA. Verdicts are the prerogative of Arafat, who according to the PA's attorney general has sole power to 'confirm, ease or stiffen' any sentence passed by the 'courts.'[51]

The legal precedent for these is found in the Mandate emergency laws, which were also invoked during Israeli occupation:

> The military security courts, established in February 1995 to deter Hamas and Islamic Jihad from attacking Israeli targets and to demonstrate to the Israeli government the PA's seriousness about combating terrorism, were based on the hated 1945 Emergency Regulations under which Palestinians were subjugated by Israeli military occupation for over twenty-eight years.[52]

These security courts have been widely condemned by Palestinians and international observers. However, international donors have not protested, and the results seem in line with Israeli expectations and perceptions of their interests.

In July 1996, a seventh prisoner died in PA custody, apparently as a result of torture. The incident provoked a riot in the victim's hometown of Nablus.[53] When unrest spread to Tulkarm, PA forces responded to the demonstrations with violence, shooting and killing one demonstrator.[54] Immediately, PA radio switched to 'emergency broadcasting' and began featuring martial music and the rabble-rousing hits of the popular Arab singer Fayrouz to highlight 'our people's triumph over all vile conspiracies.

The radio report went on to claim that Hamas militants had been responsible for the indiscriminate shooting, and that an investigation was underway.[55] Regime 'securitization' seems clearly to have taken precedence over liberalization.

Rabin had been clear in predicting such tendencies in 1993, noting that such a trend would be in Israel's interests:

> The Palestinians will be better at it than we were,' he said in September 1993, 'because they will allow no appeals to the Supreme Court and will prevent the Israeli Association of Civil Rights access to the area. They will rule by their own methods, freeing, and this is important, the Israeli army soldiers from doing what they will do.[56]

In June 1996, Dr Eyad Sarraj, human rights activist and commissioner general of the Palestine Independent Commission for Citizen's Rights, was arrested several times without charge and severely beaten while in detention. Sarraj has openly criticized the PA, decrying the 'corrupt, dictatorial, oppressive' nature of the regime, the arbitrary arrests of Palestinians, and has referred to 'an overwhelming sense of fear' amongst Palestinians.[57] Political outspokenness was openly stated as the reason for his arrest. Following a national and international outcry against his arrest, police suddenly found illicit drugs on his premises and thereby charged him with possession and sale. Dr Sarraj stated, however, that not once during his interrogation was he asked abut drugs or drug dealing, but rather about a letter that he had sent to Arafat outlining criticisms and critical remarks he had made in an interview with the *New York Times*. The judge in the Palestinian Magisterial Court in Gaza dismissed the charges against Dr Sarraj, who was released fifteen days later in the middle of the night before a scheduled hearing in front of a security court.[58]

In another case in August 1996, the Palestinian High Court responded to a petition submitted on behalf of ten Birzeit students detained without charge or trial starting in March 1996 by ordering their immediate release. The High Court ruled that there was no legal basis to justify continuing the students' detention, especially given that no charges had been brought against them.[59] However, the next day the attorney general Khaled al-Qidra stated that the students would not be released before he had conferred with President Arafat.[60] Commenting on the case, LAWE – The Palestinian Society for the Protection of Human Rights – noted that:

> The attorney general has interfered with the functioning of the court and violated Palestinian Laws, which require that the High Court's decision be

immediately acted upon ... An independent judiciary is guaranteed by Palestinian law. According to the relevant Jordanian legal system, article 97 guarantees government respect and execution of the High Court's decisions. Article 101/1 ensures that no authority influence the free and fair functioning of the courts. The refusal to release immediately the students represents a violation of the law and provides a dangerous precedent against the free functioning of the Palestinian legal system.[61]

By late August 1996, Arafat had pressured the judges involved in both the case against the students and the case against Eyad Sarraj to resign. Furthermore, 'excesses' and abuses by the plethora of different Palestinian security agencies have undermined public faith in the ability of the PA to administer and enforce justice humanely and impartially. Violations include prisoners kept for periods in excess of their sentences, bad and violent treatment, detention without trial or hearing, the taking of hostages to pressure another wanted family member to turn him or herself in, arrests due to Israeli pressure, food shortages in the prisons and prisoners being forced to pay for necessary medicines while in detention.[62]

Hilal also notes the trend to rationalize repressive practices under the heading of 'national interest.'

This is apparent in the initiation of ... imprisonment and the reported torture of political opponents, the undermining of the independent judiciary by setting up 'state security' courts, the obsessive concern with the symbols of sovereignty rather than its real powers, the proliferation of police and security organs controlled by the head of the PA, his adoption of presidential functions (before elections) and his refusal to devolve powers to the ministries of the autonomy areas. All this is taking place before any legal safeguards of basic human and democratic rights have been formulated and approved in a Palestinian constitution.[63]

Palestinians themselves are wary of this trend. According to an exit poll conducted by the Centre for Palestine Research and Statistics:

When asked whether they supported unrestricted freedom of the press and human rights versus national interests as defined by the Palestinian Authority, about two-thirds selected unrestricted freedom of the press and human rights. This clearly indicates that voters are not giving the president an unquestioning carte blanche.[64]

Palestinian voters also expressed concern at the trend toward personalization of power:

> ... the responses to one of the questions on the exit poll provide an important qualifier for Arafat's mandate: 40 per cent of the voters polled on the election day said they wanted Arafat to have less power than the council; another 40 per cent said they wanted the council and Arafat to have equal power, and only 20 per cent thought that Arafat should have more power than the council.[65]

This also demonstrates Palestinian scepticism toward the unaccountable use of power in general, the consequences of which they were made only too aware under occupation. Usher notes that such a 'securitization' of Palestinian culture might have long-term effects:

> The emergence of an increasingly authoritarian PA has contributed to a process of depoliticization of Palestinian society in which many of its most able members have 'collectively withdrawn,' reverting to individualistic or clan based (rather than political) solutions for their needs and aspirations. This is not only regressive in itself, but erosive of the essentially modernist and political national identity that the PLO – via its political factions and for all its faults – had brought into being.[66]

By way of summary, it can be said that the PA lacks effective jurisdiction in several crucial domains. According to Raja Shehadeh 'in three key areas, the arrangements imposed on the Palestinians by the Israelis (during occupation) were either preserved or augmented.'[67] These three areas are: legal jurisdiction, jurisdiction over water, and jurisdiction over land. The PLO seems to have bungled the water rights issue by giving jurisdiction to the Israeli Mekoroth Water Company and agreeing in effect to keep water use distribution at the same levels.[68]

In the area of legal (civil) jurisdiction Shehadeh argues that the agreement gives Israeli courts wider authority to matters related to disputes and offences involving Israeli citizens than the pre-intifada occupation jurisdiction did. The jurisdiction of Palestinian courts has been undermined at the current stage of the negotiations. Current zoning schemes allow settlers the freedom of movement in areas populated by Palestinians, but they are in no case accountable to Palestinian jurisdiction. The security of individual Palestinians is thereby threatened as settlers have continued leeway to harass and attack Palestinians and vandalize their property. By putting the issue of Palestinian rights in Jerusalem under negotiation, the PLO has threatened to undermine a right that belonged to the Palestinians by international law.[69] Shehadeh makes the argument that the PLO has failed to pay attention to and recognize the short and long-term significance of the legal components of the changing relationship with Israel and the transition period itself. The impact of clear and understood law to the healthy functioning of Palestinian civil society and long-term economic and social development has also been ignored.

> The leadership must understand that, significant though the political transformations inaugurated by the PLO certainly are, the law also has a vital role: first, as a tool for achieving better success in future negotiations, and second, as a tool for peaceful and effective social transformation and economic and political development.[70]

Electoral Legitimacy?

On 21 January 1996, the PA's lack of substantive powers was obscured by the conduct of elections. Andoni argues that: 'While elections generally indicate a democratic process, in the Palestinian case, a democratic right has been permitted in order to legitimize a political process that could well lead to the perpetuation of Israeli control.'[71] Shikaki is somewhat more generous, but also notes the deviation from the standard meanings of elections:

> For the PLO, since the old Palestinian consensus was gone, the elections were needed to give Arafat a mandate and to give legitimacy to a new political order. Therefore the democratic agenda is absent, and elections should not be seen necessarily as the start of a transition to democracy but in their role of nation building and peacemaking. This explains the attempt to manipulate the elections to serve both Israeli and Palestinian needs ...[72]

The intended framework and scope of the elections was stated within the interim agreement: 'These elections constitute a significant interim preparatory step toward the legitimate rights of the Palestinian people and their just requirements and will provide a democratic basis for the establishment of Palestinian institutions'[73] In fact, many Gazans who spoke enthusiastically of having taken this 'significant interim preparatory step' became very cynical when asked what they expected the politicians to accomplish in the way of improving the basic conditions of life in Gaza.[74] Elections that lead nowhere may only delegitimize the idea of election. Haydar Abd al-Shafi, a strong critic of undemocratic tendencies in the Fatah leadership, the director of the Red Crescent Society in Gaza, and a prominent independent representative of nationalist politics, did not spend a single shekel on his campaign for the Palestinian Legislative Assembly. His only campaign statement (according to word on the street) was that he would not make any promises since, if elected, he would not have the power to keep them. He was far and away leading vote winner in Gaza. Elections restored a sense of pride, but hopes for substantive and qualitative change remained dim.

Before the elections, Shikaki had noted that 'while the peace process had dealt the final blow to the old consensus, it provided the basis for a new source of legitimacy: the popular will and the elections through which that will could manifest itself.'[75] Elections, however, have seemingly failed to mould this new consensus. The subordination of the elections to the peace process in practice rendered them invalid as an arena for ideological contestation. The result is that national elections have in no way represented a foundation for popular rule, nor a safeguard in the Palestinian street against the insinuation of external interests and abuses of power.

In spite of reports of free and fair elections from international observers, several Gazans told the author that Palestinian police threatened them with harassment and denial of vital permits for travel and work if they failed to vote. Reinforcing this anecdotal evidence, a poll conducted February 1996 found that slightly over 20 per cent of Gazans reported harassment at the polling stations and 48.1 per cent of respondents either knew of vote-buying or had heard of it.[76] There is also further evidence that the PA used what powers it does have to ensure a desirable outcome to elections from their perspective. Arafat used his control over resources and privileges, as well as over the timing of the elections and campaigning, to make sure that preferred candidates stood the best possible chance of election.[77] All in all, only 41.5 per cent of respondents to the above mentioned (February 1996) poll felt that elections were 'free and fair.' Arafat's meddling with local Fatah slates of candidates before elections was discussed in Chapter 3. In spite of these attempts to manipulate the outcome, it is interesting to note that:

> Some of the largest margins of victory went to prominent nationalist independents such as Haydar Abd al-Shafi, Abd al-Jawad Salih, and Hanan Ashrawi ... Another point of significance is the fact that eighteen or nineteen of the Fatah people who won as independents – the so-called 'Fatah rebels' – are very critical of Arafat and sometimes also of the peace process and therefore cannot be counted on to tow the party line.[78]

The Palestinian Legislative Council, in spite of its effective powerlessness, has used its platform to criticize corruption and human rights abuses under the PA.[79] However, Beyer reports that when a group of Palestinian councillors were asked 'what percentage of their resolutions were implemented by the PA, they broke out laughing. The answer was zero.'[80] It seems that the council's main task was to give the agreement the veneer of popular legitimacy.

Election results may reflect attempts to connect oneself to the benefits associated with the PA apparatus more than anything else. While Shikaki offers evidence which cautions against the use of clan as a factor explaining voting preferences,[81] Andoni points out that the ability to access basic needs is still a primary factor of political allegiance rather than a good taken as a given:

> One interesting aspect of the Fatah results was that while many local Fatah activists lost, the traditional leadership returning from exile all won without exception, seeming to counter the perception of strong popular resentment concerning the bureaucracy and corruption of the 'imported leadership.' One possible explanation for their success could be that the officials returning with Arafat relied heavily, perhaps even more than most Fatah candidates, on the PA's structures, including security, in their campaigns. In some areas, they were called the 'authority's candidates,' a description denoting some resentment but also *implying connections and the ability to deliver services.* Given that people's daily lives are still under Israeli control and that the PA virtually acts as agent between the constituencies and the Israeli authorities, this represents an important advantage ... others suggest that violations ensured the victory of the exile leadership.[82]

Elections supported the façade of self-rule, but Palestinians remain frustrated over the powerlessness of their politicians. Most probably, elections have been incorporated into an early stage of the transition period in line with the currently hegemonic argument that democracy yields peace in terms of a simple, causal correlation. However, this basic assumption is dubious – especially, as pointed out here, considering the difficulty of defining democracy as a variable (not to mention the questionability of the directionality of the correlation: what if it is peace that yields democracy, or perhaps there is a third variable that contributes to both, such as, to name only one possibility, deeply integrated economic interaction).[83] But elections that lead nowhere may in the long run only serve to delegitimize the idea of elections. Accordingly, there might be good reason to question the wisdom of insisting on party based institutional elections at a time when so little is resolved and the future remains unclear. When there is no context for voters to make rational long-term decisions about proposed policies, and elected politicians lack real legislative and regulatory function, one can expect that voters are making decisions based on other concerns and opportunities.

In democratic states, elections contest power. The essential thing is that each time people go to the polls they are not simply reaffirming their identity or acknowledging a lack of alternative to the status quo. Rather, they attempt to influence the impact of power on personal and collective interests. If the elections were intended to serve as a referendum on a peace process, as was so often claimed in the press, then why not hold a referendum on that question instead of holding elections? The election results in Gaza – especially in so far as they demonstrated localized and factionalized outcomes – can be interpreted as people trying to position themselves as well as possible in a new order which is grudgingly accepted as a *fait accompli.* The economic situation for many Palestinians at the time of the elections was such that any pondering of 'to be, or not to be' as far as the peace process as a whole was concerned was less important than trying to get someone in office who might remember them when it came time to distribute the crumbs of autonomy.

Nor have states historically been born by elections, but through the consolidation of power. From an elitist perspective, the boundaries of rule have been determined by the ability of elites to use power and influence to shape the interests of society in ways that conform to their own interests. Elections might be a tool used in such an endeavour. Elections – as implied in Chapter 3 which noted that democracy requires already clear boundaries – do not create or delimit states, but existing states can use elections to solve problems and re-vitalize legitimacy. Elections in the occupied territories have given the Palestinians the rituals and obligations of self-rule with few of its associated rights and privileges. The context of the elections of January 1996 allowed the Palestinians to go to the polls, but the politicians they elected do not have the necessary powers to deal directly with problems facing society. Furthermore, elections are a means and not an end. They work well when broadly defined goals of the society have been identified and when the basic consensual arrangement between state and society has been institutionalized, but they are less useful if the fundamental premise on which elections are held are still being deeply challenged within society.

Elections tend to work well when all parties agree on the ends and only disagree as to the means of pursuing the goals of social consensus.

In other parts of the world, continuing unrest after 'free and fair' elections show that legitimacy is not merely the superficial and ritual observance of democratic practice. In cases such as Bosnia, elections must be backed up by the presence of international force. If a power vacuum exists, chaos and violence might break out as groups find advantage in challenging the results with violence. Hence perhaps the concern with coercive force as the cornerstone of PA rule.

Elections also imply that voters have a rational basis for evaluating the correlation between proposed policies and their consequences. In Palestine today, polling tends to be unreliable and volatile precisely because opinions are necessarily informed in the uncertain and volatile context of the peace process. Elections are determined by information, and in its struggle to consolidate its position from above the PA has been hard-pressed to control information on the street. Indeed, the PA's attempts to control the street by closing independent newspapers and intimidating journalists constitutes a worrying trend.[84] In the run up to elections, opponents were denied airtime and journalists publishing reports critical of the PA or the peace process were by various means denied access to their media of communication. Throughout the interim period, journalists have been arrested and beaten. Newspapers have been closed down or ransacked after publishing reports which failed to place the PA in a positive light (and even for failing to put the PA in a positive enough light).[85]

The Islamist press has in particular been subject to closings and harassment. On 30 September 1996, the PA police insulted and severely beat the president of the Palestinian journalist syndicate outside of Khan Younis refugee camp in the Gaza Strip after he had accompanied television journalists from the British television network ITN who were reporting from Gaza. When the author was in Gaza in mid-1995, the PA was actively repressing and shutting down the Islamist press after rumours concerning immoral behaviour by prominent PA figures and their families were repeated in dailies with ties to Islamist organizations.

Khalid Amayreh reports a tendency of the new leadership and their agents to 'view all 'non-conformist elements' within the Palestinian society as impeding the 'national plan' and 'aborting the Palestinian new-born.'" Amayreh continues:

> ... many of the newcomers or returnees, as they are called, view the slightest gesture of dissatisfaction with Arafat and his regime as a potential threat to their newly earned and previously undreamt of achievements. At a recent seminar in

Beit Sahor on 'Press Freedom Under the Palestinian Authority,' a high ranking military official said that Palestinians should concentrate on 'bread winning' not 'western-style freedoms' as their top priority. When confronted with 'man does not live by bread alone,' the official simply said 'this is Palestine, not Sweden.' This anti-democratic outlook, coupled with a scandalous lack of accountability and absence of discipline, [often with acquiescence from] the highest political echelons, [may have] tragic consequences.[86]

In both democracies and dictatorships, leaders and societies communicate with and manipulate each other by adapting each other's terms to serve their own ends, but however vague and transcendental that dialogue may at times seem, it is a dialogue that has almost certainly responded to the survival needs of each.

The future of democracy in Palestine is in no small way connected to the devolution of powers in ways which make them accountable and contestable within Palestinian society.[87] Elections that do not lead to change may only exacerbate frustration and highlight the emptiness of the exercise in the current environment. Democratization in its most vital sense refers to a context for social mobilization and not only to ideals of tolerance, individualism and compromise.[88] Ideally, democracy is not only a ritual that is invoked at one particular moment to ratify or reject a particular process, it would be a way of insuring that socio-political and economic processes are held accountable to and protect the rights of those who are participating in that process. The framers of the agreement have called for democracy, but have separated it from popular empowerment. Inasmuch as national elections represented any popular will, they were manipulated in service of social mobilization orchestrated from above. Effective democracy would demand that Palestinians be allowed to mobilize to influence issues over which the PA or the Palestinian Legislative Council have no authority at present. In short, real democracy in Palestine would amount to allowing the Palestinian street to contest the form and content of continued Israeli control over life in the OT.

Conclusion

In short, the distribution of rights, obligations and powers in the Palestinian self-rule areas is not in line with popular expectations/aspirations. The low degree to which the PA is able to govern under the terms of the agreement threaten to get the process of building stable Palestinian autonomous institutions off to a bad start. The PA has been given an essentially negative, coercive role during the interim period. The powers, rights and obligations associated with Palestinian autonomy have not allowed Palestinian subjects to break free of the relationship between political compliance and basic needs. In this context, systemic, institutional legitimation from above seems unlikely. The lack of power might in the end serve only to de-legitimize the social and political contexts of the elections more than simple elections might legitimize the current set of elites who must function within the limits of the Oslo agreement. The limited autonomy may prove in the short-term to be cost effective for the elites responsible for the signing of the agreement, but produces few tangible benefits for the population of Gaza. In other words, PA powers, as they reflect both agreements and personalities who bear power, have not yielded what might be described as preconditions of effective Palestinian citizenship in any meaningful civil sense

Graham Usher implies that the nature of and limitations on authority as accepted by the PA represents a 'culture of defeat.'

> This is not just due to the fact that the Palestinian political leadership has and is lowering Palestinian's national claims to a series of disaggregated parts of the West Bank and Gaza. More corrosively, it is borne out of an obsessive ethos of 'national security' and 'national interest' that, once their political and ideological content is unpacked, turn out to be no more than the practical implementation of Israel's territorial and security ambitions in the occupied territories.[89]

The limited repressive scope of power thus far granted to the PA by successive agreements only serves to highlight the degree to which the current project represents an attempted social mobilization from above as opposed to a response to popular or grass roots social concerns.[90] Given the limited powers granted to him by the agreement, Arafat is posed with a tremendous challenge in terms of truly co-opting the population into accepting the current order. As the cases of both post-colonial and post-Soviet nationalist movements show, state building and the creation of a stable political order following such a transition is tricky under more ideal circumstances. Given the relative weak position of Arafat in relation to resources and the ability to manipulate 'sovereignty' to his advantage, the prospect of the 'interim' transition leading smoothly to a 'final status' seems unlikely. In particular, the ritualistic emptiness of elections and the tendency of external forces supporting the political transition to focus on technical and procedural issues rather than issues of social substance and effective power was highlighted. People become citizens not by electing a *ra'is*. They become citizens when they discover and appropriate the power to throw a *ra'is* out. The social dynamic which lent the PLO grassroots legitimacy might not easily or automatically conform to the situation of self-rule, as the designers of the agreement perhaps wrongly assumed.

Finally, the meaning of Palestinian powerlessness cannot be understood without understanding the context of Israeli power. When considering the immense gap between the words and deeds of the peace process, one does well to consider that in Orwell's 1984, the Ministry of War had been renamed the Ministry of Peace. As the media, in their (perhaps misguided) notions of balance, are careful to point out that neither side has really been able to match in deed their apparent verbal commitment to peace, one must ask just what deeds can and should be expected of the PA given their very limited power and the need to use this limited power to somehow hold it accountable to their subjects and not to the moribund (and perhaps dying as I write) peace process or an Israeli conception of security which excludes the very real security concerns of Palestinians.

The Palestinian Authority is powerless to do other than sit by as settlements are expanded; Palestinian land is confiscated for security reasons or occupied by radical settlers who try to provoke a situation in which the Israeli military will be forced to step in and take the settler side; homes built by Palestinians on their own land are demolished because of the lack of a proper building permit (Palestinian land is subject to entirely different zoning restrictions and Palestinians are forced to go through a winding bureaucratic process in order to obtain a building permit); and the Israeli government cordons off entire Palestinian cities – denying medical care to the sick and even denying food shipments from getting in – for the acts of individual Palestinians while Israelis who have killed or attacked Palestinians (often in cold blood or for political reasons) are given light sentences if they are sentenced or arrested at all. The images of IDF recruits clubbing elderly PA ministers during the unrest in late September early October 1996 are perhaps emblematic (although they might also encourage greater solidarity between elites, who perhaps experienced the physical presence of the continued occupation for the first time for the first time, and the grassroots). The Netanyahu government seems intent on showing Palestinians the full extent and effective meaning of their collective powerlessness within the context of arbitration and negotiation established by Oslo.[91] In doing so, they are provoking (perhaps intentionally) people to respond in the only way they can, however disorganized, violent and desperate that might be.

The ultimate limitation of PA power has been summed up by a senior Israeli military officer: 'The Israeli Army is prepared to move back into the PA territories any time it wants.'[92]

6

The Crisis of Authority: The Spectre of Superfluous Man

A pun commonly heard in the streets of Gaza after the signing of the Oslo Accords transformed the PLO slogan 'revolution until victory' into the ironically more appropriate 'chaos until victory.' Indeed, the often arbitrary and unaccountable intrusion of authority into daily life in Gaza over many decades has encouraged chaos as a mode of resistance. If the occupier could not be challenged head on, it could be frustrated. Ironically perhaps, chaos thus represented potential for social mobilization and expression of popular will. Even as various contingencies and interests were fragmenting the organizational structure underlying the uprising, the intifada showed the Palestinians themselves, and the world, that the inhabitants of the OT would not remain passive or submissive in the face of an increasingly unaccountable and economically disenfranchising military rule. The Palestinian street proved capable of initiating change.

The intifada arose because the Palestinian population found it increasingly difficult to justify passivity while political and social rights were denied in the face of increasingly acute economic hardship. Recognition of the link between economic hardship and political unaccountability, and the lack of institutional channels for redressing this link, forced Palestinian protest into the street. That the external leadership seemed less capable than ever of providing a sustainable solution increased the sense of urgency.[1] The uprising was a sign that the younger generation in the occupied territories had lost faith in the PLO's ability to effectively challenge the Israeli occupation through military means or in games of politics and diplomacy.[2] This suggests that Palestinians are not necessarily complacent in their loyalties to social and political fixtures associated with the nationalist movement. However, the local environment was able to sustain few – if any – alternatives.

The Arabic words used to describe the Palestinian resistance againstIsraeli occupation carry connotations of geological inevitability and uncontainability:[3] *thawra,* a term associated with PLO-led resistance since the mid 1960s, means revolution, insurrection, and rebellion, but it also means fit of fury or despair and volcanic eruption; *intifada* has been described as the 'shaking off' but it also means 'tremour' in the sense of an earthquake. Another word used to describe the activities associated with resistance, *jahada,* means to endeavour, strive, take pains. However, it also means to exhaust one's self. Similar to the trajectory of events during the 1936–1939 Palestinian uprising, by the time an occupying power was driven to the point of making concessions, Palestinians were in many respects too exhausted and too fragmented to take advantage of new opportunities.[4]

Their emotional and material resources depleted, and the object of their ire distanced by the Oslo Accords, Palestinians, initially euphoric at the arrival of Arafat, sat back to take a wait-and-see attitude toward interim self-rule. There has been a clear tendency of withdrawal from civic activism in Gaza during the interim period. Today, the struggle associated with paradigms of resistance has been replaced in the official rhetoric by the struggle of *al-salaam* (the peace). But under the interim regime, the demands upon popular civility have been extreme while the benefits of 'self-rule' have been minimal. Despair may once again breed conflict.

The chaos of the intifada, as it developed into a general condition rather than a tactic for undermining Israeli control, also reflected the trauma suffered by the structures of authority in Gaza over several generations. Its institutionalization into ingrained modes of behaviour that threaten the stability of any future order now poses a serious challenge to the construction of material and psychological linkages encouraging society's identification with PA elites. This chapter looks at how these pressures and trends manifest themselves in terms of 'social mobilization from below.' It suggests that a persistent crisis of authority at various levels of Gazan society has complicated meaningful definitions of self-rule from below, and threatens to summon a 'spectre of superfluous man.'

Internalization and Externalization of Authority: Accommodations with Power

Occupation conditioned Gazans to resist even the most mundane restrictions imposed and enforced by occupation authorities. The structures and attitudes regulating social life developed in the absence of a broadly based legitimate authority, a factor which reinforced the fragmentation characteristic of Gaza's life structures in general. Loyalties became localized and personalized, and insecurity and general disorder created a climate of suspicion. The coercive authority of Israeli occupation, at least so far as its ability to restrict, regulate and punish superseded that of the family, faction, neighbourhood elder, gang or clan, perhaps also engendered ambivalent attitudes toward abstract, institutional expressions of authority in general.

Conscientious behaviour with respect to authority, according to Freud, always represents a contradiction to the ego.[5] In Gaza under occupation, this contradiction could not be rationalized away in the name of any transcendent social value. This tended to create a situation where popular assessments of right or wrong were made in terms of who was enforcing the rule and who was the transgressed rather than 'traditional' or 'legal' criteria. Almost all rules enforced or all disputes arbitrated by the occupying authorities were viewed as inherently illegitimate. An anecdote from the author's personal experience illustrates the problem in the post-Oslo context.

Arriving for my second stay in Gaza on 21 January 1996 – the day after the first Palestinian national elections in the occupied territories – I was almost immediately confronted with evidence of a tense relationship between Gazans and the PA. Omar Moktar Street is the main east-west thoroughfare linking Palestine Square in the centre of Gaza City with the beach-front. Most of the community improvements initiated since the signing of the Gaza–Jericho Agreement seem to be located on or within a few blocks of this road and the work was creating traffic chaos and frustration. Cab drivers worked to dodge the attention of police who were struggling to maintain traffic order, a difficult task in a society which has been conditioned to resist even the most mundane manifestations of authority. My north-west European prejudices concerning traffic etiquette aside, such scenes – being the most visible meeting point between manifestations of authority imposed from above, and expressions of the norms and forms of life as understood and organized from below – offer clues as to how the relationship between the new organs of authority and Gazan society is emerging.

Starting two blocks below Palestine Square, and continuing about ten or so blocks beyond, Omar Moktar was closed for repaving. This forced traffic into side streets and created an obstacle to north-south movement through the city. A Palestinian policeman directing traffic stood at an intersection where Omar Moktar Street became once again usable.

He directed all traffic coming out of the side street to turn right (west) toward the beach front, not allowing them to swerve a little to the left over the area under repair and continue on the most direct south-bound path. One cab driver, however, refused to make the right turn, and began to argue with the policeman, who then stepped into the south-bound path Instead of turning right as directed, the car drove at the policeman who was forced to jump on the hood. It stopped and the policeman rolled off putting his boot-heel angrily through its front grill. He then grabbed the driver and a shoving match ensued until several other Palestinian policemen standing nearby intervened. A crowd began to gather, and a Palestinian armoured vehicle (the same as those earlier used by the Israeli occupation forces, only now painted blue instead of military olive green) arrived on the scene. The crowd grew bigger, and more police arrived.

It soon became apparent that the crowd was rallying to the support of the cab driver and the security forces were quickly forced to turn their attention from calming their offended colleague to pushing it back. The driver was finally driven quickly off in the armoured vehicle. With the object of popular ire gone as quickly as it arrived, the crowd dispersed; but resentment obviously remained, even if now fragmented. A group of young men, passing by as they walked away from the scene, looked towards me: 'F— Arafat,' one of them said, emphasizing the sentiment with a gesture that often accompanies it. His friends backed him up with similar sentiments in Arabic.

Freud posits the superego as a kind of internalization of the limitations which power and external authority place on the individual ego. 'By means of identification (one) takes the unattackable authority into himself.'[6] In order for civic restrictions to make sense to the individual, this submission to authority must provide some benefit in terms of security or material comfort. The exercise of authority must conform to the expectations of the superego; and in changing environments that demand the reinterpretation of social norms, the superego may gradually reset the parameters of discipline itself within changing bounds of authority. If the restrictions on the ego are manifest in civilization, within the triangular boundaries of the relationship between individual, society and power, they are compensated somewhat by increased stability, predictability and security of the licit objects of desire. If the Authority does not supply the stability and the framework which allows for compensation to the ego, the conflict will force the individual to reject the authority. The superego will rationalize the restrictions on the ego in relation to other social and ideological configurations besides the state. Larger groupings, religion for example, influence the individual's conscience in relation to authority; as does belonging in smaller groups – the nuclear family, the *hamula*, the camp or even a gang.

Punamaki-Gitai's research notes ways in which expressions of authority in the street during occupation shaped popular attitudes and responses to authority, and determined the arena within which confrontational impulses could be released:

> Descriptive data on Palestinians' stress responses showed that there was an ongoing 'psychological war' between the Palestinians and Israeli soldiers on matters of endurance and weakness, power and submission, pride and humiliation. For instance, the presence of enemy soldiers moulded the expression of grief, because its free expression would have meant revealing the weak point to the enemy. Psychoanalytic research has taken the importance of the enemy into account, by giving it the function of being the focus of fear and hate, as well as the target to displacement and projection of one's own undesired impulses ... Both (psycho-analytic and cognitive phenomenological approaches to social stress and trauma) agree that no occurrence is stressful or traumatic of itself, but by virtue of psychological processes, especially by the meaning given to the experience.[7]

The sexual harassment of women by Israeli soldiers during the intifada is a case in point. According to one report, 'politically active and experienced women are usually more prepared to talk about sexual harassment during occupation. But most of the young women and minors feel deeply ashamed, and if they are willing to report it do so 'hesitantly, shyly and very mild[sic].'[8] The same report also notes: 'The intifada has accelerated changes in [Palestinian] attitudes toward women prisoners. Preservation of national honour is increasingly seen as more important than personal honour [sexual integrity].' Stress and uncertainty still characterize life in Gaza. Concurrently, however, the mechanisms which they used for coping – have been distanced or are threatened with irrelevance. Al-Jarbawi refers to 'contradictory double talk' and a 'painful schizophrenia in the Palestinian collective pyche' as the prevailing post-Oslo political discourse employs 'revolutionary slogans and rhetoric of the past' in the context of establishing a political entity overtly subject to Israeli constraints and harsh realities on the ground. Such conditions might contribute to socio-political disorientation at the grassroots.[9]

Certainly, self-identification informs, and is informed by, socio-political demands and available options. The individual identifies with, rationalizes, and seeks to protect a variety of sheltering and empowering structures. Georg Simmel, one of the founders of modern sociology, described the reinforcing characteristics of such multi-layered structures of identification and coping in terms of intersecting concentric rings of social affiliation. Interestingly, invoking a trope also used by Nasser and Heikal (as ideologues of Arab unity) and Hassan al-Banna (the ideological father of the Muslim Brotherhood), Palestinian Islamists expressed their various social and ideological loyalties in terms of a model based on 'circles:'

There are many circles, all of them in one circle. I am from Gaza, nobody can deny that. I am very proud to be a Gazan. Gaza is part of Palestine, so I am very proud to be a Palestinian. Palestine is part of the Arabic land, so I am proud to be an Arabic man. And the Arabic nation is part of the Islamic nation, Islamic *umma*, so there is no contradiction. As regard region I am from Gaza, as regard state, I am from Palestine, as regard nation I am Arabic, as regards all these, [they are] in one system which is called Islam.[10]

Bassam Jarrar, a prominent Islamist activist in Palestine, uses the same image for more local (and also intimate), civic relationships: ' ... there are some people that I have duties for ... like father, brother, wife, neighbour, a human being, Arab Palestinian, just like circles. The Palestinian circle is very important, we share many things that make us close to each other.'[11]

The primacy of any given circle is in the first instance dependent on circumstances in society at large. According to Punamaki-Gitai, 'Psychological processes, like appraisal and coping, do not only follow intra-psychological rules, but also the rules of the military, political and nationalistic atmosphere.'[12] The strategies of resistance – ideological responses and the social support networks which emerged to sustain the population through years of deprivation and instability – served to give meaning to events and propose a longer term significance and reward for current deprivations. 'When excessive and taxing internal/external demands are placed on an individual a person has to mobilize psychological counter forces to deal with these demands.'[13]

Analysis of the FAFO data gathered at the tail end of the intifada showed that only 20 per cent of the respondents were free of mental distress.[14] Interestingly – given that living conditions were worse in the Strip, and confrontation with occupation forces generally more intense – Gazan respondents reported fewer symptoms of psychological stress than respondents from the West Bank. According to Giacamen et al., this might reflect

> ... a clearer sense of collective meaning and common purpose [amongst Gazans]. A greater sense of cohesiveness, originating in a more traditional family structure, may also contribute as a protective factor. The population in Gaza may enjoy greater protection against distress as the perception of an external enemy becomes exceedingly strong. Then again, the explanation could be that Gaza residents are less prone to recognizing and expressing symptoms of psychological distress.[15]

Some studies have gone so far as to suggest that mental health might even improve during times of war.[16] Resistance, even if chaotic, offers an active sense of shaping one's social and psychological space in an environment otherwise characterized by a loss of control over personal destiny. However, if social cohesion and thus mental health are based on the common identification of a clear external threat, what might be the effect if many of the objective conditions of hardship remain while the object against which active coping was defined is suddenly distanced? In Gaza, it can safely be said that both the occupation and the initial realities of self-rule have created traumatic and stressful situations in society at large. At the same time, the environmental resources and the orienting factors which helped people to deal with that stress have changed.

> Lazarus and his colleagues have defined two processes that mediate the person environment relationship: appraisal and coping. Primary appraisal is the process of perceiving a threat to one's self, and secondary appraisal is the process of evaluating the ability of resources and options of response to the threat. Coping is defined as the process of executing that response, which refers to cognitive and behavioural efforts to master, reduce and tolerate demands that are created by the stressful transaction.[17]

Ironically perhaps, the individual's primary appraisal of occupation in many cases may not differ too much from appraisals of threats to personal survival under self-rule. The options informing secondary appraisal, however, have been significantly altered leading to increased stress in the population. Two responses to this stress can be observed: making one's self 'go boom' (i.e. glorification of the fate of the *shahid*, or holy martyr) and absolute withdrawal from a political process that seems to be going nowhere.

Resignation or Revolt?

> Fatalism in the guise of docility is the fruit of an historical and sociological situation, not an essential characteristic of people's behaviour … the oppressed, [in adapting] to the structure of domination into which they have been immersed, become resigned to it, [and] are inhibited from waging the struggle for freedom so long as they feel incapable of running the risks it requires [including the risk of greater repression]. (Paulo Freire)[18]

Punamaki-Gitai's empirical study suggests an explanation for the current withdrawal from political activity in Gaza that reinforces one that could be derived from Paulo Freire. Her evidence implies that while cumulative exposure to uncontrollable stressors might encourage active oppositional coping strategies when ideologically supported, when ideologically deflected and made dependent on the new source of authority, stress might lead to resignation and withdrawal. As Punamaki-Gitai notes:

> … only in the conditions of very active and visible collective resistance against foreign occupation was it possible that personal exposure to hardships, such as detention in the family or destruction of the home, were associated with increased active and courageous coping responses. On the other hand, the exposure led to passivity and helplessness after the Lebanon War, which brought about Palestinian military defeat and the frustration of nationalistic aspirations. The decisive factor encouraging the employment of active and courageous coping when exposed to political hardships may thus be the degree of nationalist optimism, social cohesion, and ideological support available in society … The results showed that in the stress group, the more the children were exposed to political hardships, the more they employed active and courageous coping modes. In the post war group, however, exposure to political hardships increased passive and helpless coping modes, as hypothesized.[19]

Today, frustration remains in Gaza, but the option of resistance has been, for a period, pre-empted by the very elites who earlier promoted its ideology and the alternatives it promised. It is no longer justified in the context of a nationalist ideology incorporated into the contours of the peace process. Freire has noted that in such conditions (ideological disorientation, horizontal fragmentation, and the removal of the object of opposition) horizontal violence – the striking out against peers for personal or petty reasons – is often manifest.[20]

The role of stress in defining the social condition of Gaza and in understanding Gazan's responses to the changing situation must be considered. Over the past thirty years, and during the past ten years in particular, Palestinians in Gaza have been exposed to a high degree of social instability and subjected to varying forms of personal and structural violence. Factors such as displacement have increased stress and depression by disrupting interpersonal relationships and inducing shortages in available material resources. Mass arrests and labour migrations are just two examples of potentially depression-inducing experiences which place demands upon one's ability to cope.

Has the structural violence of occupation left Palestinians more likely to resort to violence to seek redress in the current order? Punamaki-Gitai notes several phenomena which could be relevant in trying to understand how the grassroots might cope with the inadequacies of the new order, and the potential for these coping strategies to coalesce into integrated opposition or grassroots activism. Empirical studies seem to indicate that, 'while criminality and suicide tend to decrease during actual wars, the rates of homicide, delinquency and suicide tend to be especially high in post-war societies.'[21] Exposure to violence tended to encourage covert aggressive responses such as an increase in patriotism and extended group loyalty which were deemed by some researchers to represent psychologically healthy responses.[22] The role of ideological factors in promoting social cohesion during times of general stress should be understood.[23] Denis Goulet has noted the important role of ideologically motivated, politically charged language in mobilizing 'collective energies around a value which is the motor of all successful revolutions [and political transitions] – HOPE.'[24] Hope seems currently in short supply in the OT. Although polling has shown significant swings from month to month, in October 1996, 56 per cent of Palestinians in the OT described themselves as generally pessimistic. A poll taken in December of the same year suggests that only 12.4 per cent of the same group describe themselves as 'optimistic towards the Palestinian future.'[25]

An individual might also channel internal stress into patterns associated with and legitimized by key terms and symbols of broadly accepted socio-ideological systems (nationalism or Islam for example). On the other hand, the demands of coping may also direct energies toward transforming existing environmental restrictions. The meaning given to events and the social cohesion which results is crucial in determining how stressful an event is to each individual.[26] It is worth quoting Punamaki-Gitai extensively on this point:

Active coping modes such as street demonstrations and barricade construction and the active helping of others have been assumed to protect the individual's mental health from the damaging impact of political violence. On the other hand, denial of threat and suppression of feelings are considered healthy ways of coping when the situation is too overwhelming and uncontrollable. Both trauma and stress approaches ignore the role of political or ideological factors in affecting psychological responses in conditions of political violence ...

The contradictory dynamics [of a 'conflict *between horror and heroism*'] form a good example of the psychological processes, which are neither a direct reflection of society nor do they solely follow intrapsychological laws. They follow both a psychological and political logic, and thus depict a meeting point between person and environment ... [The Palestinian intifada], for its part, provided new ways of healing psychological stress and trauma. New modes of collective coping are created, such as politically organized mass funerals, army like rituals and dramatic plays that ventilate sorrow and anger, and organized study activities in prison and underground that prosper the nationalistic self esteem. The motive of these new coping activities is to increase endurance, and they share both a psychological and a political function. These examples show a close transaction between the psychological and political processes ...

Finally, what is special about the psychological processes in conditions of political violence is that their aim is not necessarily to restore the equilibrium between person and environment. Thus, the assumption of homeostasis between person and environment found in the stress and trauma models should be re-evaluated. It is more realistic to emphasize the goal oriented and collective activity of people, the aim of which is to change the environment, rather than adapt oneself to it.[27]

Simmel describes conflict, and the associations that people form to pursue conflict, as the tool they use to define and redefine the social arrangements in which they live.[28] The instability and the impotence of authority – its inablility to contain and channel conflict – may give rise to calls for sweeping change. However, the ineffectualness of existing structures that contribute to the impotence of leaders similarly undermine efforts at organization and mobilization from below. In the absence of effective civil avenues in which to pursue public competition, violence may be invoked in a last resort to effect change. Perceptions of what these changes should be and how they should be pursued and implemented are determined by the individual's economic and social situation and the various forms of affiliation and identification available to him or her. In the absence of apparent structural or institutional alternatives, attempts are made to resolve fundamental psycho-social disorientation by appeals to authenticity. In many cases, authenticity is resorted to as a last hope for order – it asserts the stability and recognizability of an imagined past, and gives the satisfaction of having solved the problem at least on paper. It seeks action as the logical extension of enforcing the myths of text and narrative, thus making a world that does not seem like the logical extension of what has been written conform.[29]

But social mobilization from below might also be based on something less abstract, such as a common economic or neighbourhood interest. In a world where individuals belong to multiple associations of varied form and content, each individual potentially possesses a multitude of bases of resistance. Thus, a monolithic call of authenticity would probably fail to serve the variety of needs of the modern individual over the long term. It is, however, with the inability to fulfil developmental imperatives, or more accurately the loss of developmental alternatives, that the call for authenticity seems to become most contentious. In the absence of meaningful change, the grassroots might be inclined to pose Denis Goulet's question: 'Liberation for what?'[30] On the other hand, the current situation might be stifling pressures which, if pent up for too long, are capable of blowing the lid off the current peace process.

'Traditional Structures' and Current Dilemmas in Mobilization

The challenges that face the grassroots of Gaza as they attempt to steer the trajectory of self-rule toward recognition of their concerns and interests cannot be understood without at least a brief overview of the repeated trauma suffered by the structure of authority and mobilization in Palestinian society. In Gaza, these have been severe, leaving society with few structures and mediators around which to organize civil opposition. This section examines the condition of social institutions on the periphery of civil society. It identifies three themes that suggest disorientation in the mechanisms through which authority is consolidated and legitimized: 1) the delegitimizing of traditional elites and the rise and fall of activist legitimacy; 2) the lessening of the inherent authority within family structures and 3) women's mobilization and the threat to patriarchal restrictions on mobilization and control. It is argued that PA rule has not been able to provide conditions which entirely restore the structure of the first two categories. Concurrently, activist channels of legitimacy have been usurped; and, in a climate of general dependence, the position of woman may be especially hard hit. While not taking the position that primary affiliations such as the family constitute in and of themselves a base of civil society, the argument does assume that they play a supportive role, and that they might also mirror the contingencies at work on social affiliation in general.

The decline of traditional authority

Hanan Ashrawi has commented on the struggle of each generation to redefine the contours of mobilization and national struggle following the perceived failures of the previous generation.

> Would we leave the next generation a legacy of failure as we had so often, and perhaps unfairly, accused my father's generation? You tried. You failed. Armed struggle and Arab nationalism had led us from one disaster to another. Innocent lives were lost and sacrificed. Perhaps, I hoped, our generation could make the supreme effort to divert its course, and leave our children the legacy of living, and redefining the future, rather than joining the dance macabre of the past.[31]

And, as Punamaki Gitai notes:

> For a Palestinian child, confrontation with an Israeli soldier does not only signify the present threat, but also the humiliation and defeat experienced by the earlier generation that was forced to leave their homeland.[32]

'Most traditional societies,' say Almond and Powell, 'have some long range promise of performance built into their norms of legitimacy;' in the face of a disaster, the traditional leadership loses some of its authority.[33] In Palestine, the authority of traditional elites was tarnished by the military defeats of 1948 and 1967. But even before that, the decline of the Ottoman Empire and the increasing contacts between the Arab world and Western Europe – contact which was to culminate in imperialist occupation – introduced new notions of politics and the state. This implied in its wake 'changed notions of person, responsibility, and political roles – notions not always accepted without resistance or providing the results intended by their carriers.'[34]

Historically, the crisis of authority in the Palestinian context can be traced to the failure of local elites and local forms of social affiliation to mobilize effectively against the onslaught of Zionism. The absorption of Palestinians into the world economy during the early decades of this century and the loses of 1948 and 1967 each in turn had a dramatic impact on the relationship between Palestinian society and its political and economic elites. Economic bonds between peasants and landowners were weakened, and the military defeats encouraged a questioning of the ability of the existing political order to ensure the security of individuals, communities and property. The large scale displacement of the Palestinian population entailed a separation from the patriarchal/agrarian order within which existing relationships of benefit, obligation and authority made sense. In spite of attempts through marriage and economic remittances, families and villages could not always reproduce and sustain in exile the conditions of proximity and economy within which the old political status quo had been rationalized.

Thus, the political, social and economic ruptures which followed 1948 and 1967 were in many respects strong enough to de-legitimize one generation of leaders and push a new group forward in its place. The take-over of the national movement by the *fedayeen* in the late-1960s capped a trend characterized by the increasing significance of the poorest in Palestinian society in defining what it meant to be Palestinian. The military defeat in 1967 and the inconclusive results of the 1973 war created despair in a political psyche whose dignity and sense of efficacy had before been stoked into feelings of efficacy and power by the rhetoric of Arab nationalist elites. So much of the legitimacy had been based on words and symbols which leaders proved not able to back up in deed, leaving a population with wounded dignity and deep suspicions. Nowhere was this suspicion of promises of redemption from above more deeply felt than in the poor neighbourhoods and refugee camps of the Gaza strip.

During the Arab nationalist heyday the rhetoric gave the Palestinian refugees a feeling of security and immanent victory. The defeat of 1967, however, created feelings of personal vulnerability which ensuing crackdowns by insecure elites outside the OT and the excess of force used by the occupying authorities in the OT did nothing to assuage. In many respects, the post-Oslo environment represents just as serious a break with the past as those represented by the political disorientation of 1948 and 1967.

The increasing significance of activism as a way of acquiring legitimate social position also posed a challenge to traditional elites, who, while they openly shared the nationalist aims, saw in such activism a destabilizing challenge to their own interests. The emergence of the nationalist movement provided a counter to the remnants of the traditional leadership at a later stage and created new avenues of social and political advancement on the basis of activism. This new dynamic provided much of the organizational underpinning of the intifada and was perhaps reinforced by it. Structural changes in the economic sphere also gave rise to new bases and notions of legitimate authority, and encouraged and even demanded activism. These changes include, firstly, the rise of wage labour; secondly, extensive land confiscation; and, thirdly, the increasing availability of university education after 1967. 'Each of these helped break traditional patron-client relations that had been the social base of the old elite and paved the way for the rise of a more extensive, better educated, more rural, and non-landed elite which had gained cohesion in the new universities ... [this] transfigured a basically peasant society.'[35]

However, the arrest, imprisonment and deportation of a generation of nationalist oriented local leadership, and the lack of economic bases for integration and class or sectoral solidarity, has crippled civil society in Gaza, placing even greater stress on the individual. Furthermore, the steadily worsening economic situation in Gaza since the mid-1980s has increased dependency on the localized and familial social coping mechanisms. The Israelis allowed only one mass political rally in Gaza during the whole of the occupation. This lack undermined the ability of any local leader to identify with a larger constituency around an activist agenda. It is also one reason why funerals became such an important political rallying point during occupation. Today, many in Gaza lament the inability of the old factions to mobilize the population.[36]

Since the deployment of the PA in Gaza, a recurring point of tension has been disappointment among the younger cadres of intifada activists who did not receive positions in the new structure. Opposition from within Fatah ranks has come from younger activists who were on the streets confronting the Israeli army while the nationalist leaders were 'off somewhere cutting deals.' The feeling was sometimes expressed in terms of betrayal: those who engaged in the 'real' struggle – those who had suffered in Israeli prisons and who had missed out on the chance for education and training – should be rewarded with meaningful positions within the new authority. A status that had been achieved by standing up to the occupier was suddenly no longer immediately relevant as narrower interests came to the fore in the context of the new order. Once the PA, representing essentially conservative interests within the context of the peace process, was established in Gaza activism was looked upon with suspicion and no longer provided the same access to privileged positions within the Fatah infrastructure.

Challenges to the family as a reference point of authority

Even as the destruction of other structures of social organization and mobilization was encouraging a retreat into the family as a primary structure providing economic and personal security, the family itself was experiencing pressures which have challenged its traditional role in social control, discipline and economy. According to Punimaki-Gitai:

> The very nature of war and political violence is such that it puts at risk the ability of parents to protect their children. The descriptive part of the Palestinian data showed some special features in the parent-child relationship owing to political violence and national struggle. There were changes in family patterns so that a child tended to assume the responsibility for caring for both parent's well being and the national fate ... In Palestinian society, for example, it is evident that long term involvement in war and national resistance has created new models of protective factors, which could not be detected by using traditional stress models ... Palestinian children tend to apply an active, responsible and 'adult' role in political resistance. In child psychiatry, too early adaptation to the adult world is considered a sign that the adults fail in providing security for a child, and thus risks the child's healthy development.[37]

The isolation experienced by children who have had parents arrested, killed or otherwise removed from the home may further encourage the acceptance of primary group affiliations outside the home. Research indicates, for example, that the forced removal of individuals from localized groups (something that was a common experience for activists under occupation) tends to encourage greater identification with abstract principles and goals.[38] Indeed, Israeli prisons were often called 'Palestinian universities'[39] and were hotbeds first for nationalist activity, and later – as Israelis allowed Islamist literature into the prisons while prohibiting nationalist literature – as recruiting grounds for the Islamist movements during the intifada. Furthermore, Punamaki-Gitai reports that children tended to 'take care' of parents who were undergoing extreme stress, and at the same time if parents were subjected to debilitating stress, that children were more likely to pursue strategies of active confrontation with what were perceived as its sources.[40]

During the twenty-seven years of formal Israeli occupation, women became increasingly involved in political and economic life outside the home and younger males moved into the forefront of active resistance and articulated the demands and expectations of the vision of a new order. Many of these young men spent considerable time in Israeli detention, which alienated them from household authority and put them in contact with alternative underground political networks which came to the forefront of Gaza's civil society during the intifada.[41] Other demographic migrations affected relations of proximity, and in some cases perhaps made elders more economically dependent on adult children than would otherwise be the case. Migrations to work in the Gulf states, deportations, the flight into and return from the diaspora of many political elites, the daily migration of a large percentage of Gazan men to work in Israel all placed tremendous strain on the effective functioning of traditional authority and community survival structures.

Another sign of the decline of traditional family-based socio-economic imperatives are the changes in the customs regulating courtship and marriage. In the previous century, marriages tended to be arranged for economic reasons (thus in most cases according to the peasant agricultural logic). Immediately after 1948 marriages were consciously designed to reproduce the ties of the previous environment; but this pattern has been declining and increasingly there is more freedom for individuals to base marriage plans on the existence of individual relations. The importance of this fact is that it denotes atrophy of the areas where elders determine the most fundamental life decisions of others in the family group.

Patriarchy and women's roles

Punamaki-Gitai notes that 'girls and boys participate rather equally in contemporary national conflicts'[42] and that girls tend to adopt more masculine (militant) characteristics while boys tend to display more feminine (nurturing) characteristics. If this is so, one might argue that exposure to sustained political upheaval might be a factor that discourages identification with traditional patriarchal structures over the long term. The rise in the number of activist women's movements in the OT and the active role of women in resistance activities reinforces images of women and girls as efficacious and conscious social actors. Indeed, evidence that politics might have irrevocably shifted from its focus on the patriarchal clan unit toward other bases of political awareness could be found in the expanding role and visibility of women in Palestinian society.

While women as a group may not have entirely transcended their traditional social and economic roles in Palestinian society, the scope of these roles has extended increasingly into the public sphere, making them visible. These are naturally preconditions to political inclusion and an expanded role for women in Palestinian society. Even while increased use of the veil seemed to denote a regressive trend in Gaza society, the contingencies of resistance forced women into new types of activities that challenged traditional constraints. (Often subtly, public tasks became appropriated within the scope of women's activities.) Furthermore, the widespread and general support across gender lines of female political figures such as, to name one example, Hanan Ashrawi, and the enthusiasm for women candidates shown by many Palestinian women with whom the author spoke during Palestinian legislative and presidential elections in January 1966, indicate the acceptance of women in politics. These feelings of solidarity of women with female candidates also bodes positively for the expansion of women's role in the political life of Palestine.

The strategy of home production during the 1980s was largely a women's income-generating initiative. Other economic and social trends also increasingly brought Palestinian women into universities and workplaces. Resources traditionally considered a means of financial independence for women (the dowry for example) have been depleted in recent years as assets have been sold off to compensate for the lack of steady income by male employment. These assets have increasingly been used to finance household investments and education of children, expenses traditionally placed upon the man. While the immediate impact of this might be to give women less external financial freedom from their husbands, in the long run it might encourage the view that women can play an active role in meeting daily financial needs. As in Egypt, where economic necessity led to greater participation by middle class women in the work force, perhaps economic hardship may in the end push more women into employment outside the home, and perhaps male attitudes would follow necessity. On the other hand – in a climate where so few jobs are available – women may be pressured to stay out of the job market in favour of men. Currently, women express that they feel themselves to be financially dependent on men.[43] While only 10 per cent of Palestinian women are employed outside the home, 77 per cent of the women surveyed declared their support for the right of women to work outside the home.[44] However, these trends should be considered cautiously. Evidence collected in the FAFO survey of living conditions in the West Bank and Gaza Strip indicates that women are still restricted in terms of economic independence and their freedom of movement.[45]

During the latter stages of occupation, Palestinian women were often singled out for abuse and insult by Israeli authorities in ways intended to mock and degrade Palestinian cultural norms and sense of honour. No longer sheltered from social confrontation, and made aware of the need to overcome their double vulnerability in the face of traditional patriarchal restrictions and the violations of dignity in the face of Israeli soldiers, women increasingly organized to declare and protect their rights and security in an unstable and insecure environment. While women were subject to the terror of occupation in some different ways than men, they were in certain circumstances less likely to be arrested if confronting Israeli soldiers during the occupation. Thus, while boys and young men involved in resistance activities were forced to run, women would come out on the streets to face Israeli troops on the front line. This 'rescuing of males' played an important role in increasing the status of women's roles during the intifada. It is also worth noting that women were there experiencing the daily impact of occupation while many men were away at work in Israel. In a significant act during the early stages of the intifada, the announcement of a 'gender agenda' by Palestinian women's groups on 8 March 1988 indicated an increasing orientation of women's organizations toward finding a more dynamic role for women in society.[46] These early initiatives have been institutionalized during the interim period in the form of a 'women's parliament' where women's organizations meet to draft and lobby for changes in laws with significance to women's lives. These efforts have been condemned by Israeli activists and viewed with suspicion by the relatively conservative Fatah PA elite.

Hammani notes that 'the problem of 'mixing' to a large extent disappeared with women's entrance into universities, the work place, and political activism – either need or changing notions of what was prestigious for women overrode fears of potential for scandal.'[47] Recently, this has been increasingly countered by Islamist calls for more traditional roles for women. Abdul-Jawwad notes that while the Islamist groups do not oppose increased education for women per se, they tend to evaluate female education in terms of its impact on improving the overall chances of men to carry out religious duties and duties of resistance. In fact, while calls for the reduced social visibility of women could be heard from Islamist quarters since the early 1970s, it was not until the later stages of the intifada, when women were increasingly included among the targets of Israeli crackdowns, that this call began to find some resonance in the population, especially in Gaza. A statement issued by the Unified National Leadership of the Uprising addressing the issue of increased harassment of unveiled women read, 'We are against excessive vanity in personal dress and the use of cosmetics during these times. This is applied to the same degree for men and women.'[48] While deferring to traditionalistic interpretations of social norms, the statement also seems to carefully avoid singling out women so as not to alienate them, which could in turn be interpreted as a recognition of their organizational significance. These attempts to more clearly delineate the social and cultural space between occupier and occupied created a fundamental shift in the ways Gazans saw their role in the nationalist movement in general – active in the clear delineation of cultural space where other forms of activism seemed not to provide results. There were seeming contradictions in the active role and cultural symbolism born by women; these trends created cleavages within the women's movement itself.

As elsewhere in the colonial and post-colonial contexts, women's movements in Palestine have never really articulated a clear feminist agenda beyond calling for more fundamental economic equality and enhancing the role of women's activities in the context of the nationalist movement. Women's liberation was subordinated to the broader goal of national liberation. The first women's organizations were the Arab Ladies Committees established in 1929. These were composed largely of the spouses and other family members of upper class urban nationalist elites. Their activities were mostly in the area of organizing charitable activities. In public demonstrations at the time, women were put in a protected position, usually surrounded by troops of boy scouts near the end of the procession. After 1948, however, women began to join the ideologically-based and nationalist parties which formed in the diaspora. While increasing prominence was given to the need to mobilize women in the context of all out national mobilization, issues of equality in economic and social life were not in the fore. With the training of women's cadres to face Israeli occupation, women became involved in activities traditionally seen as the domain of men. The result was that women increasingly ended up being tortured in Israeli prisons; many who refused to cooperate in prison became romanticized as part of the mythology of the resistance.[49] Leftist political parties paid particular attention to the mobilization of women[50] and the formation of the national front in 1973 saw the unprecedented participation of women at higher levels. Later, during the intifada, the mass arrests of males (especially younger males) led women to the front lines of protest. 'All these things had an important impact on changing the traditional views of society toward women as being weak creatures incapable of surviving the burdens of political activities and their problems.'[51] The mobilization of women was becoming seen as integral to national mobilization generally.

Ultimately, the dependence of the women's movement on the nationalist political structures tied to various political factions means that it might find itself with less official support now that male nationalist leaders feel they have achieved their limited aims. Accordingly, PA elites might feel compelled to build a nationalist consensus by giving in to more conservative demands, while feminist demands might be viewed by nationalist leaders as destabilizing and radicalizing in a situation where they no longer benefit from 'radical' activities. This is especially true given that the nationalist leadership, and Fatah in particular, have never had any real social content in their political agenda.[52] Furthermore, Deniz Kandiyoti has argued that, 'as the state itself uses local patronage networks and sectional rivalries in its distributive system, citizens also turn to their primary solidarities both to protect themselves from potentially repressive states and to compensate for inefficient administration. This reinforces the stranglehold of communities over their women whose markers as boundaries become heightened.'[53] It remains to be seen whether the women's movement can counter the reactionary trends in society, sustain themselves, and transcend these political and social constraints.

Authority in the Street

A society that has for twenty-seven years experienced almost all manifestations of institutional authority as illegitimate is maintaining a sceptical stance toward the Palestinian Authority. When asked over the latter half of 1996 which Palestinian personality and political (or religious) faction they most trusted, around one quarter of OT residents either reported that they trusted no one or did not fill in the question, while close to 50 per cent reported in August 1996 either that they did not trust any political grouping or did not feel strongly enough to answer the question.[54] The consequences of this lack of trust are exacerbated in Gaza by a pandemic social insecurity and growing cynicism. Gossip – often malicious and directed against leading politicians as well as neighbours – seems rife in Gaza.[55] In part, this seems driven by economic insecurity; particularly dependence on the PA for jobs that are secured through connections as opposed to qualifications. Given the external and internal restrictions on productive action within the PA, people compete for positions and influence by putting each other down. Furthermore, while polling has indicated increased feelings of personal security in areas from which Israeli troops have redeployed,[56] continued high rates of quasi-criminal activity and the abuses or excesses of an insecure security force conspire to engender feelings of personal insecurity within the population at large. The rise in crime may in itself indicate contempt for authority within the new order.[57]

In many respects, the demoralization and powerlessness reflected in these phenomena were influenced by the disintegration of the internal and external of public discipline during last years of the intifada. Specifically, it can be traced to the measures taken by both the IDF and the Palestinian 'strike forces' in their battle to control the street during the intifada – measures which became increasingly violent as the intifada wore on. The prolonged chaos of the intifada as a tactic for undermining Israeli control and increasing Israel's costs of occupation took its toll on the institutions of the movement – not to mention the nerves of many Palestinians living in the OT. While achieving this tactical aim, the eventual militarization of the intifada also heightened a sense of insecurity on the Palestinian street. Gradually, the strike forces began to more openly wield guns and knifes and increased the scope of their activity to include a campaign of retribution against those who were seen as breaking the discipline of the uprising. Even today in Gaza, people speak nostalgically of the first two years of the intifada, before things lost direction.

One early act of solidarity with the uprising's intended aim of shattering Israel's grip on the OT was the mass resignation of the Arab police force (responsible for monitoring traffic and petty crime and not any matter related to internal security) in March 1988, at the behest of the UNCU. This move was compensated by the formation of 'popular guard committees.' These were originally formed to protect the shops which had been damaged by Israeli soldiers as retribution for refusing to open.[58] The UNCU leadership also set out to organize other participatory structures to make up for the sudden vacuum of authority. These initiatives included people's courts which invoked *shari'a* law and local notables were mandated to mediate in a broad range of local intra-Palestinian disputes. The initial success of these initiatives was undermined by a severe Israeli crackdown against the committees, including mass arrests, with the result that gangs of young men began to play a larger role in enforcing the directives of the external UNCU without the supervision of local civic leaders, and without accountability to the severely damaged institutions of the popular committees.

The uncertain situation heightened feelings of insecurity and suspicion. Roy discusses the traumatization of the young and their inability to recognize or accept the difference between illegitimate and legitimate authority.[59] As Ashrawi notes, the population became obsessed with the thought of collaborators. The UNCU preyed upon such fears, continuously warning the population of the 'repercussions' of collaboration. The excessive violence of many of the factional gangs 'enforcing' the uprising through summary punishments including assassination led to local disgust with the turn of events and a general withdrawal of identification from the bearers if not the aims of the uprising. Shop-owners selling Israeli products were roughed up and bonfire campaigns (burning offending products) were organized to intimidate shop-owners.[60] These developments were to gradually alienate the conservative merchant class, whose active participation in the resistance had been important to the coherence and street level unity of the intifada's early stages. As Israel's grip on the Palestinian street weakened, the chaos turned inward as various groups competed to fill that vacuum, or people sought to take advantage of the uncertainty of the situation for personal gain.

The increased repression in the wake of Israel's policy criminalizing all forms of popular organizing from 1988 onward:

> ... set in motion the process of removing the mass population as the front-line of the intifada to be replaced by militarized underground cells of male youth. These 'strike forces' operated with little ideological direction or oversight, since the massive and constant imprisonment of activists meant that the mature nationalist leadership was continually being replaced by younger, politically uneducated and inexperienced activists. Added to this, the Israeli secret services stepped up the recruitment of collaborators in order to contain the intifada, now that the popular committees had been made illegal. By 1989, confronting collaboration had become the dominant resistance activity of intifada activists of all factions and had become an obsession of society as a whole.[61]

And according to Don Peretz:

> Moderates among the Palestinian leadership who opposed the use of violence seemed to be losing to militants who were unwilling or unable to calculate the possible impact on the Palestinian community of armed resistance ... Equally worrisome was that young zealots were taking the law into their own hands ... violence seemed to take two forms, armed robbery or murder by Palestinian criminals and clashes between nationalist factions ... masked youths knocking on doors in the middle of the night ... robbing and attacking in the name of the intifada.[62]

The strike forces became the provenance of individuals who used their power to settle personal and political vendettas. The intifada began to eat its own, overtaken by rival gangs engaged in an increasingly violent struggle for the Palestinian street. The original policing role of the strike forces had degenerated in an environment where Israeli policies, significantly, provided an example of authority by raw power. The paramilitary gangs were increasingly cloaking their self interest in terms of protecting the 'purity' of the intifada.

With Israeli redeployment in the middle of 1994 and the arrival of the PLO elite in Gaza, the PA regime was not able to consolidate order in the street, and was seen by many as contributing to disorder rather than taking steps to counter it. According to a correspondent in *The Guardian*, the new forces looked ill prepared upon their arrival in Gaza: 'not [like] a police force at all, but an army; a small lightly armed and ramshackle army, but an army all the same.'[63] This grouping had been put together with recruits from among local militant activists, many of them who have received their 'human rights training' in Israeli prisons.[64] An aura of 'foreigness' surrounding the security forces is not only reflected in the recent diaspora histories of many of its members; it is reinforced in the fact that they have received their training not locally, but in The Netherlands, Britain, Egypt and elsewhere. This has contributed to confusion in style and approach and also distanced training from conditions on the ground in Gaza. Moreover, the political groups were not successful at disciplining their armed cadres who had been engaging in Mafia like activities. Gun and drug smuggling are rife, perhaps with the tacit approval of the Israeli authorities who would like to see Arafat forced into a situation of greater dependence on Israel.[65]

Sara Roy describes conditions at the outset of the autonomy which did nothing to endear Gaza's population to the new order.[66]

> Fatah, which is still the largest faction in the Gaza Strip, is increasingly seen as a reactionary force promoting social discord, not harmony ... Feelings of irreversibility have left the population defeated, vulnerable and fearful.[67]

One disturbing anecdote relates that immediately after the withdrawal of the IDF from Gaza, the *shabab* adopted the fashion features of the Israeli soldier or agent – an American style baseball cap and sunglasses.[68] The symbolism of power in the street had been reduced to style, but its content remained raw force. Many human rights activists complain that the security cadres, having experienced the exercise of authority only through being tortured in Israeli prisons or in the types of summary justice of unstable situations in southern Lebanon or collaborator assassinations in the late phases of the intifada, now have little understanding of human rights or the legally restricted and humane exercise of authority.[69]

Much of the open political conflict on the Gaza streets has flowed into the contours of the Islamist/nationalist divide – notably between Fatah and Hamas. During the intifada, days were set aside to commemorate the start of the intifada and other national achievements. The ninth day of every month was held aside as a day to commemorate the outbreak of the intifada. The Islamist movements, on the other hand, commemorated the start of the intifada on the sixth, which they claimed was the date of its inception. According to Lindholm Schulz, after the arrival of Arafat and the PA, these events seemed to take on less significance:

> The yearly intifada day used to gather huge crowds of celebrators, but in the aftermath of the establishment of self-rule, celebrations took on lesser proportions. Another day was added to the national calendar during the intifada, the Day of Independence (*yum al-istiqlal*) on 15 November, which was also widely celebrated during the years of the intifada. In 1994, its meaning, at least temporarily, seemed to have eroded from popular nationalism. Yasser Arafat made a speech in Gaza, but the enthusiasm was gone, and [apart from in the schools] there were only dispersed and small-scale celebrations.

So called Islamist v. nationalist conflict was carried into the post-Oslo autonomy from the latter stages of the intifada, and reached a climax on November 18, 1994 with an event that became known as 'Black Friday.'[70] Early on within the Autonomy, hard liners within Fatah had accused Arafat of being soft on Hamas. In order to show the resolve of the PA, Gaza security chief Colonel Nasser Yusuf made repeated calls on the Islamic groupings to disarm.

The Islamists, however, rejected the call to disarm as 'unpatriotic,' and organized protests against the call and against Palestinian police. 400 Palestinians were arrested by Palestinian security forces between August and November 1994. On 3 November 1994, Gazans ejected Arafat from the funeral of activist Hani Abed, as thousands took to the streets protesting Arafat's leadership. Later (after an incident on the border between Israel and Gaza) the tension came to a head as PA police fired on protesters after Friday prayers on 18 November, killing twelve and wounding

200. Arafat's response to the tumble of accusation and denial that followed was to establish and arm seven plainclothes 'emergency committees' – composed mainly of local Fatah hawks – to assist Palestinian police in the campaign against Hamas. Tasks included the removal of pro-Hamas graffiti from the streets and replacing it with pro-Fatah graffiti. This seems to reflect the insecurity of the PA regarding the street level legitimacy of its institutions.

Palestinian consternation after the election of Benjamin Netanyahu in May of 1996 (leading to a slowdown in the implementation of agreements), and the increasingly active interference of the IDF and Israeli settlers in the daily lives of Palestinians, heightened tension and led to Palestinian calls for retaliatory measures. A dramatic indication of the crisis of authority in the street (and the way it results from a general crisis of 'authorization') was the unrest in late September/early October 1996 which followed the Israeli government's decision to open a controversial tunnel under the al-Aqsa mosque. The unrest climaxed when Palestinian security forces returned fire against Israeli troops who were firing on unarmed Palestinian civilians inside the self-rule areas.[71] In this case, however, the popularity of Arafat and the security forces actually increased as they for perhaps the first time acted in a protective role, covering Palestinian civilians who were being fired upon by Israeli troops.[72] According to *Jerusalem Post* reporter Jon Immanuel,

> Hamas supporters at one end of the spectrum admired what they saw as the political acumen with which Arafat took advantage of an Israeli blunder. Oslo Accord supporters admired the masterful way he ran with popular feeling for awhile and then reined it in forcefully, creating the impression of control without kowtowing to Israeli demands.[73]

However, control is not authority, nor is the ability to rally public sentiment in a time of external threat. In fact, the incident highlights Arafat's effective weakness by showing how contingent his ability to mobilize the population remains on what essentially amounts to active resistance.[74] This was not a position he was capable of sustaining for any length of time. Within days, Arafat's forces were taking 'active measures with riot sticks to quell further unrest,'[75] and Israeli authorities were demanding that between one and two hundred Palestinian policemen involved in the clashes be immediately dismissed. No disciplinary action was called for against the Israeli participants in the incidents, a fact which can only leave Palestinians feeling that authority in the streets is not serviceable to their security interests. Furthermore, the inability to sustain any political gain made during that week, confusion in the ranks of the Palestinian security forces during that time, and the fact that the earlier status quo (with the tunnel still open but no Palestinian gain on the ground or politically) was restored, could only heighten Palestinian despair.

In spite of popular exhaustion, a poll taken after the clashes in late September 1996 between Palestinians and Israeli troops showed that almost 70 per cent of Palestinians supported a continuation of the intifada, including many who advocated military operations against Israel.[76] These clashes mobilized national sentiment, and temporarily resuscitated the flagging reputation of the PA security forces. Slogans of the intifada reappeared on walls whitewashed after the PA's return in 1994. An employee in a shop in Gaza City reported that, 'The people's demand for national songs has increased. They are also buying songs of the intifada and this shows you how they really feel deep within.'[77] On 3 October 1996, Hamas issued a communiqué urging the Palestinian people to go to 'total confrontation' in mobilization against Israeli forces and settlers. However, the outcome of the Washington Summit (4 October 1996) between Netanyahu and Arafat to deal with the crisis was disappointing from the Palestinian perspective, and the euphoria that had bubbled up during the collective action of the previous two weeks seemed to dissipate. During a protest against the sentencing of three PFLP activists on 20 December 1996, one could hear once again the accusation being made that Palestinian police were agents of the Israeli security services.[78]

The continued frustration at the grassroots is clear. In early 1995, 57 per cent of those responding to a survey conducted in Gaza 'expressed dissatisfaction with the functioning of the PA, 69 per cent complained about a lack of democracy, and 90 per cent expressed the view that PA positions are filled unfairly.'[79] Since then, the objective conditions upon which such opinions were founded have got worse. The ritual of elections served to defer some of these complaints in the early months of 1996, (the grumbling about a new occupation seemingly more difficult to justify), but incidents of street protest and violent clashes between, *inter alia*, students and Palestinian security forces, testify to the ongoing suspicions. Many complaints stem from the perceived inability of the Palestinian authorities to ensure the security of individuals from incursions by Israeli troops. This was especially the case during the Israeli army roundups of Palestinian students after the suicide bombings in March 1996; and again in April 1997 when four were killed in a Tel Aviv cafe.[80]

The crisis of authority in the streets cannot be separated from the failure of the new order to satisfy the short term needs and expectations of the population of Gaza. The debate is no longer one of ideology, but one of competition for control. Politics is seen as irrelevant as it no longer seems to serve any economic, social or humanitarian purpose,[81] a perception which this author found again and again when talking to young Palestinians in Gaza.

The abrupt transition from general participation in a movement of national resistance to life in an elitist/accommodationist status quo left many Gazans disoriented. The feeling that the new elites did not understand their concerns or sympathize with local values serves to fuel the resentment and disillusionment growing from the grassroots.[82] The interaction between the new security forces and the population in the street has been one of mutual suspicion and at times outright hostility.[83] Hamas founder, Sheikh Ahmad Yassin, offered a relevant word of caution: 'I would advise the Palestinian Authority not to copy the methods resorted to in the Arab countries in dealing with people. The authority should be careful not to bring down the bridge over which they crossed into this land.'[84]

Statistics reinforce the notion that the lack of viable alternatives may increasingly push opposition toward desperation and violence. 'Gazans are … supportive of the opposition's right to violent expression, with a September 1993 poll showing that 28 per cent of Gazans (40 per cent for Gazan refugees) approve of the use of 'violence if necessary,' with only 6 per cent of West Bankers holding this view.'[85] During the height of the crisis in the peace process in April 1997, CNN refered to a poll suggesting that 50 per cent of all Palestinians 'supported' individuals who carried out suicide bomb attacks inside Israel.[86]

Political Islam in Gaza: An Alternative Basis of Civil Society?

It should be remembered that the crisis of authority in Gaza occurs in the context of a crisis of authoritarianism generally in the Arab world, and that the responses to the kind of apparatus being built by Arafat might be similar to responses seen elsewhere in the Arab world.[87] The legacy of one party authoritarian states has crushed or marginalized many of the ideological and political options available to groups and individuals as they seek political and social expression of their interests and/or attempt to legitimize a project of political opposition or social change.

While the alternatives which have emerged have often been grounded in 'ideologies of last resort' that propose extreme and final solutions to all social and historical injustice, one must not overlook the degree to which their support is gained not only by feeding on hopelessness, but also in the building of constructive alternatives and offering services – in short, by constructing the types of structures that in a different political environment might easily be identified as full fledged 'civil society.' While isolated, Gazans are not uninfluenced by these trends. Given the apparent personal and collective hopelessness found in the streets of Gaza, the extremist ideologies have their appeal, and there may always be a segment of the population who reject uncertain long term solutions when ideologies proposing alternative means of more immediate and transcendent gratification are available.

In this context, the grassroots trend that would come to have the most profound impact on civil society in Gaza rose to prominence in 1988 bearing the banner of political Islam. Indeed, the rise of Islamism in Gaza can be seen in direct relation to frustration with the ineffectualness of the nationalist elites at addressing issues of fundamental concern to the population of the territory. In the late 1970s, creeping disillusionment with the diaspora nationalist elites began to affect the population of the territories, leaving them amenable to ideological and strategic alternatives.[88] Islamic revolution in Iran captured the popular imagination and while the Israelis were focusing on repressing the nationalist movements, the Islamists, who at the time were not involved in active resistance, were allowed to build their organizations.[89] Most importantly – using the resources of its parent organization, the Muslim Brotherhood – Hamas began to develop real linkages in society during the intifada, largely unharassed by the Israelis in the beginning becuase they saw this as a way of undermining the PLO's ability to establish a foothold in Gaza through the organization of social activities. Also, Israeli authorities banned most political books and allowed only religious literature in the prisons.[90] The mass appeal of Hamas – in contrast to the tepid support previously shown for the Muslim Brotherhood – lay in its militant and essentially nationalist stance at a time when the old nationalist institutions seemed increasingly inaccessible or irrelevant to many activists. Its access to the resources of the *waqf* and other sources of patronage offered new opportunities for professional activism at a time of increasing unemployment.

The origins of the tilt in the balance of power in Gaza that has ended up making Islamism an important political and social force can be found in both local and regional political factors. The most important include the PLO expulsions from Jordan and Lebanon that weakened the movement and highlighted internal problems such as emerging factionalism. These events brought into question the PLO's conduct, its efficacy, the quality of its leadership, and the soundness of its strategy, its tactics and its political programme as a whole. The resulting change in PLO strategy included more limited and short term goals. These often undercut the more sweeping rhetoric of liberation and triumph which had characterized its earlier discourse. Institutions as well as leaders were negatively affected in the minds of the masses. 'The PLO seemed to be going nowhere,' and the boundaries of its bureaucratic factionalism seemed to be 'finalized.'[91] Many younger potential activists sought alternatives in the Islamist movement. In turn, Hamas created an active discrepancy between old and young within the Muslim Brotherhood.[92] Its avenues of recruitment included mosques, the Islamic University in Gaza and the *waqf* administration.[93]

In a tactic akin to divide and rule, the Israelis had nurtured the Islamists as a counter to nationalist institutions and to thus blunt the effectiveness of PLO-related organizations in Gaza. After leftist successes in organizational elections in the late 1970, the 'Israelis, Gazan rightists and the Muslim Brotherhood set about its destruction ... In 1980, a mob marched from the Islamic University to the Palestinian Red Crescent Society [which, as a stronghold of the leftists, had been successful in organizing a variety of activities and mobilizing grassroots support] and set fire to the building' as Israeli troops stood by and watched.[94] The PLO suffered from repression at the hands of the Israelis while the Brotherhood was laying back and not taking an active role in resistance activities.[95]

> PLO groups believe, and openly argue, that the Israeli authorities opened the door for the Palestinian Muslim Brotherhood ... so that they could compete with, oppose and undermine the PLO. Certain nationalist circles go so far as to claim that Ahmad Yassin, the leader of the Islamic Centre in the Gaza Strip, swore on the Koran, before the Israeli investigators, that weapons seized in his possession in 1984 were meant to be used against the leftist factions.[96]

This legacy has meant that nationalist and Islamic trends continue to view each other with suspicion. Each accuses the other of working on behalf of Gulf regimes. The Muslim Brotherhood emphasizes the failures of the nationalists, and PLO will occasionally accuse the Muslim Brotherhood of collaboration with the occupation by attempting to undermine national unity. The Muslim Brotherhood views the PLO as the construction of failed, corrupt, illegitimate and morally bankrupt Arab regimes who created the PLO for its own manipulative purposes. The Muslim Brotherhood also attacks the PLO connections with liberal Israelis and outside powers (ironic given Hamas' pragmatic alliances with the secular nationalist opposition – while the Brotherhood denounces all contact with the Israelis and the West, records exist showing that they have in fact at various times had such contacts).[97] Such bickering has certainly contributed to Gazan's frustration with politics.

Just prior to the outbreak of the intifada in 1987, support for the PLO had reached its lowest ebb.

> Apart from their growing alarm at the PLO's increasingly obvious military weakness, the Palestinians in the West Bank and Gaza were further alienated by the PLO's persistent attempts to bypass them politically and to abort what ever national gains they had made over the previous twenty years.[98]

Hamas, formed as an activist front for the Muslim Brotherhood in the early stages of the intifada, was the only Islamic movement to combine the activities of resistance with the building of a structurally significant social base. It drew its initial support from those who saw in the PLO's secularism the same rank materialism which they analysed as the cause of much of the corruption and arrogance of regimes elsewhere in the Arab World. Hamas benefited from the social links and material resources of the Muslim Brotherhood. This infrastructure included schools, universities and other social services networks as well as waqf resources.[99]

Where other Islamist groups proved dogmatic in their approach to using Islam as a tool and vision for political and social change, Hamas has been dynamic and active in the community in a variety of ways and in response to perceived needs of the population. They were 'there', active in Gaza, when the PLO leaders in exile were not. Hamas, in spite of its being an organization containing many personalities and sometimes tensions, seems to have always perceived itself as a party which sought to compete politically for primacy in Palestinian internal politics. Al-Jarbawi writes:

> ... by means of this far reaching network in Palestinian society, many developing segments of that society grew into relationships of dependence upon Hamas. In turn, this was transformed by Hamas into a means for political mobilization ... In open contrast to the excellent performance and clean reputation enjoyed

by the organizational network connected to Hamas, the factionalized organizational structure of national powers within the occupied territories suffers from a poor record of performance and an even worse record for corruption, nepotism and political patronage'[100]

Abu-Amr adds that 'Hamas's rejection of the PLO's political platform and its call for the establishment of an Islamic society in Palestine and for the establishment of an Islamic leadership to spearhead the popular struggle are all manifestations of its rivalry with the PLO for leadership.'[101] Just as importantly, however, Hamas proved its ability to work with political and social delicacy under the 'umbrella of what became known as 'national unity.' This was very important in a political arena which, with the relative demise of the PLO during the 1980s, was fraught with differences.[102] It managed to achieve a structural base for legitimacy in spite of its open rivalry with the PLO.[103] It did so largely because of its ability to be perceived as an impartial mediator in social disputes. Even Palestinian Christians accepted Hamas judgments. Abu-Amr notes that:

> People resorted to such informal mediation because of the absence of authority structures that are usually entrusted with this role, or because of the lack of credibility on the part of those structures. During the intifada, most of the Israeli controlled government structures and institutions, including courts, were practically shut down. The secrecy of the PLO factions and the fact that they do not enjoy spiritual authority increased the demand for the arbitration of the Hamas leaders. While the resort to these leaders undermined the authority of the Israeli occupiers, it also undermined the authority of the PLO and the nationalist institutions.'[104]

While most Fatah activities were militant in thrust (combined with network-building based on patronage rather than problem solving on a grassroots level), Hamas managed to balance militancy with activities that responded to people's broader institutional needs. While Fatah organized camps where they dressed up boys in uniforms and marched them around a field, Hamas organized computer camps.[105] The Muslim Brotherhood accuses the PLO of wanting power for itself rather than in the interests of all the community – 'You should be the first to sacrifice if the goal was the liberation of your country and your people. But if their goal is to seize power, then there is no blame on you for not sacrificing yourself.'[106] The leadership and organization of Hamas, while growing and becoming compartmentalized, is still small and unbureaucratic in comparison to the PLO. The overall leadership is entrusted to consultative councils.[107] However, Hamas has repeatedly been plagued by losses in its ranks through deportations and imprisonment. However, a high point in Hamas' visibility came after Israel deported 415 alleged Islamists at the turn of the year 1992–93, depositing them in southern Lebanon after a Hamas campaign in December had killed six Israeli soldiers. This was also the time when the Labour leadership began to openly advocate a policy of withdrawal from Gaza. In Shimon Perez's words, it was time to get 'Gaza out of Tel-Aviv.'[108] Such mass deportations left the OT bereft of leaders with activist bases. Abu-Amr argues that the arrests and deportations only opened the door for more militant younger leaders who are less interested in social concerns.[109]

Hamas has also benefited from being able to act as the opposition, a situation which for awhile even allowed them to ally with Christian secular nationalist George Habbash.[110] 'Following their participation in the intifada, the Muslim Brotherhood began to realize that actual involvement in politics requires more than romantic stands.'[111] Still, however, Hamas has not had to make difficult decisions or concessions, and was able to pick up the militant slogans of the PLO at a time when the nationalists were abandoning them – a moment which also coincided with increasing disillusionment and economic hardship.[112] In fact, the formal enlistment of Hamas in the secular leftist-based Palestinian Forces Alliance (an attempt to construct an alternative PLO?) in January 1994 underlines the pragmatic political ambitions of at least one important part of its leadership.

As of 1993, Hamas began paying less attention to the enforcement of social codes and more to attacks on the Israeli army. This probably reflects Hamas' success in attracting militant defectors from the mainstream nationalist movements and the context of acute economic hardship which made the focus on the veil as an alternative to Arafat's khafiyya as a symbol of identity and resistance seem less immediately relevant. Iyad Barghouti argues that Hamas has found its support more as a 'nationalist alternative' than as an Islamic movement ... Hamas is popular among young more because of disillusionment with nationalist generation than religious conviction.[113]

The PLO and the Muslim Brotherhood continue to compete with each other in terms of taking credit for accomplishments and in uncovering contradictions between words and deeds. They each try to be seen as legitimate heirs to historical movements and figures.[114] During the intifada, this competition went so far as contentiousness over whether the monthly date for celebrating the intifada should be the sixth or the ninth.[115] Violent factional clashes have occurred at the Universities, including competition for control of the agendas of the Islamic University in Gaza.[116] Clashes have not only been between the Islamic groups and Fatah, but also between some of the Islamic groups themselves.[117] The Islamic tendencies have in turn been affected by PLO/PA attempts at divide and control. 'The PLO leaders made persistent attempts to co-opt the Islamic movement in the OT through coordination and offers of support;'[118] sometimes doing so even at the expense of their own (particularly the local) candidates. At present, the combination of repression and co-optation at the hands of the PA has blunted the effectiveness of independent Islamist social mobilization in Gaza as an alternative to PA authority.

While coercive measures against the Islamist groupings have left them down for now, they are certainly not out, and Arafat's 'good cop, bad cop' attempts at co-opting them into the pro-Oslo camp have only been marginally successful.

> Arafat cannot, as he can with the PLO opposition, keep the Islamists in line with his enormous powers of financial and political patronage, for the Islamists are not and never have been financially dependent on him. Hamas in particular represents a mass, indigenous, and authentic political constituency in the occupied territories by virtue of having its own finances, structures, organization, and, above all, ideology. It is because Hamas represents a genuinely independent force outside the PA's sway that it is perceived as the main internal threat, the most difficult of all Arafat's internal and external oppositions to 'tame.'[119]

Other recent reports suggest that as of the summer of 1996, Hamas has been making a comeback among Palestinians. This is not reflected in polls, which show popular support for Hamas at steady 6–10 per cent in the OT. Its current tactical objectives have been largely organized and articulated from the diaspora, a situation which suggests the physical and ideological fragmentation of the Islamic movement in general. This fragmentation is reflected in a press release from Hamas' central leadership blasting statements made by Mahmoud Zahar, one of Gaza's most prominent Hamas figures, who had publicly questioned the wisdom of 'martyrdom military operations' by Hamas' military wing the al-Qasim brigades. The same press release accused the PA of being a threat to national unity and warned of the 'consequences' of the PA's continued detention of hunger-striking Islamists in poor conditions.[120]

However, that Hamas remains able to mobilize mass demonstration is supported by events over the latter part of 1996 and early 1997. A protest on 13 December 1996 commemorating the first anniversary of the assassination of Hamas militant Yehia Ayyash drew massive crowds. Frustration with the lack of progress in the peace process, and an increasing feeling that the eventual final status will not satisfy needs and aspirations have been cited the main reasons for this limited resurgence. At the same time, people appreciate Hamas' low key stance during this time (before April 1997) in regard to terror operations that might lead to an indiscriminate punitive response from Israeli authorities. Still another element of this comeback appears to be an apparent tactical accommodation with the PA aimed, as Khalid Amayreh notes, at sending a 'tacit but unmistakable message to 'whom it may concern' that Palestinians have options other than the peace process.'[121] The PA, at Arafat's instruction, released hundreds of Islamic activists from PA detention in late 1996, and media reports suggest that more were released in the wake of Israel's decision to build at Har Homa in March 1997.

As a closed, secretive, organization which always placed more emphasis on dramatic actions than on institutional mobilization, the Islamic Jihad has perhaps maintained its unity as an opposition actor. The organization makes no bones about its feeling toward the Israeli authority. In September 1996, a senior official in the Islamic Jihad noted that, 'there is no alternative to returning to the path the Zionist state understands: the holy *jihad*. Painful blows to the heart of the Zionist entity will embarrass the Netanyahu government and the corrupt, weak and shameful Palestinian Authority.'[122] However, by mid-November, an Islamic Jihad leader was forced into a more apologetic mode for not having been able to carry out his threat: 'Palestine has been transformed into a fortress in an unprecedented manner. Naturally that has created some difficulties and delayed our action.'[123]

Islamist movements such as Hamas and the Islamic Jihad, while presently on the defensive in the PA-controlled areas, offer ready made contours within which the spectre of superfluous man might coalesce in Gaza. As a socially mobilizing force, it can find the subject of resistance both in external enemies and in internal illegitimacy (as cases in other predominately Muslim countries demonstrate). That said, there seems to be a secular current in Gaza that is all too often overlooked. While secular and nationalist, individuals in this trend have been alienated by worsening economic conditions and by the dismantling of much of the nationalist activist infrastructure of the intifada, and if they have not yet lost their affinity for the PA, they appear to be rapidly losing it. This group would be comprised mostly of young men who have withdrawn from the PLO factional structures that emerged in the OT during the intifada and who don't see a viable alternative to, or at least no immediate connection to, opposition groupings based in Damascus and elsewhere. For example, Fatah's Hawk and Falcon wings have been disbanded, leaving many young men unemployed and without an active social role.

Although sentiment varies with the ebb flow of negotiations and events, no Gazans spoken to by the author in early 1996 spoke of a return to the intifada, people wanted peace and jobs. On the other hand, at present there is no secular ideology capable of appealing to extreme sacrifices, unity or 'steadfastness' in an environment currently characterized by extraordinary hardship and constraint.

Conclusion

Any new order inevitably creates conflict over issues of legitimacy, control, and the basis for redistributing resources and power. This kind of competition in Gaza has been stifled by the incontestability of issues that are in fact amenable to ideological debate or democratic contention. The conditions described throughout this work have suggested the difficulties facing any attempt by the Palestinian street to appropriate self-rule and shape it in ways that reflect their interests and aspirations. Things are simply too regulated, restricted or limited by the terms of the agreements. Neither the struggle for peace within the new order, nor for that matter an existential grounding defined in terms of resistance before it, has thus far proven capable of providing the scaffolding for a productive and participatory project of Palestinian national reconstitution.

Sara Roy has given poignant expression to the predicament in Gaza:

> Many increasingly see a connection between emerging Palestinian authoritarianism and Israel's security led interpretation of autonomy. Gazans say they will resist. But how? What mechanisms of social and political mediation, other than violence, do Gazans really have at their disposal? Put differently, what does it mean to be a socially engaged person in Gaza today, in an environment characterized by continuing occupation, waning security, warring factions, a moribund economy, diminishing water and land, a traumatized population, and an uneducated generation of children?[124]

Tragically, in the current context of Palestinian autonomy, the

Palestinian people have been seen as a threat to the PA, a perception which encourages the marginalization of the grassroots in the building of the post-Oslo Middle East order in general. The Palestinian street might once again be pushed to strike back, and to take an active role through the only opportunities given to it: the incitement of confusion and, perhaps, violence which though related to political demands and economic superfluousness also reflects desperation, the lack of structurally-informed organizing principles and of a clear target against which to vent frustrations. While political withdrawal seems to have been the dominant tendency within the grassroots thus far, the positions of Prime Minister Netanyahu, and the resulting loss of popular faith in the will of the Israeli government to reach a settlement, have inspired periodic convulsions of protest that have the potential of becoming generalized.[125]

The introduction of PA rule has shattered the contours which moulded popular political expression and integrated society, at least on the level of outward manifestations of protest and opposition.[126] It is doubtful that individual Palestinians have struggled to throw off the shackles of Israeli repression only to be repressed by others because they speak the same language or wear the same hats. Sooner or later the promises of the new order will have to be redeemed or delivered or overwhelming force will have to be used to weld a subdued population to a state built from the scrap heap of Palestinian political and economic institutions – institutions which have been torn apart by occupation, neglect and inertia. As Paulo Freire has argued, 'Freedom is acquired by conquest, not by gift. It must be pursued constantly and responsibly. Freedom is not an ideal located outside of man; nor is it an idea which becomes myth.'[127]

Gaza is not too far from the edge of total disorientation, from fragmentation within fragmentation, and if the new order proves unable to service needs, hopes and interests, the 'spectre of superfluous man' looms imminent. The Palestinian elites who have not backed up their rhetoric with deeds, nor offered real strategies for anything other than a very relative and limited vision of liberation, might in the end be put on trial in the Palestinian street. Alternatively, in the absence of a dramatic turnaround in the course of the peace process, they may be reduced to policing masses united by little more than disillusionment.

Clashes between Palestinians and Israelis in September of 1996 and March/April of 1997 demonstrate, especially given the failure to ameliorate economic conditions, the fragile balance between accommodation and the spectre of superfluous man. They illustrate that it is ultimately 'the people,' and not only leaders, who must accept the new order.

7

Sustaining the Polity: Towards Autonomy on the Street?

As the peace process slips deeper into crisis and contradiction, Albert Hourani's comment on developments in Arab politics following the Suez War of 1956 seems apt to today's situation: 'Although it was clear that things would never be the same, it would take some time before we could really see how they had changed.'[1] Similarly, Palestinian politics has entered a new and uncertain era. This book has suggested an imbroglio in the socio-political development of Palestinian self-rule. The resulting predicaments – grounded in the conflicting interests being pursued within the peace process, in a problematic methodology of transition to Palestinian 'self-rule' outlined by the DoP and subsequent agreements, and in the dependent and de-institutionalized trajectories of Palestinian socio-political life – threaten the potential meaningfulness and viability of autonomy on the Palestinian street. In so doing, they diminish the likelihood that the current trajectory will lead to a 'just and lasting peace.'

The new order in the 'Palestinian areas' has proved unable to allow tensions arising in a time of economic hardship and political change to be mitigated either by grassroots innovation or through the legislative and executive efficacy of the PA. That this has not lead to even greater social unrest in the OT than has already been seen is in large measure due to an artificial decoupling of political and economic developments – a situation that has been made possible by massive donor funding. Civil society is left to fend in a structural vacuum without any sustainable platform from which to influence the course of the peace process or the character of emerging institutions. Interventions aimed at procuring short-term stability in the autonomous areas have incorporated Palestinian social atomization, economic paralysis and vulnerability to coercive incentives into authoritarian modalities of social control. In short, stability has been conceived in a negative, static sense. It is a model of pacification that is likely to require substantial external input and the continuous, ad hoc mediation of minor crises. It is within this context that the long term effectiveness of interventions designed to promote stability in the Palestinian areas (particularly those that have coalesced in the securitarian and neopatrimonial characteristics of the PA reviewed above) must be evaluated, and the responses and challenges that emerge form the Palestinian street understood.

Stability versus Political Order: The Question for the Long Term

A corporatist, neopatrimonial dynamic is clearly emerging as a major pillar of stabilization in the relationship between the PA and society in the self-rule areas. It is, however, a model that arises from and is likely to perpetuate the fundamental structural malaise that threatens Palestinian acceptance of the emerging order. In form, this dynamic resembles both that invoked by Israel to ensure the 'quiescence' of the Arab population left within its borders after the 1948 war,[2] and those mechanisms of syndical co-option utilized by other states in the region such as Egypt, Syria and Jordan. It also finds precedents in the factional organization of the PLO, and in the traditional dependent power relations between peasants and indigenous elites in Ottoman Palestine.

Corporatism as a social pillar of political control thus finds a certain resonance in the political culture of the Middle East; one cannot, however, reasonably argue that it represents the limits and expectations of politics in Palestine. Its persistence is a response to specific socio-economic conditions. At an immediate and practical level, factionalism and neopatrimonialism are unlikely to create an environment conducive to the kinds and degree of economic growth that will satisfy expectations and demands associated with self-rule. On the contrary, the neopatrimonial framework is likely to encourage non-productive forms of social competition which neither advance the cause of nation-building nor promote national political and economic integration over the long-term. By reducing the number of organizations and social formations that might serve as mediators or buffers between the individual and the state, and by limiting the civic frame of reference, factionalism pushes those who remain uncommitted to the existing framework out of the given political order. In other words, it does not diffuse or absorb isolated poles of frustration and anger.[3]

The dependency inherent in factionalism limits the efficacy of civic discourse. It thus leaves opposition to the order as a whole, perhaps violent opposition, as a seemingly necessary and reasonable alternative to those excluded from the political process. The other potential response – withdrawal – merely reinforces abject dependence and nominal compliance as ways of surviving in the margins.[4] At present there seems to be no mass-based Palestinian constituency which has benefited from Oslo. While a dependent factionalism might be able to co-opt and provide basic needs and benefits for large segments of the population, its fundamental inadequacy is that the stability of the factional order depends not on an integrated and reinforcing internal dynamic, but on the willingness of external benefactors to reward the political compliance of the PA. PA resources are not extensive enough to placate the population if current levels of unemployment continue (especially given the fact that most of the aid which has come to the PA is in the form of loans and not grants). The economic situation and the repressive base of PA rule threaten to widen the realm of the marginalized over the longer term.

Butressing the neopatrimonial tendency in the PA is what might be described as security authoritarianism, or securitarianism. Put in a straightforward way, the securitarian paradigm insists on the immediate containment of Palestinian activism and the disciplining of the Palestinian population, even if this must be at the expense of institutional development and the nurturing of structural bases of cohesion and stability. It is the security function of the ruling apparatus that is used to discipline those who fall outside of the corporate framework or those who challenge its limited political vision.

Gaza's history of external dependence and reliance on limited, vertically organized coping strategies has left society with little experience of either channelling social competition into more productive, integrated and self-sustaining developmental activities, or mediating ideological disputes through large scale organs of political arbitration. However, it must not be forgotten that Palestinians have been shaped as individuals and as a collective by responding and accommodating to the challenges of life in a modern world. Hanf and Sabella conclude that Palestinians have to a significant degree 'internalized the language of human rights and the rule of law in their struggle to bring down an efficient army of occupation.'[5] In a survey conducted by these two political scientists, four-fifths of the respondents agreed with the statement: 'the time of family/*hamula* politics is over. Leaders should be chosen on their own qualifications and merits.'[6] As noted in Chapter 2 above, other writers, notably Hilterman and Robinson, have emphasized the role of nationalist politics and the emergence of a group of young, university educated 'modernizing' elites in overturning the stultifying role played by traditional elites in pre-intifada Palestinian politics (a role characterized by narrow interest affiliation and dependency). However, as this book has argued, the structural underpinnings at the social, political and economic nexus were not transformed in ways capable of sustaining pluralist developments in Palestinian society. Indeed, a donor agenda that attempts to impose a pluralist framework in the absence of such a supporting environment might legitimately be questioned both in terms of its effectiveness and intent.[7]

The Netanyahu administration has been recklessly unapologetic over the insinuation of its ideologically determined interests and demands into Palestinian affairs under the cover of security interests. Whereas the Labour government which negotiated and signed the Declaration of Principles (1993) and the Interim Agreement (1995) sought stability in the territories as a precondition to meeting its strategic aim of viable separation, Likud and the right-wing parties in its ruling coalition do *not* seem to view instability in the territories as anathema to their ideological and strategic aims. Indeed, a convincing case can be made that the current Likud government is provoking instability in order to justify its intrusions into crucial spheres of Palestinian life. The strategy is apparently to isolate instability within pockets of resignation, denying Palestinians the spaces that might allow frustrations to lead to mass mobilization.

The inability of the PA/PLO to resolve issues of daily existential concern to Palestinians only heightens awareness of the regime's inadequacy in other respects. The Israeli retreat from negotiations suggests that the timely resolution of the issues still subject to final status negotiations – *inter alia*, the sovereign boundaries of self-rule and the fate of the Palestinian diaspora – is unlikely. This contributes to Palestinian anxiety over, and impatience with, the impotence of emerging 'autonomous' institutions. The lack of progress on the diplomatic front, the desperate economic situation, and the increasing awareness in the OT that lines of accountability (culpability) still lead to Israel increase the potential for violent attacks against Israeli targets. Such attacks, however, further weaken the PA position, which is inherently more dependent on a quick progress in negotiations, and on delivering the benefits of self-rule. Attacks also undermine the willingness of the international community to arbitrate and place diplomatic pressure on Israel on the PA's behalf. Given the imbalance of power built into the bilateral negotiating framework, the PA is dependent on such pressure. The Israeli responses to Palestinian violence are exacerbating the conditions which inspired the violence in the first place.

The contradiction does not seem entirely lost on the Netanyahu government, which even as it stalled the progress of negotiations granted 18,000 new permits for Palestinians from the OT to work on the other side of the 'green line,' bringing the number of Palestinians with permission to work in Israel back up to 50,000 (as of Autumn 1996). This indicates a subtle trend toward re-establishing the pre-Oslo status quo. It increases Palestinian dependence on access to Israel for basic needs, while using the de facto imbalance of power to expand the Jewish presence in the OT and consolidate control over productive land and water resources. Delay therefore seemingly serves the strategic interests of the Netanyahu regime, while any delay for the PA only further emphasizes its impotence in addressing past and future Palestinian concerns. As of the middle of September 1996, a majority of Palestinians still supported the peace process, but 51 per cent of Palestinians in the West Bank and Gaza reported that they no longer trusted or held any opinion about Palestine's political factions.[8] Perhaps reflecting the 'pessoptimstic' attitudes so often attributed to Palestinians in the past with regard to their national struggle, a poll conducted before Israel's decision to begin construction at the 'Har Homa' housing project on the outskirts of occupied East Jerusalem showed that 62.3 per cent of Gazans are 'somewhat optimistic about the Palestinian future.'[9] Concurrently, while a robust 82.5 per cent of Gazans expressed their support for the peace process in the same poll, a majority expressed only 'cautious support' for the interim agreements, and a plurality described the performance of the PA as only 'average.' After 'Har Homa,' general Palestinian support for the peace process sank to 60 per cent, while 40 per cent expressed sympathy for acts of armed resistance (as opposed to 21 per cent in a pre-Har Homa poll).

Palestinian apathy and cynicism plays into Likud's strategy of subverting the viability of Palestinian political representation, perhaps leading to the re-establishment of Palestinian society's direct dependence on Israel (as opposed to dependence mediated through a Palestinian Authority, which will always be troublesome from the perspective of Likud ideology because of the broader national claims that a PA, in theory, represents). Palestinian political analyst Ghassan Khatib argues that the current balancing act amounts to 'trading Palestinians' national rights for jobs.'[10] At any rate, Likud seems to be trying to set the boundaries of Palestinian autonomy in terms of a Palestinian '*millet*' in which a PA would be given 'vassal' status in exchange for quelling and deflecting popular discontent from Israel.

At this stage of the peace process it can be said that neither the PLO or the contours of power and mobilization which informed the intifada can resurrect the energy and unity of the Palestinian past to build the Palestinian future. The fact that the Palestinian polity is made up of disconnected bits and pieces (tragically it seems to have been many of the most undesirable bits and pieces which have persisted into the new order) makes it that much more easy for Israel to determine the contours, uses and meanings of power within Palestinian autonomy. The ideal of the Israeli administration seems to be a Palestinian autonomy which preserves the benefits of occupation with fewer of its costs.

Palestinian patience is at present being sought with the promise of eventual control over land and resources. Long term economic viability depends on access to resources and an environment of greater individual and national economic autonomy. Ideologically and tactically, the Likud regime has put itself in a position where it will have great difficulty taking steps forward in negotiations on these issues, while for the Palestinian leadership (and its hope of realizing even the limited aspirations of Palestinian nationalism in the near term), significant reversals of the peace process may prove fatal or even apocalyptic.[11] Palestinians thus face a dilemma. A rush to entrench the 'final status' quo might mean that Palestinians are forced to accept something far short of the hopes engendered by self rule. On the other hand, delays or reversals could lead to the de facto fulfilment of the Likud vision of a 'Greater Israel.' The prospect of the peace process' disintegration at this stage – a stage in which historic institutions have been dismantled or distanced from constituencies while effective alternatives have not been put in place – might mean disaster for the Palestinian cause. However, such a 'catastrophe' might one day be looked back upon as the only way in which alternatives to a corrupt and factionalized PLO could have been built. If Palestinians are forced into pressing for civil rights in the OT and in the diaspora, such claims might become a more integral part of any movement of national reconstruction and mobilization that were to emerge from a failed peace process. Alternatively, civil society in the OT might be pushed to find new ways of challenging the contours and uses of Israeli power. While it is unrealistic to assume that many Israelis would accept a political trend that would threaten the exclusivist Jewish character of the state of Israel, variations on a bi-national theme might generate interesting alternatives from within Palestinian circles if the two-state solution envisioned by Oslo fails to mature and stabilize.[12]

The peace process has encouraged superficial realignments within the politico-economic processes of occupation without fundamentally challenging its structural foundations. The donor countries contribute to this problem by making distortions viable in the short-term (substituting external aid and grants of legitimacy for an internal dynamic of mobilization and legitimacy) rather than contributing to structural transformation that would encourage the development of a sustainable Palestinian polity, the trend is toward making the occupation viable and palatable. The result has been be a political entity that operates incongruously with regard to political and economic development. The authoritarianism and violent responses to the new order that are likely to result must not be viewed in terms of any innate cultural tendency, but rather as the product of peculiar socio-economic contingencies and political constraints. The peace process has inherited these conditions from the past, but rather than addressing the structural roots of these problems, it seems to be ironically entrenching them and offering them a veneer of legitimacy. The failure of the autonomy to consolidate processes of, *inter alia*, territorialization and institutionalization mean that the boundaries of any future Palestinian polity will be externally determined and constrained.

For the time being, we can only assume that some sort of autonomy based on Oslo will remain the model of rule in Gaza. The nature of PA power is such that it must respond with coercion to the frustration that arises when the demands of the peace process exceed the new order's ability to provide. At the same time, the PA lacks the power to initiate socio-economic reform and provide positive incentives to encourage popular identification with the new order. The opinion of many was expressed in a Hamas press release of 16 September 1996: 'Arafat's promises of "prosperity and well-being" had proved to be "nothing more than an illusion aimed at covering up the failure of the police regime" of his Palestinian self-rule authority.'[13]

One wonders whether, in the face of Israeli intransigence and mounting Palestinian frustration, Arafat will be tempted to just let loose his tenuous authority over society in the OT and take his chances on riding out the potential upheaval. At present, it is possible that an outright rejection of the peace process as a hopeless pantomime might even revitalize his broad-based legitimacy among Palestinians.

The current stalemate leaves 'official' Palestinian national reconstitution in a state of suspended animation, and thus prone to being overtaken by events in the Palestinian community whose activities may increasingly fall outside the scope of existing national institutions. That socially significant opposition groups are currently not attempting to take over the autonomy, but are rejecting it altogether as a basis for polity highlights a crisis of legitimacy in the order established by Oslo. Indeed, the trend as of early 1997 is for even Fatah figures to distance themselves from the PA, which further undermines the organizational base of the PA, and thus its ability to mobilize the population with reference to the apparent institutions of autonomy. Arafat is thus left as 'the system' personified.[14] The specific conditions of Palestinian autonomy have not encouraged the building of a polity capable of sustaining itself, protecting the security of its citizens, or promoting their interests in all but the most symbolic or dependent of ways. If future negotiations fail to achieve the limited national objective of a state in part of Palestine, it will be in part because the PA was all too successful in the task – delegated to it by its Israeli 'partners' in the negotiations – of neutralizing the Palestinian street.

Bringing the Street Back In

An irony of Palestinian 'self-rule' until now is that the fate of the Palestinian street remains largely in the hands of political forces that it may only peripherally or negatively influence (e.g. through violence). This has occurred largely because stability has been envisioned as an issue separate from the building of an integrated socio-economic and political order. Ultimately, however, the viability of the Palestinian polity and its ability to contribute to a productive stability in its region demands that the Palestinian street be brought meaningfully into the production of political order. Political order demands the room for a hopeful and productive instability if it is to be sustained without resort to coercion or the infusion of large amounts of donor patronage for the long term in any society. By this is meant a situation in which people may participate in and respond to socio-economic change from within the sphere of daily life without being forced to resort to overt political activism (perhaps violent) or base political compliance to meet the challenges associated with change.

In spite of the often simplistic and misleading application of the concept to Middle Eastern polities, those features traditionally associated with a vibrant civil society may also prove crucial to Palestinian success in negotiations and to hopes of Palestinian statehood. Azmi Bishara has eloquently stated the case:

> … the Palestinian ruling elite does not understand that the issue of empowering the legislative council is no longer a luxury but a dire necessity, as is freedom of the press, the rejection of the use of torture against prisoners, and orderly democratic life. The Palestinian ruling elite will not have a power base unless these conditions are satisfied … recent events have shown that only Palestinian civil society can make an impact on the international situation.[15]

More than just representing the ability to speak out or attract donor funding, civil society must be able to respond directly and immediately to the actual sources of power in society. While there have been many brave and outspoken responses from within a Palestinian society calling for greater democracy and transparency within the ruling institutions, fragmentation, economic dependence, and psychological exhaustion have undermined the building of a concerted and mobilized response representing the interests of the Palestinian street. In other words, even if society is speaking out about issues and interests classically associated with civil society, it has been distanced from the (Israeli) power that has the ultimate authority to affect these interests, and its ability to organize and mobilize in active and integrated responses has been, to say the least, problematized. Dramatically demonstrating the weak position of Palestinian civil society vis-à-vis the national leadership, PLC member Rafiq al-Natsheh, has accused the PA of 'even monopolizing people's food.'[16] Quiescence is imposed on the street while a small clique of PA 'VIPs' – their interests and actions conditioned by the need for permits and approvals from Israeli authorities – have used their powers and Israeli connections to accumulate personal wealth. While the nature and extent of this corruption has been the subject of debate amongst Palestinians,[17] and is by its nature difficult to document, the commitment of these elites to the constituency of self-rule has been increasingly questioned on the street.[18] Such developments have greatly undermined Palestinian steadfastness and communal cohesion.

The PA may indeed need to keep society weak and involved in internal conflict in order to channel civic energies and frustrations away from challenges to the regime itself. The PA's hostility to a nascent civil society in the areas under its administration stems precisely from its inability to affect, respond to and shape issues of traditional concern to civil society in its purest political and economic senses. In other words, the limitations on the PA's ability to exercise non-coercive powers and its officially granted monopoly on violence determine that it responds to independent political initiative using those powers it has – force and administrative co-optation. Spatial fragmentation and abject economic hardship and dependence place severe constraints on society's ability to respond.

Meanings, Visions and Political Order

The notion of 'a political economy of meaning' has been elaborated upon in this study to suggest that future stability in Gaza must be evaluated in terms of the agreements' paradigmatic impact on society, not the ability of an elite to 'protect' the peace process from the attacks of a sceptical society. The alignments and incentives of the new order indicate that the political entity implied by 'Oslo' will not be able to sustain and reproduce a political order corresponding to the needs and aspirations of the Palestinian people. A Palestinian Authority that remains unable to either reflect or instigate socio-economic change will almost certainly be forced to continue to resort to externally bankrolled dependence and coercion to manage its relationship with society. To return to Apter's concepts, a new 'mytho-logic' is not emerging. A clear disjunction can be seen between the Palestinian world as it is, and the ability of Palestinians to mobilize and shape that world in accordance with ideological vision and meaning. This is of course not new to Palestinian life, but the prospect of immediate accountability is.

At the level of nationalist ideology, some of the instability within emerging authority/society relationships might therefore be understood in the context of the national movement's transition from a transcendent context of ideological (nationalist) idealism to a context of immanent accountability.[19] What will happen as the nationalist ideology becomes embodied in real structures representing finite restrictions on the meaningfulness of interpretations? And what will happen when promises – promises made by a supposedly accountable administration – remain unfulfilled? Authority must reconcile its own demands with those of society; and, in order to promote and sustain a political economy of meaning, it must uphold what is perceived as a balance between rights and obligations. Authority shapes, and is in turn shaped by, the variety of perceptions society holds in this regard. This study has suggested that within the current Palestinian political framework, the stability of the Gaza Strip will depend more upon the external backers of the agreement than the structural and institutional features which characterize today's autonomy. It will be this inability of the new order to generate developmental or ideological legitimacy (beyond the tautology of nationalism as the reference point of the national leadership), and the inability of the new order to accommodate alternatives within its own framework, that reveals the deficiencies in the current political economic order.

Prescriptively, however, the general feeling that the Oslo process represents a *fait accompli* suggests that current challenges can at present only be addressed with reference to current agreements and the trajectory which they imply – an administratively segregated (perhaps in the form of a two state) solution. Protection of the new order must be envisioned not in terms of the protection of a particular elite, but through the institutionalization of new relationships between politics and economic possibilities, between the socio-economic structures that might underpin civil society and efficacious political institutions, and between aspirations for justice and actual interests underlying manifestations of power. This can only take shape with the entrenchment of institutions and rights. It should not be based on personalities associated with a given administration, but on the ability to really govern, and the ability to account for and incorporate social mobilization in the Palestinian street.

Accordingly, Hanan Ashrawi has described the challenge of self-rule for the Palestinians as one of translating an agreement on principles into a mechanism for the transformation of reality.[20] Such a transformation would entail, *inter alia,* the reforging of a document that transfers limited powers and responsibilities from Israel to a Palestinian political faction into a basis for the rule of law,[21] the consolidation of a given apparatus of rule – today primarily administrative and disciplinary – into integrated social, economic and political processes that confirm and continuously assert the boundaries of a distinct and viable polity[22] and the development of structural bases of accountability (to which ritual bases such as elections are merely useful complements) between civil society and the exercise of political power.[23] Whether or not the Palestinians will have a real chance at meeting these challenges in the future depends in large measure on the outcome of negotiations with Israel over the 'final-status' of the Palestinian polity in the OT.

Forced smiles and handshakes between Arafat and Netanyahu aside, the stability of any future order will depend on the perceptions those who live within it have of their own situation. Gazans (and West Bankers) may lack both the resources and the will for patience. If the fundamental problems suggested by this work are not addressed, there is a danger that the current process could merely institutionalize the conditions of future conflict. Perhaps only an alliance between coercive force, dependence and social disorientation postpone it for now. Unfortunately, there is little in the content of previous agreements and Israeli statements to inspire confidence that future negotiations will in fact lead to effective Palestinian statehood; and little in the early behaviour of the PA suggests that it is truly committed to the establishment of the democratic and open society that Palestinians seem to expect after a century that has seen the development of Palestinian national consciousness under conditions of dispersal and repeated occupation. While the new order has effectively deconstructed the comprehensive nationalist message, little has appeared in its place to encourage (or even allow) Palestinians to participate in the production and reproduction of political order. In spite of a genuine desire for peace and normalcy in the streets of Gaza, the contrast between current restrictions, hardship, hopes and needs remains great.

If the current order represents the practical boundaries of Palestinian citizenship, then Palestinians may find that it was easier to imagine a nationalist world than it was to build and live in one.[24] If Palestinians are not allowed to re-imagine and effectively reshape their world within the framework of the emerging institutions – if alternative visions remain excluded and repressed – the spectre of instability may become omnipresent, and the response to the limited vision and empowerment of the new order just might be violent.

Notes

Preface

1. Sayigh, p. 29.
2. Cited in Lindholm Schulz (1996) pp. 20–1.
3. Usher (1995c) p. 45.
4. Gilen et al. (1994), p. 9.
5. Murphy (1995), p. 38.
6. Roy (1996), p. 70.

Chapter One

1. Hobbes, Thomas. Behomoth, or the Long Parliament; IV.

2. 'Oslo' refers to the 'Declaration of Principles on Interim Self-Government and Principles' (Sept. 13, 1993). Other agreements referred to and analysed here include: the 'Gaza Strip and Jericho Agreement' – a.k.a. 'Cairo agreement' (4 May 1994 with Annex IV of this agreement – the 'protocol concerning economic relations' or Paris protocol signed on 9 April 1994); the 'Agreement on Preparatory Transfer of Powers and Responsibilities' – a.k.a. the 'Erez agreement' (29 August 1994); and the 'Interim Agreement on the West Bank and Gaza Strip' – a.k.a. 'Taba agreement', 'Oslo II' 'Cairo II' (approved at Taba on 11 August 1995 and formally signed in Washington on 28 September 1995). At least one reference is made to the protocol concerning Hebron signed on 15 January1997.

3. Many Palestinians insist on the use of Palestinian National Authority (PNA) to emphasize national Palestinian aspirations as represented within the current peace process. I choose PA not to express hostility to these sentiments, but to reflect what I feel are unavoidable realities. I list two technical reasons and one more subjective: (i) technically, the PLO – and not the PA – represents the Palestinian people in the negotiations with the Israelis. The PA does not have any jurisdiction over those Palestinians who remain in the Palestinian diaspora and the PLO remains the 'approved' advocate of their rights and claims. (It should be noted that other groups competing to represent these claims are emerging as forces in Palestinian diaspora politics.) (ii) The texts of the agreements refers to the Palestinian Authority, so this in fact represents the official designation. (iii) The PA as currently constituted and empowered should not be taken as the boundaries of Palestinian national rights, obligations and aspirations; and it should not be confused as being a final national

political entity.

4. See Whitbeck (1996), pp. 19–20. Even seemingly self-evident claims such as one made by Lindholm Schulz (1996) (p. 1) – that 'official Palestinian nationalism is now firmly territorially based' – are problematic. The relationship of the PA/PLO to actual ground and to various Palestinian constituencies seems in some ways as complicated as ever. A firm territorial base in political terms naturally must also mean a firm base with a constituency in that territory. In this sense, apart from a degree of international recognition and support, the PLO were perhaps more firmly territorially based in Lebanon in the late 1970s than they are in Gaza and the West Bank today. It remains to be seen whether 'official Palestinian nationalism' has actually achieved such a situation in Gaza and the West Bank.

5. One of the peace formulas most invoked by commentators is 'security for Israel and economic viability for the Palestinians.' This totally ignores that if the process is to be viable, the security and rights of the Palestinians must be addressed, while there is a strong economic rationale pushing Israel to make peace.

6. *De Standaard* (Belgian newspaper), August 17–18, 1996, p. 6. (Citing Israeli daily *Ydioth Achronoth*.).

7. The Palestinian Central Bureau of Statistics put Gaza unemployment in April/May 1996 at 39.2 %. A figure widely quoted in late 1996 / early 1997 put unemployment at over 60% (statement of Palestinian Monetary Fund governor Fouad Bseiso, late Jan. 1997). Doughty (1996, p. 73) puts unemployment at 70–80% and underemployment at 90% but gives no source for this. Olmsted, p. 12, notes that 'the lower figures should be considered very conservative measures of unemployment given that they do not take into frequent closures' or widespread underemployment. See Chapter 4 below for analysis.

8. The relationship between security and economic protectionism is addressed in Chapter 4 below.

9. Interview with human rights worker Gaza City, September 1995.

10. Oslo II: Art. XVII; 2a.

11. Oslo II: Annex III; Art. I; 1c[2].

12. Oslo II: Annex I; Art. II; 3d.

13. Oslo II: Annex III; Appn. I; Art. 24, 6 and Art. 40, 3a-c.

14. Oslo II: Annex III; Appn. I; Art. 40, 9b.

15. This issue is dealt with in greater detail in Chapter 4.

16. Rabbani (1996), p. 4. For a couple of egregious examples of arbitrary violence see 'Prosecute undercover soldiers responsible for death in Hizmeh' B'tselem press release of 5 March 1997; and Amayreh, Khalid. 'Sexual humiliation of Arab women in the name of security' *Palestine Times* issue no. 67, Jan. 1997 (as well as B'tselem's press release on the same events). Events as of late March 1997 concerning the Israeli settlement plans for Har Homa (Jebel Abu-Ghnaym) dramatically highlight the shortcomings of the agreements from the perspective of ensuring good faith and the security of Palestinian interests. While the Israeli government confiscates land for heavily subsidized Jewish only housing and development, Palestinians cannot get permission to build on lands that they already own. B'tselem and LAWE are reliable sources for those wishing to investigate the land confiscation issue further.

17. See reports from LAWE, Gaza Center for Rights and Law, Amnesty International, B'tselem, and the U.S. Government.

18. See, for example, *Jerusalem Post* 4 February 1997, p. 2.

19. In an interview with the author, a human rights field worker in Gaza argued that Palestinian police had received their 'human rights training' in Israeli prisons or in the factional wars of Lebanon. Arafat's new security cadres thus do not have any conception of what a human right might be. It is also worthy of note that many of the first troops to return to the occupied territories had received their training in Southern Egypt – hardly an auspicious place for human rights training.

20. The present situation, by introducing the liberator as an apparent mechanism for imposing social restriction, perhaps undermines ideological psychological strategies for coping with hardship and uncertainty (see Chapter 6).

21. Abu-Amr (1995), p. 41.

22. Press release of Makassed Islamic Charitable Society, received via *Middle East Realities*, 27 February, 1997.

23. In a neopatrimonial regime, relationships of dependency are cultivated in order to offset the potential for instability created by the failure to alleviate pressures associated with economic development and accompanying structural changes in society. Neopatrimonialism personalizes political and economic relationships as opposed to institutionalizing them, thus facilitating cronyism and other forms of corruption. For an excellent overview, see Brynen (1995b).

24. In his keynote lecture at the 'Conference on Citizenship and the State in the Middle East' held in Oslo, Norway 22-24 November 1996, Ibrahim Abu Lughod noted that the transition to independence of most states in the Middle East went through this same process of limited autonomy before being achieving sovereignty. The potential for drawing parallels in terms of the way the interim period seems to be conditioning elite strategies of consolidation and control in those cases and the current Palestinian case are apparent.

25. Eickelman (1985), p. 135.

26. Ibid., p. 136.

27. Indeed, there is something mind-numbingly Orwelian about the 'peace-process,' as if by changing the vocabulary we might change reality, or at least induce a stabilizing paralysis. The 'iron-fist' has become 'self-rule,' and one of the most significant differences is the paralysis induced by the latter on the Palestinian public in the OT.

28. Quoted in Schwedler (1995), p. 5.

29. Quoted in Ibid., p. 4.

30. Ibid., p. 5.

31. Peter Mansfield quoted in Schwedler (1995), p. 9.

32. It should be noted that the concept of neopatriarchy is not an un-controversial addition to the debate over 'orientalist' approaches to studying Middle Eastern societies. The concept as used here is not intended to refer to any inherent cultural tendency or notion of mind in Arab societies. Rather, it is seen as important to understanding how elites secure their position in a relatively unproductive economy dominated by the daily struggle to meet basic needs. Indeed, the problem is that the factionalism that is prone to neopatrimonial tactics of manipulation is *rational* given the social

breakdown and lack of economic alternatives in Gaza today.

33. Sharabi (1988a), p. 4.
34. Ibid. p. 35.
35. Ibid. p. 31. These issues are dealt with in Chapter 6.
36. Ibid. pp. 31-2.
37. Sharabi (1988b), p. 153.
38. Ibid., p. 152.
39. Sharabi (1988a) p. 7.
40. Ibid.
41. Externalized is emphasized because the direct confrontation between Israeli force and Palestinian society was able to encourage such organization even if the context of repression and external co-optation broke it down. With ultimate power distanced by the peace process, such efforts become strangely delegitimized.
42. Sharabi (1988a), p. 19.
43. Apter (1987), p. 298.
44. Ibid. p.308.
45. Quoted in Schwedler, p. 22.
46. Ibid., pp. 22–3.
47. Sharabi (1988a), pp. 13–14.
48. Simmel (1964), pp. 98, 19.
49. Ajami (1992), pp. 146–7.
50. Usher (1994a), p. 13.
51. Tamari, (1995), p. 10.
52. Roy (1995b).

Chapter Two

1. i.e. alternatives to the PLO factional base of the previous era.
2. Muslih, pp. 65, 66 (emphasis added).
3. From an elitist perspective, social stability is grounded largely in elite consensus.
4. Hilal (1993), p. 55.
5. Above quotes are drawn from Ehteshami and Murphy (1996), p. 3.
6. Cited in Brynen (1995), p. 24.
7. Ibid., p. 25.
8. Moghadam (1993), p. 113.
9. Ehteshami and Murphy (1996), p. 1.
10. Khalaf (1991), p. 2.
11. The non-productive character of social competition distinguishes factional bickering from the positive sides of social competition which have been outlined by, for example, Simmel.
12. Sharabi (1988), pp. 28–9 (emphasis added). Virginia Woolf asserted that 'economic dependence has always locked women into the reproduction of patriarchal values.' See Morag Shiach's introduction to Virginia Woolf's *A Room of One's Own and Three Guineas.* (Oxford: Oxford University Press [Oxford Paperbacks], 1982, p.

xxi). Very much the same might be said for the situations which lock Palestinians into the reproduction of factionalism and enforce Arafat's current position as the patriarchal reference in Gaza society today. The analogy could even extend to the lack of a forum in which grievances could be addressed and the lack of power to press grievances.

13. Hilal (1993), p. 54.

14. Hilal (1995), p. 9. The dynamic by which Fatah manipulated this situation is described by Hilal on p.14. of the same article.

15. Elmusa and Butler (1995), p. 83.

16. Usher (1995c), p. 46.

17. Ibid., p. 45–46.

18. Ibid., p. 46.

19. Roy (1996), p. 68.

20. Nakleh, K. (1977), p. 52.

21. Sharabi (1988a), p. 31.

22. Eickelman (1988), p. 155. Heiberg, discussing the house as an indicator of boundaries and units in the interaction between private and public sphere, notes that 'members of each *hamuleh* lived in a group of adjoining houses grouped around one or more interconnected courtyards. To a certain extent the spatial relationship between the houses was an indicator of the kinship relation between households' p. 82. Heiberg goes on to point out, however, that marginalization of agriculture, the massive shift toward wage labour, and new architectural styles have led to greater prevalence of nucleated family organization.

23. Nakleh, K. (1977), p. 53.

24. Eickelman (1988), p. 156. Bourdieu 'argues that anthropologists easily forget that genealogies are the product of multiple strategies and thus treat the meaning of kinship relations as a resolved question. Instead, anthropologists should seek to specify the types of situations in which the use of genealogies and relationships defined by them are particularly dominant ... individuals who have something to gain by imposing their interpretation of genealogies upon the social order will strive to do so.' Ibid., p. 178.

25. Cossali and Robson (1986), pp. 27, 46.

26. Ibid., p. 48. These issues are discussed in detail in Chapter 6 below.

27. In an interview on Israeli television, Arafat said that the Palestinian people are his first wife. He said of Suha: 'It is very difficult. I know she is suffering. Still, she is my second wife. My first wife is my people.' Posted on *MSA News* (August 12, 1996): Original sender: Al-Quds interfax (alquds@palestine-net.com).

28. Nakleh, K. (1977), p. 54.

29. Lindholm Schulz (1996), p. 6.

30. Robinson (1992), see esp. pp. 45–55. Discussions with a wide variety of informants in Gaza loosely support the notion of the *hamula* as an organizing structure of factionalism in Gaza under the PA. One foreign aid worker in Gaza went so far as to attribute to some family based groupings 'mafia-like features' with notions of territoriality both on the ground and within PA institutions. NGOs working in Gaza have been known to hire locals on the basis of their relevant 'family' connections.

31. Robinson (1992), *passim*. See pp. 11–15 for his typology of 'modern and

traditional' leaders.

32. Tamari observes that: 'the dismal performance of the PA relates to the unwarranted expectations regarding systems and institutional patterns of governance that were inherited from the intifada 'in embryonic forms,' as the prevailing expression had it. It also related to the absence of a strong civil society which can monitor, steer and temper the repressiveness of (PA) institutions' Tamari (1995), p 12.

33. Usher (1996), pp. 28–30.

34. This fact tends to reinforce the notion that Arafat is organizing his power base along lines similar to those in Lebanon. The original agreement called for 9,000 PA internal security personnel, of which up to 7,000 were to come from the diaspora. Such a ratio cannot have been maintained as the number of Palestinian police has climbed above 30,000 while Zureik notes that only 30,000 Palestinians have returned to the OT since the signing of the agreements (Zureik, p. 54).

35. Bergman, Ronen and David Ratner. 'Israel has transferred 500 million shekels to secret Arafat bank account since 1994' *Ha'aretz* February 2, 1997. See also Bainerman, Joel. 'Corruption: A Thorn in the Palestinians' Side' IMRA Review, 20 Jan. 1997; and Byrne (1996a).

36. See for example Kimmerling and Migdal (1994), p. 221. Obviously, however, the relationship between the Palestinian peasant and the Palestinian notable was an exploitative one. See esp. Khalaf (1991) pp. 234–5.

37. The *musha'a* is discussed by Zureik, p. 107.

38. Khalaf (1991) p. 235.

39. Although by the mid-and-late 1940s, such a movement was beginning to take shape – in the form of the Arab Nationalist Bloc, the Arab Front – and demonstrate a willingness to mobilize along side labour – for example the Federation of Arab Trade Unions – to express national and class demands in the context of an Arab League of National Liberation.

40. Khalaf (1991), pp. 148–9.

41. Khalaf (1991) is citing communications from Gaza DC to CO dated 16 Feb. 1948 and 1 Mar. 1948. Significantly, a major tactic used by the Islamists to attempt to undermine the authority of the PA is to spread rumor and gossip concerning the various figures of the PA and their families. Examples of the continuation of extreme localism can also be found in Gaza politics. For example: after the arrival of PA authority in the Gaza Strip, the entire South Gaza village of Dahaniya was collectively accused of collaboration and most of its families had to be evacuated. During Palestinian elections, at least one candidate loaded up the entire *hamula* village structure into busses and delivered them to the polling stations.

42. 'If a refugee in Gaza is asked where he comes from, he will answer with the name of his original village whether or not that village still stands.' Kimmerling and Migdal (1994), p. 202. This conscious effort to reconstruct along old social lines is reflected also in marriage patterns and barriers as well as the fact that the names of new diaspora settlements and organizations were often named after places in Palestine. Zureik (pp. 54, 60) makes similar points.

43. The overall response should be understood in its context. It reflects the tendency of a peasant/lumpen-proletariat society to view personal security and the ability to

meet basic needs in terms of the mediation of traditional elites. Palestinian society before 1948 had not developed in relation to strong state institutions. Social order was instead predicated on local, familial and neighborly bases of social control and assistance. Thus it not surprising that people sought to recreate these modes of social stability in the uncertain situations of diaspora and refugee camp existence. The conservatism embedded in this response, and uncertainty about the future, certainly discouraged integration.

44. Before 1948, 'the Gaza province included the districts of Gaza and Beer Sheba. In 1947, Gaza province covered 13,688,501 dunums and had a population of 303,500. After 1948, all but 2.5% of the province was lost. The Gaza Strip was isolated and 80% of its population lost their livelihoods.' Abu-Amr (1988), p. 101.

45. Summarizes Chapter 3 in Roy (1995a), see esp. p. 79.

46. Cossali and Robson (1986), p. 62.

47. Kimmerling and Migdal p. 234.

48. The above three paragraphs paraphrase information and arguments adapted from Roy (1995a), chapters 2 & 3.

49. Hilal (1993), pp. 44–60.

50. Kimmerling and Migdal (1994), p. 217.

51. Hilal (1995), p. 1.

52. The battle of Karamah being perhaps the most dramatic manifestation of this.

53. Kimmerling and Migdal (1994), p. 227.

54. Cossali and Robson (1986), p. 102.

55. Kimmerling and Migdal (1994), p. 216.

56. Gowers and Walker (1990), p. 130. A few months earlier, the PLO had declared a shift in tactics calling for recognition of UN resolutions 242 and 336 as part of a transitional solution, and expressing a desire and willingness to set up a Palestinian state on any parcel of liberated Palestinian territory. This theme is discussed in the next chapter under the heading of inside/outside tensions in the Palestinian national movement.

57. Hilal (1995), p. 2.

58. Cossali and Robson (1986), p. 118.

59. Ibid., p. 111.

60. Ibid., p. 112.

61. Kimmerling and Migdal (1994), p. 227.

62. Arafat has also tried to play traditional leader and revolutionary at the same time. He thus has many counterparts in other ethno-specific nationalist revolutions.

63. For a general overview, see Zureik, pp. 74, 98, 124–5.

64. Hilal (1995), pp. 10–11.

65. Ibid., p. 12.

66. Ibid., pp. 10, 12.

67. Gowers and Walker (1990), p. 189.

68. Ibid., p. 203.

69. Brynen (1995b), p. 35.

70. Gowers and Walker (1990), p. 137.

71. Cited in Kimmerling and Migdal (1994), p. 232.

72. Cited in Ibid., p. 233.
73. Brynen (1995), p. 28.
74. Ibid., p. 53.
75. Gowers and Walker (1990), p. 181.
76. Ibid., 154.
77. Ibid., pp. 181, 223, 228.
78. Ibid., (1990), p. 229. In a footnote (#16) Brynen (1995b), citing Schiff and Ya'ari, (1995) notes that 'Complaints arose when Arafat appointed Colonel Ghazi 'Atallah and Colonel Hajj Isma'il to command Palestinian forces in Lebanon. Both had deserted their units during the Israeli invasion (the latter stopping only to commandeer an ambulance in which to carry his unit's funds), but both were loyal to the PLO leader.'.
79. The violence in Lebanon included violent clashes between the Palestinian military factions themselves.
80. For and overview of these services, see Rubenberg (1983) and Cobban (1984). For discussions of how these services were politicized and broken away from their original constituencies, see Hilal (both 1993 and 1995), and Sayigh, esp. p. 31 for more recent detachment of the PLO from the refugee community in Lebanon.
81. Hilal (1993), pp. 49–51.
82. Hilal (1995), pp. 7,12.
83. For an overview of the roles of and restrictions placed upon the Chambers of Commerce, professional associations and other public institutions, see Roy (1995a), p. 268–70.
84. Cossali and Robson (1986), p. 150–8.
85. Hilal (1995), p. 7.
86. Cossali and Robson (1986), p. 55.
87. Tamari (1990), p. 27.
88. Hammami (1995), p. 54.
89. Ibid. p. 54.
90. Brynen (1995b), p. 28.
91. Roy (1995a), p. 269.
92. Locke and Stewart, pp. 13, 20.
93. Hilal (1993), p. 54.
94. Cossali and Robson (1986), p. 105.
95. Ibid., p. 155.
96. Ibid., p. 149.
97. See Ibid., p. 107.
98. Tamari (1990), p. 36.
99. Ibid., p. 37. Tamari offers an excellent description of the crucial part the bourgeoisie played in the early effectiveness of the intifada and the forces which caused this class to identify with the conditions of daily life for most Palestinians under occupation. However, caught between Israeli tactics aimed at the enforcement of occupation policies and the increasingly unprincipled, unorganized and unsustainable demands on the merchants by the Unified National Command of the Uprising (UNCU) – which were in later stages enforced by the often overzealous 'strike forces,'

the merchants gradually began to retreat from their role.

100. See Tamari (1995).

101. Cited in Lindholm Schulz (1996) p. 11.

102. Ibid. p. 11.

103. Connel (1995), p. 7.

104. Ibid., p. 6.

105. Hilal (1993), p. 50.

106. Cossali and Robson (1986), p. 101.

107. Lindholm Schulz (1996), p. 7.

108. Hammami (1995), p. 55.

109. Ibid.

110. Moughrabi (1997), p. 8.

111. Ibid., p. 55.

112. Cossali and Robson (1986), p. 72.

113. Fischer et al. (1994), p. 102. The authors go on to describe the composition of aid into the OT as 'unusual;' '42% went into the health sector, 18% into education, and the rest of about $200 million annually went into 'other developmental objectives,' Ibid., p. 152. Not surprisingly, Fischer et al. conclude that the aid structure which arose under occupation might not be appropriate for self rule; Ibid., p. 153.

114. Roy (1994), p. 94.

115. Hammami (1995), p. 59.

116. See for example Barghouti, M. 'Palestinian NGOs and their role in building a civil society' (Union of Palestinian Medical Relief Committees, n.d.) or Dr. Iyad al-Sarraj in *PNGO Network Newsletter* vol. 1, no. 1; 1994.

117. Hammami (1995), pp. 59, 60.

118. Abed, (interview 1994), p. 46.

119. Ibid., p. 45.

120. See for example Palestinian Center for Human Rights. *Critique of the Second Palestinian Draft Law Concerning Charitable Societies, Social Bodies and Private Institutions of 1995*, Series Study 3, Gaza: 1995. At present, the major donors to the PA, particularly the EU, seem to have removed most performance criteria from the conditionality placed on aid, indicating perhaps a political desire to see the peace process continued for its own sake.

121. See Roy (1995a), pp. 281–3.

122. Interview of Jan. 6, 1970 cited by Gresh (1985), p. 50.

123. The mechanism of selective empowerment has been very interestingly elaborated by Judith Palmer Harik in 'Principles and Mechanisms of Political Inclusion and Exclusion in Postwar Lebanon; Parliamentary Elections in the Governate of Mount Lebanon, 1996.' (unpublished paper presented at the 'Conference on Citizenship and the State in the Middle East' November 22–24, 1996).

124. Hilal (1993), p. 56.

125. Said, Edward. 'The politics of memory' *Al-Ahram Weekly*, 26 September–2 October 1996, p. 13.

126. See Kuttab, Daoud in *The Jerusalem Post*, Jan. 5, p. 7. See also: Brown, Derrick. 'Arafat Lambasted for Poll Meddling' *The Guardian Weekly*, Jan. 7, p. 3. Before the

national elections in January 1996, local elections were held to determine candidates for the official Fatah slate. When many of Arafat's preferred choices were not elected, he voided the results and put his own favourites on the list. Usually, the replacements were diaspora figures or local notables. Arafat's stated reasons were to make sure that Fatah in elections still represented the broad national movement. However, many of these candidates were seen by locals as having not participated in the resistance (some I spoke with in Gaza even referred to them as collaborators) and were usually people with money or clan connections that Arafat might find useful.

127. Brynen (1995b) discusses this on p. 30.

128. Roy (1993), p. 25.

Chapter Three

1. Connel (1995), p. 7.

2. Naim (1995), p. 18.

3. For an excellent analytical review of the literature on the refugee issue in the context of current negotiations, see Zureik. If the eventual Palestinian entity is declared to fulfill the 'right to self-determination' and thus constitute a homeland to which refugees might return, does this preclude the 'right of return' of refugees to land and property owned before 1948 within what became the state of Israel?.

4. This has meant that, for example, Palestinians in need of health care have often been unable to travel to receive it. One issue which received considerable attention through an international campaign in late 1996–early 1997 was Israel's denial of travel permits to Gazan students and academics who study and work in the West Bank. Other significant consequences are discussed in later chapters.

5. Ashrawi (1995), p. 261.

6. Abu-Amr (1994), p. 80.

7. Ibid., p. 80. This is reinforced by Hilal: 'The problem of who exercises authority and how has become particularly acutHHHHe with the refusal of the majority of the Palestinian political groups to take part in the PNA.' The PLO is charged with the double function of building viable state structures in the OT while at the same time representing the 'unity, interests and aspirations of the Palestinians, as a people, in all their communities and gatherings.' Hilal (1995), p. 15.

8. Cited in Bergman and Ratner (1994). Interestingly, Khader is a Fatah representative and himself a returnee. His stated priorities as a council member include: 'democracy and freedom, public control over the Executive Authority (stop mismanagement), affirming the principle of separation of powers, and maintaining the PLO as a political resource for unity;' all of these issues are traditionally associated with the 'inside' agenda. Cited in JMCC 1996, p. 71.

9. Al-Jarbarwi (1996), p. 31. This is clearly seen in the stated agenda of many PLC members as outlined by the various representatives – see JMCC (1996).

10. Interview in Gaza City, September 1995.

11. Lindholm Schulz (1996), p. 42.

12. Personal interview, 26 November 1997

13. Cited in ibid., p. 40. Interview with Izzat Abdel Hadi (Oct. 4, 1994).

14. JMCC (1997), poll no. 18, Q. 16, December 1996.

15. Ibid., Q. 17.

16. Hilal (1995), p. 2. Al-Jarbarwi suggests that this contradiction arises in part because the Palestinian left 'never got beyond the contradiction between their political Marxism (espousal of Marxist jargon) and their social and economic contexts – the fact that they were Arab, traditional and frequently from the upper and middle classes ... [as well as the their] tendency to remain aloof from everyday life, preferring instead to dwell within the abstract realm of ideas.'

17. Ashrawi (1985) (1995), p. 282.

18. Naim (1995), p. 18.

19. Roy (1994), p. 88.

20. Al-Jarbarwi (1996), p. 35.

21. Cited in Lindholm Schulz (1996), p. 24; (date of interview 28 Aug. 1994.

22. Moughrabi (1997), p. 8.

23. Shikaki (1996a), p. 17. Perhaps consciousness of the historic role played by the diaspora in legitimizing the PLO in ways which gave it the authority to come to the bargaining table has encouraged Arafat to absorb the new Legislative Council (PLC) created by recent elections into the larger Palestinian National Council (PNC). It offers a way of ensuring the inclusion of diaspora interests in an agreement which largely ignores them. Disturbingly, it might also represent an opportunity for Arafat to play the two groups off of each other.

24. See Zureik, esp. pp. 45, 61.

25. Shikaki (1996a), p. 8.

26. Jadallah, Muhammad cited in an interview with Lindholm Schulz (1996), p. 20; (italics added).

27. Hilal (1995), p. 1.

28. Cited in Harelde. (this quote has been edited from the original for grammatical reasons).

29. Tamari (1995), p. 11.

30. Interview with UNSCO official who wished to remain anonymous on this point (September 1995).

31. During the time of the 1996 Palestinian elections in the OT, I spoke with an EU diplomat who was part of the observer team. He said that he had been assured by leading figures in the Labor party that Israel would redeploy forces and settlers from Gaza following a supposed Labor victory in May of 1996. Since the 'surprise' Likud victory, however, there seems to be more talk from Israeli authorities of reinforcing the settlements in Gaza than of redeployment.

32. JMCC 1997, poll no. 18, Q. 14; December 1996.

33. See Usher (1994a), p. 13; Abed (1994), p. 43; Kuttab (1996), p. 7.

34. Abed (1994), p. 49.

35. Ibid., p. 51.

36. Butler and Elmusa (1995), p. 80.

37. Usher (1995c), pp. 47–8.

38. Schnell, Izhak. *Perceptions of Israeli Arabs: Territoriality and Identity*. Aldersot:

Avebury, 1994. Cited in Hareide. Political identities must ultimately respond in some ways to the connection between territory and the governing institutions against which or within which political identity is expressed.

39. Lustick (1993), p. 3.

40. Another way of saying this is that the state represents the institutionalization and territorialization of social and political processes. Political geography tends to focus on three different understandings of human territoriality: territoriality as power, territoriality as mobilization, and territoriality as perception. A useful overview of the literature concerning these themes as they relate to Palestinians and Palestine has been presented by Hareide.

41. Fatah has always emphasized blood unity as opposed to building structural bases of unity. As Abu Adnan of the PDFLP told Alain Gresh, 'We first met Arafat in 1964. At that time he had no mass support, but he asked us to co-ordinate the action of Fatah and the Arab National Movement (ANM). We agreed, on the condition that we could agree on a common political platform. Yassir Arafat then said it was not worth the bother, that the problem was one of joint armed action, 'blood unity', as he put it. The negotiations failed.' The rest of the quote is also worth a look. See Gresh (1985), p. 24.

42. Gowers and Walker (1990), p. 112.

43. Gresh (1985) provides a thorough overview.

44. Kimmerling and Migdal (1994), p. 245. Incidentally, it was not until 1987 that the communists gained a seat on the PNC. Since the DoP, the Communists have changed their name to the Palestinian People's Party (PPP).

45. See Roy (1995a), p. 106–7. Shawa resigned in 1972, only to accept Israel's offer again in 1975, a tenure which was terminated as Israel took direct military control of the municipal structures in August 1982. Ibid. p. 109.

46. This resulting from the oil price rises in the wake of the formation of OPEC and the oil crisis in 1973.

47. Gowers and Walker (1990), p. 115. This also exemplifies the tendency of Arafat to try to co-opt ideas that have a social appeal in the OT after having first undermined any alternative leadership that might have introduced the idea to begin with. This strategy has led to quite a piling on of contradictions in the PLO's stated strategy.

48. Hilal (1993), p. 55. Suggesting an elitist focus, Elmusa (1994) adds that 'There is not a single present or former (refugee) camp resident in the Palestinian authority's cabinet, whose composition has been explained in terms of a carefully calibrated balance among regions, factions, families and so on.' Elmusa (1995), p. 98.

49. See Gowers and Walker (1990), pp. 273, 280.

50. Hilal (1995), pp. 7–8.

51. Tamari (1990), p. 31.

52. Gowers and Walker (1990), pp. 280–2.

53. Abu-Amr (1994a), p. 72.

54. Hilal (1995), p. 8.

55. This refers to the United Nations resolution passed on 11 December 1948 which, *inter alia*, '[r]esolves that refugees wishing to return to their homes should be allowed to do so at the earliest practicable date' and specifies compensation for property

damaged or to which the owner did not wish to return.

56. Zureik, p. 89.

57. Hilal (1995), *passim.*

58. Roy (1995a), p. 7.

59. Hilal (1993), pp. 56–7.

60. Andoni (1991), p. 57.

61. Ibid., p. 62.

62. Gowers and Walker (1990), pp. 280–2.

63. Andoni (1991), p. 62.

64. Ibid., p. 57.

65. Kuttab (1992), p. 103. Previous two sentences also based on observations from Kuttab.

66. Kuttab (1993), pp. 80–90.

67. Ibid., p. 86.

68. Ibid. p. 86.

69. Ashrawi (1985), p. 186.

70. Hilal (1995), p. 8.

71. According to one observer, PLO institutions fell victim to their own bulk: 'An inertia ridden system is seen as having lost its dynamism. Criticism is leveled against the omniscient attitude of the organization's leadership, the personality cult, and the modes of conduct and styles of work these aspects encouraged. Organizations are criticized for showing little or no interest in democratic practice, for turning a blind eye to public corruption, and for practicing favoritism, patronage, demagoguery, elitism and so on. Much has been said of the need to rid the intifada of unpopular and gangster like practices that have attached themselves to it through factionalism and unprincipled conduct. Yet little is done by the political organizations to stop such practices.' Hilal (1993), p. 59.

72. See Kuttab (1996), p. 7.

73. Immanuel, Jon. 'Independent candidates lend carnival air to elections' *The Jerusalem Post* (Jan. 1996).

74. Ashrawi (1985), p. 260.

75. See Kimmerling and Migdal (1994), pp. 252–3.

76. Usher (1995a), p. 22.

77. Ibid. p. 22.

78. Roy (1995a), p. 285n.

79. Usher (1995a). p. 22.

80. Rabbani (1995), Interview with Chomsky.

81. Usher (1995c), p. 43.

82. The word refugee appears twice in the *Interim Agreement on the West Bank and Gaza Strip,* both times in a list of issues to be dealt with in final-status negotiations (Art XVII, 1a; and Art. XXXI, 5). For examples of the current PLO/PA restraint in confronting the issue in negotiations, see Zureik, pp. 73, 87, and 94. The RWG was established to gather data on the refugees to inform negotiations.

83. Zureik, p. 87.

84. This number is Zureik's own estimate (p. 116). Zureik's work also provides

estimates and statistics from other sources.

85. See *Interim Agreement* Annex VI, Art. I, 1 where this is explicitly stated as a goal of negotiations.

86. For details see Zureik, pp. 65–87, 115–27.

87. Ibid., p. 125.

88. Graham Usher, 'The fire next time?' *Al-Ahram Weekly* 6–12 February, 1997.

89. Some expression of this was mentioned above based on the author's own observations. See also Zureik, pp. 54, 57, 125.

90. Personal interviews, Gaza; February 1997.

91. Gassner-Jaradat, p. 8.

92. See *Muslim World News* 15 Oct. 1996, 28 Oct. 1996 and 4 Nov. 1996.

93. Also, for the nationalist, it contradicts the notion of national 'self' determination. It should also be noted that the Israeli state is currently manipulating its legal and coercive apparatus to undermine these demographic trends (e.g. denial of residency status to Palestinian inhabitants of Jerusalem who have left the country for a period of time or have married foreign nationals – LAW and B'tselem have produced excellent reports on this. The Israeli Ministry of the interior has countered such claims.

94. See for example Usher 1995c; and Daoud Kuttab 'Palestinian State or Bi-nationalism but no Apartheid' (posted on Daoud Kuttab home page).

95. Cited in Lindholm Schulz (1996), p. 21; interview with PFLP activist Walid Salim.

96. Ibid., p. 22. The brackets are those of Lindholm Schulz (1996).

97. Accordingly, while it is beyond the scope of this work to address the issue in direct detail, one cannot fully understand Palestinian autonomy, or Palestinian responses to it, without understanding Israeli politics.

98. Some people in Gaza argue that if the PLO had returned to govern in Gaza in the early 1980s, it would have been welcomed. Now, however, things have changed. The experience of the intifada and the experience of the less appealing and efficacious elements of Fatah and PLO tendencies has left a gap in the ability to identify with each other. Also 'returnees' spoken to by the author reported that they felt uncomfortable in Gaza.

Chapter Four

1. David Bar-Ilan of the Jerusalem Post has argued that such assertions are falsehoods, noting that central Cairo and even parts of Tel-Aviv are more densely populated than the Gaza Strip. What this fails to account for is that while these cities are economically and socially integrated into much larger environments, the Gaza Strip is an isolated, densely inhabited and economically depressed ecological and social unit. It is in a losing competition with Israel for access to common resources. It does not have equal access to inputs from the regional environment and even under more politically ideal conditions the proper comparison is not between a territory and an inner city but between two regions subject to distinct geographically delineated political regimes. An appropriate comparison would be one between Gaza and Israel or Egypt

and not between Gaza and Tel-Aviv or Cairo. Statistics presented by Roy (1995a: p. 178) bear this argument out: 'Gaza has one of the highest population densities in the world: 5,929 people per square mile Only the populations of Singapore and Hong Kong (6,734 and 14,763 respectively) exceed Gaza's, although not if one considers Arab built up areas alone [and after the interim agreement Israel still reserves 44 per cent of the Gaza Strip as either for Jews only or is militarily in control] ... the population density for the Gaza Strip more than doubled when calculated on the basis of Arab owned land alone.'
The Palestinian Central Bureau of Statistics put the population in the Gaza Strip at 963,026 as of mid-1996. Byrne (1995a) notes that 'with an overall population growth rate of 4.5%+, the economy would need to grow at this amount just to maintain current levels.'

2. The ability of states like Taiwan and Singapore to invoke economic sovereignty to construct and manipulate a niche in the global capitalist system and access world markets in spite of a relatively weak political position has played a crucial role in their success. The ability to plan, set monetary policy and subsidize have played important roles in the development of these economies.

3. Cossali and Robson (1986), p. 157. Sara Roy reports that changes in the tax laws applicable to Palestinians in the OT meant that Palestinians paid much higher taxes than their Israeli counterparts. 'Based on a direct tax per person, the average family in Gaza (consisting of seven persons) owed a relatively higher tax than the average family in Israel (four persons).' Most sources indicate that taxes paid by Palestinians far outweighed funds invested into the administration and development of the Gaza Strip's Arab areas. Hilterman notes that the proceeds of the $10 identity card imposed on all Gazans who sought employment in Israel went to the installation of protective windows on the cars of Gaza's Jewish settlers. Cited in Roy (1995a): p. 297. The Israelis further bureaucratized every feature of life in Gaza imposing various licenses and mandatory documentation to extract funds from Palestinians. See Roy (1995a): pp. 298–302 for a revealing summary of the various fines, taxes and licensing requirements imposed on the Palestinians of Gaza and their impact on the economy.

4. Roy (1996a) p. 176.

5. Ibid. pp. 230–1.

6. Roy (1995a), p. 136.

7. 'In 1985, Yitzak Rabin, then defense minister, put it bluntly: '[T]here will be no development in the occupied territories initiated by the Israeli government, and no permits given for expanding agriculture or industry, which may compete with the state of Israel.' Cited in Roy (1995a), p. 222.

8. By creating relative individual prosperity without reference to the need to develop and integrate Gaza's devastated economic infrastructure, current patterns of aid giving are reinforcing dependent relations, and distancing any socio-economic or developmental agenda from the content of Palestinian autonomous politics. Uncritical aid giving might only serve to make effective Palestinian disempowerment under the guise of autonomy bearable over the short term, while Israel pursues its strategic interests of procuring sovereignty over the land and its resources. The irony is that in order to sustain a process which claims to be leading towards the building of a

Palestinian state, the tactics which are being used to sustain the process undermine the future ability of that state to sustain itself.

9. See 'Paris Protocol' Article III, paragraph 12. Riding between Jerusalem and Gaza on Jan. 21, 1996, I sat next to a Palestinian-American man on his way to visit family in Gaza. He informed me that Gaza was the cheapest place in the world to buy a new Mercedes, and that he was thinking about buying one there and having it shipped to the states.

10. Byrne (1996a).

11. Roy (1996), passim.

12. JMCC poll no. 18, December 1996. More details concerning personal economy in Gaza are offered in the section *Economic Realities of Self Rule: The View From Below; Restructuring from Above* later in this Chapter.

13. See Gaza–Jericho Agreement: Annex II, Article IIB, sub-paragraph 24b. See also Roy (1995a), pp. 268, 325. While the donors are building a new electricity grid for Gaza, the strip still has no autonomous source of energy production.

14. See 'Gaza–Jericho First,' Annex I, Article XI, especially paragraph 4. The Hebron protocol signed on 15, Jan. 1997 promised advancement on the port and some of these other issues, but this essentially means that the joint committees will finally meet, and does not guarantee that progress will be made.

15. Sewage and solid waste disposal continue to be among the most serious environmental/health problems facing the Gaza Strip. The German government has made available $90 million for joint Israeli water and sewage projects; however, PA Director of Environmental Planning Dr Mohammed Ajjour has complained that the Israel has refused to convene the necessary expert and ministerial joint committees which are supposed to plan and implement these projects. For an overview of sewage treatment and the development of the relevant infrastructure under occupation, see Roy (1995a): p. 164. Not only must the PA contend with building a new sewage network from scratch, but they must (as of Dec. 1996) also deal with Jewish settlements which continue to dump untreated sewage into the Palestinian run areas. (source: IMRA review – interview with Mohammed Ajjour, PA environmental planning, 1 Dec. 1996). Dr Ajjour: 'This has been going on all the time. The whole area is spoiled by misplanning and neglect. I can tell you that many of the Israeli settlements are releasing their waste in a way that is dangerous even for the Israelis. This is caused by the lack of control over waste disposal by settlements which are not controlled by the Ministry of the Environment.' Yiftah Kramer, Spokesman for the Ministry of the Environment responds: 'There is a problem with the sewage of some of the settlements. Around 60% is treated and 40% is not.' (cited in Ibid.).

16. Shehadeh (1994), p. 21.

17. Ibid., p. 22. Furthermore, Palestinians have consistently accused the Israelis of 'stealing' water. According to Riyad el-Khoudary, '[The Israelis] are pumping our water from areas along-side the border with the result that about 30% of the water used in Israel comes from Arab sources. In the Gaza Strip, the [1 to 5 thousand] Israeli settlers use between 5 and 20 million cubic meters of water per year, while the rest of the population, one million Palestinians, must make do with 100 million cubic meters.' Cited in *Muslim World News*, 'Palestinians say Israelis stealing water' Nov. 26, 1996. It

should be noted however that ownership of water in aquifers which cross boundaries is complex, in terms of usage and needs, however, it is clear that Israeli policy undermines both the quality and quantity of Palestinian water supplies, and leads to radically unfair distribution along ethnic lines. For an overview of water use and policy preceding autonomy, see Roy, (1995a): pp. 162–75.

18. Byrne (1996a). Informed sources spoken with by the author in early 1997 have put the number of persons employed by the security forces alone at 40,000, with up to 90,000 employed by the PA.

19. Fischer et al. (1994), p. 94.

20. See for example Gaza–Jericho Agreement, Annex II, paragraph 19c.

21. However, a map signed together with the agreements in Cairo fixes the boundaries in which Gaza fleets are allowed to operate at twenty miles from shore and excluding the area off the coast from one and a half miles in the north and south. See Roy (1995a): p. 373(unnumbered page). For a mention of the importance of fishing in Gaza before, see World Bank Report, p. 8. See also Abu-Amr (1988), p. 105.

22. Roy (1995b), p. 74.

23. 'Paris Protocol' Article III, Paragraph 3. Article II of the protocol outlines the formation of 'the Joint Economic Committee' and various sub-committees are called for and referred to throughout the text.

24. See especially 'Paris Protocol' Article III paragraphs 2, 5, and 10 as well as the referred to appendices (lists of relevant goods).

25. For a thorough review, see Palestinian Center for Human Rights, *The Israeli Policy of Closure: Legal, Political and Humanitarian Evaluation,* series study 6 (Gaza: Mansour Press, 1997). This issue is discussed in greater detail below.

26. IMRA review. 'Interview with Dr. Mohammed Ajjour' Dec. 1, 1996. (note: the grammar of the original has been touched up a bit in this quote). Yiftah Kramer of the Israeli Ministry of Environment responds: 'As for impact statements, the PA is supposed to prepare them for every project, not just the airport.' (Ibid.). While the airstrip and control tower of the airport have basically been completed as of early 1997, construction of the terminal has been held up and Israeli authorities have not allowed the airstrip to open for traffic. (See 'Interview: Businessman Mahmoud El-Farra: We are going to make it' *Palestine Business Report,* vol. II, no. 1 (January 1997), p. 17.

27. Roy (1996), p. 61. Olmsted also offers an insightful overview of the impact of travel restrictions on Palestinians wanting to move between Gaza, the West Bank and Jerusalem, and within the West Bank.

28. See for example *Interim Agreement* Annex I, Art.XII.

29. See Gaza–Jericho Agreement, Annex II, Article II B 25.

30. See also paragraph 3a.

31. See Interim Agreement Article IX, this re-establishes a situation grounded in the Gaza–Jericho agreement, see Gaza–Jericho agreement Article VI, paragraph 2a. Israel must approve all visitors from countries not having diplomatic relations with it Annex II, Article II B 27g1.

32. See 'Paris Protocol' Article III, paragraph 9. The way in which these licenses become in effect subject to Israeli standards is clear from a reading of the protocol.

33. For some examples, see 'Paris Protocol' Article VI, paragraph 3, and Article III, paragraph 12.

34. This is usually done by invoking security concerns. A usual tactic is to place on or two recruits to inspect all of the thousands of trucks leaving Gaza. These individuals usually take their time about the inspections, delaying exit from the strip for as much as days. See Kuttab, 'How Can Anti-Israeli Attacks from Gaza be Lessened?' (Summer 1996) *Daoud Kuttab Home Page.*

35. Muslim World News 'World Banks slams Israeli embargo on Palestinian economy' Nov. 12 1996. In another article in the same issue ('EU blames Israelis for hardship in Gaza, West Bank') Irish Foreign Minister Dick Spring is quoted as saying, 'We feel very strongly there are opportunities in the economic sphere which the Israelis have not been very helpful to.'.

36. Elmusa and El-Jaafari (1995), p. 23.

37. See Interim Agreement Article IX, or Gaza–Jericho Agreement, Article VI, paragraphs 2a. and 2b.

38. Ideological and ethno-historical factors, which are discussed at length by Roy and others, must not be discounted when analysing the reasons for Israel's continued hold on the land which seems marginal to Israel's economic interests. Concerning use, the World Bank Report notes that Palestinian water use in the OT was capped at pre-1967 levels while reserves available for Israeli farmers were expanded ... these limits on water use and quality, together with restrictive regulations placed on Palestinian farmers by Israel and limited land area have stifled the possibility for growth in the agricultural sector ... increasing salinity of water resources has all but halted agricultural production in parts of Gaza (World Bank, pp. 7–8).

39. Byrne (1996a), p. 1.

40. 'Immediately after the June 1967 war, Israel banned Gazans from exporting to all Western markets in order to prevent competition with Israeli agricultural producers and then to limit Gaza's access to foreign economic and political circles.' Roy (1995a), p. 232. See also esp. Ibid. pp. 242–246. More than just symbolic of this isolation is the 53 miles of security fences erected around Gaza in 1971 under the direction of Ariel Sharon. See Roy (1995a), p. 105.

41. Most notably Locke and Stewart (1985).

42. Roy (1995a), p. 4.

43. Al-Jarbarwi (1994), p. 141.

44. Usher, (1994), p. 11.

45. Peled (1995), *passim.*

46. Roy (1993), p. 26.

47. Rabbani (1995), p. 96.

48. Roy (1995a), p. 120.

49. Kimmerling and Migdal (1994), p. 198.

50. Abu-Amr (1988), p. 101.

51. Roy (1995a), p. 78.

52. Elmusa and El-Jaafari (1995), p. 16.

53. This was particularly the case for many Bedouin, who while sometime classified as residents of the strip, were cut off from their traditional grazing areas in the Negev.

54. Roy (1995a), p. 80.

55. Abu-Amr (1988), p. 113. For a concise overview of the role of smuggling and the reliance on service and administrative bureaucratic sectors for employment in the Gaza economy under Egyptian administration, see Roy (1995a), esp. pp. 85,90–91. See also Kimmerling and Migdal (1994), pp. 200–1.

56. Abu-Amr (1988), p. 115.

57. See for example Kimmerling and Migdal (1994), pp. 200–1.

58. Abu-Amr (1988), p. 103.

59. Abu-Amr (1988), p. 103.

60. See Marx for the role of UNRWA in the local economy. Zureik offers a useful critique of Marx's analysis; Zureik *inter alia,* p. 74. Kimmerling and Migdal (1994), summarize, (citing the Clapp commission report; Issa Naman Fakhoury; and the *Report of the United Nations Conciliation Commission for Palestine*): 'A key factor in reinforcing the isolation of the refugees was UNRWA. Established by the UN in late 1949 as a response to the refugee crisis, the agency rapidly became a kind of overpowering paternal force. Most camp dwellers depended on it for their sustenance ... .', p. 192.

61. Roy (1995a), p. 87.

62. Hilal (1995), p. 7. Even as incomes increased, for many, occupation meant taking jobs that were of lower prestige. Inflation also skyrocketed by the middle 1970s.

63. Taylor (1995), p. 99.

64. World Bank Report, p. 8.

65. Roy (1995a), p. 172. For a comprehensive review of Israeli water policy in the Gaza Strip and its impact on the local economy and health, see Ibid., pp. 162–175.

66. Roy (1995a), pp. 136–7.

67. Øvensen (1993); Brynen (1995a); World Bank Report; Abu-Amr (1988).

68. Øvensen (1993), p. 12.

69. Roy (1995a), p. 138.

70. Davidi (1993), p. 25.

71. See Fischer et al. (1994), pp. 60–2.

72. World Bank Report, p. 5.

73. Elmusa and El-Jaafari (1995), p. 18.

74. World Bank Report, p. 7.

75. Roy (1995a), p 126.

76. World Bank Report, p. 5.

77. Ibid. p. 6.

78. Fischer et al. (1994), p. 74.

79. Øvensen (1993), p. 11.

80. Shadid and Seltzer (1988), p. 16.

81. Water use was capped at pre-1967 levels in spite of the growth of the population. See World Bank Report, pp. 7–8.

82. See Roy (1995a), pp. 162–175. This section gives an excellent overview of water issues in the Strip. The degradation of the drinking water was a common complaint of residents of Gaza spoken to by the author. Ironically, refugee camp residents who live bordering settlements often have purer supplies of water because they get the run-off from the settlement (anecdote relayed by a resident of one of the middle

camps).

83. See Ashrawi (1985) on this episode.

84. Peretz (1991), p. 18.

85. Zureik, p. 54.

86. Elmusa and El-Jaafari (1995), p. 19.

87. See Roy (1995a), pp. 150–3 for an excellent overview of these issues. There is an irony: while the external funding kept Palestinians alive and in place, it deflected the urgency of the increasing alienation of Palestinians from ecological resources, any means of production and in general locally sustainable means of economic survival and thus facilitated the process of Israel's effective consolidation over the economy of the Gaza Strip.

88. Roy (1995a), p. 294.

89. Cossali and Robson (1986), p. 157.

90. Roy (1995a), p. 294.

91. Tamari (1990), *passim*.

92. Fischer et al. (1994), pp. 60–1.

93. Kimmerling and Migdal (1994), p. 268.

94. Elmusa and El-Jaafari (1995), p. 75.

95. Roy (1993), p. 21.

96. See Fischer et al. (1994), chapter 6.

97. BRT 'Journaal' (Belgian television news), March 30, 1996.

98. Reported in Mennonite Central Committee press release of Oct. 11 1996.

99. Roy, Sara. 'Speech given at Brown University's Watson Institute for International Studies' 30 Jan. 1997. Summary available via *Middle East Realities* web-site.

100. Hass (1995), p. 28.

101. *Palestinian Central Bureau of Statistics* (PCBS), 'Palestinian Territories Statistical Brief 1996', Gaza City, 1996. The labour force is measured as every individual above 15 years of age who is capable of and actively seeking work. According to the PCBS, Gaza's population as of mid-1996 includes 341,154 persons between ages 20 and 64. The same census recorded 102,500 people between the ages of 15 and 19, and 586,693 persons under the age of 15. Salah Abd al-Shafi offered the number of 130,000 as the size of the labour force in late 1993 [Usher (1994): p. 12]; Roy (1995a: p. 212) offers a figure of 120,000 for 1993.

102. See Olmsted, p. 12.

103. See USAID Congressional Presentation for Fiscal Year 1997 (available via http://www.usaid.gov).

104. Hass (1995), p. 26.

105. Fischer et al. (1994), p. 74.

106. Hass (1995), p. 27.

107. Fischer et al. (1994), p. 76.

108. Rabbani (1995) pp. 93–8. Also personal interview with Palestinian human rights worker in Gaza, September 1995. Roy (1995a) reports that between 1986 and 1990, 'the amount of area under Israeli control [in Gaza] increased to approximately 58 per cent, largely due to confiscation'(p. 175). A high level EU official told the author in January 1996 that sources within the upper echelons of the Peres administration had

assured him that withdrawal from areas of Gaza still under direct military occupation would be carried out following Israeli elections in May of 1996. This was of course assuming a Labor victory. Netanyahu's policies show a completely different approach.

109. Byrne (1996), np.

110. Elmusa and El-Jafaari (1995), p. 24. (Sections on exports and the diversification of trade partners follow in this article).

111. Byrne (1996), np.

112. Bergman and Ratner (1997). See also *Jerusalem Report* 22 February 1996.

113. Byrne (1996), np.

114. Cited in Bergman and Ratner (1997).

115. Connel (1995), p. 6.

116. Several interviewees with UNRWA connections expressed fear and dismay at the prospect of UNRWA functions being turned over to the PA. Tamari (1996) notes that these fears have led the Europeans and the Japanese to rethink their push to have UNRWA responsibilities transferred to the PLO and bail UNRWA out of its budget crisis (as of 1996).

117. Øvensen (1993), pp. 13–14.

118. Cited in Byrne (1996), n.p.

119. The above in this paragraph draws entirely on Byrne (1996a).

120. Murphy (1995), p. 36.

121. Shehadeh (1994), p. 30. Ashrawi (1985) makes similar points.

122. Murphy (1995), p. 36.

123. Shehadeh (1994), p. 31.

124. Roy (1995a), p. 22. Article IX, paragraph 9 of the Gaza–Jericho Agreement states that: 'Laws and military orders in effect in the Gaza Strip and Jericho area prior to the signing of the agreement shall remain in force unless abrogated or amended in accordance with this agreement.'.

125. Shehadeh (1994), p. 31. A glance at the agreement shows that the development of tourism basically means that the PA can issue licensees for tour companies, hardly the basis of a thriving sector regulated by autonomous institutions.

126. Abed (1994), p. 42.

127. In fact, Sadan noted that 'severance of the [Israeli and Palestinian] economies means immediate poverty for [the Palestinians], deep poverty, no hope for development.' Sadan, Ezra. 'Investing in Peace' *Jerusalem Post,* May 14, 1993. Cited in Roy (1995a) p. 313.

128. Palestine Ministry of Information. Web announcement 4 December 1996. Israel has arrested about 13,700 laborers for attempting to enter Israel to work without a proper permit.

129. Beyer (1996), p. 26. For an analysis of the articles concerning safe passage from a 'minimalist' Israel perspective, see Lerner, 'Safe Passages - The Next Challenge' in *IMRA Review* 27 November 1996 (Internet posting dated 28 November). Lerner points out, that since Israel has a veto right over who might be allowed to use the safe passages from Gaza, Israel might technically keep the 'safe passage route open, but simply deny all individuals access to it.' See Annex 1 of the interim agreement, especially Articles VIII, IX and X.

130. *Muslim World News*, September 19, 1996. Palestinian 'industrialists' issued an announcement on Monday 2 November1996 calling for a boycott of the Economic Summit in Cairo in order to protest the restrictions on Palestinian goods (Source: *Muslim World News*, 5 November 1996).

131. Agreements clearly stipulate that Israel has control over borders, leaving the PA only able to counter with rather desperate measures.

132. *Muslim World News*, 28 October 1996. Other features of the agreement give Israeli civilians great scope to disrupt the Palestinian economy. In early November 1996, and experimental farm that had been turned over to the PA under the agreements was destroyed in an attack by settlers while Israeli troops looked on. (See *Muslim World News*, 12 November 1996 – 'Jewish settlers seize Palestinian experimental farm.') Under the agreement, PA security forces have no mandate to arrest or detain Israeli citizens if Israel security forces are near by, and no scope to punish or discipline Israelis under any circumstance. There are numerous reports of settlers destroying Palestinian agricultural property and physically intimidating, often using firearms, Palestinian agricultural workers as they try to work in their fields. IDF confiscation of productive Palestinian land for the pretense of building 'security by-pass roads' and the like pose a further threat to the viability of Palestinian agriculture.

133. *Muslim World News*, 'Palestinians hold large protests near Gaza settlement' 25 November 1996.

134. *Muslim World News*, 9 Nov. 1996 'Gaza City.' The same article notes that the Palestinian GNP has fallen by 23% and average earnings per person by 39% in the previous four years. Given that statistics from four years ago reflected the economic crisis following the Gulf War and the prolonged impact of intifada repression, these figures seem especially dire.

135. Davidi (1993), p. 25.

136. Taylor (1995), p. 99.

137. Usher (1994), p. 12.

138. Based on conversations with source within the IMF, and a Gazan flower producer, February 1997. The producer, who stated that timely delivery of his flowers to markets in Holland would mean a profit of $12–15,000 per greenhouse of 100 square meters, had absorbed a considerable loss for 1996. This is one reason why Gazans are very concerned about the opening of the air and sea ports in Gaza.

139. Roy (1995a), p. 327.

140. Byrne (1996a), n.p. For other perspectives, see also Roy (1996), pp. 72–3; and *Palestine Business Report* 'Germany to Support Palestinian Industry' Vol. II, no. 1 (Jan. 1997) p. 9.

141. Usher (1994), p. 12.

142. Israel Shahak. 'Translations from the Hebrew Press' September 1995; cited in Byrne (1996).

143. Byrne (1996).

144. Reported in *Ha'aretz*, 8 January 1997. The report also noted that the Israeli Ministries of Industry and Trade, and Defense support the establishment of an Israeli park on the Israeli side of the border.

145. Elmusa and El-Jaafari, pp. 14–32.

146. Rabbani (1995), p. 96.
147. Murphy (1995), p.36.
148. Shehadeh (1994), p. 30.
149. Murphy (1995), p. 38.
150. Shehadeh (1994), p. 30.
151. Abed (1994), *passim.*
152. Salama, Salama A. 'The bogus nuptials', *Al-Ahram Weekly.* 26 September - 2 October, 1996, p. 13.
153. Usher (1996), p. 31.
154. Ibid., pp. 31–2.
155. See statement by Netanyahu advisor David Bar-Ilan reported in 'Netanyahu aide vows to continue settlement expansion' *Muslim World News,* 21 Nov. 1996; and '50 per cent hike in spending on Jewish settlements' *Muslim World News*, Nov. 22, 1996.

Chapter Five

1. It also seems to ignore the power content of legitimacy, reducing it to recognition.
2. Usher (1995c), p. 44.
3. A reading of the agreements refers to joint committees in almost every area, from establishing basic needs to deciding where on the Gaza sea-front the PA might be allowed to build. Even where the PA has apparent direct powers, they are usually carried out or overseen with reference to rules and laws drawn up by one of the many spheres that are regulated by joint committee. PA authority is circumscribed by the need to consult with Israel on almost every issue that might be considered an expression of sovereignty – PA functions are primarily administrative. Particularly worthy of note is the degree to which any future expansion in the scope of PA power is linked to fulfilling the demands of external actors rather than to its performance in addressing the concerns of the inhabitants of the self rule areas.
4. MKs from Labour and Likud, headed by Yossi Beilin and Michael Eitan respectively have attempted to draft a common document toward future negotiations (a.k.a. the Eitan-Beilin platform). In some case where there is not agreement, there are two versions given as in the case noted here. See *Ha'aretz* (8 January 1997) cited in *IMRA*, 'News and observations from Israel' (8 January 1997).
5. Roy (1996), p. 74.
6. In the same interview with *Der Speigel* (21 Sept 1996), Netanyahu, apart from this reaffirmation of his opposition to a Palestinian state, also reaffirmed his refusal to allow Palestinian access to subterranean water reserves in the West Bank. (Source: *Muslim World News*, 22 Sept 1996).
7. Two postings in *MSA News* summarized the article. *IMRA* 8 November, 1996. See also *Muslim World News* of 9 November 1996.
8. Usher (1995b), p. 22.
9. Cited in Lindholm Schulz (1996), p. 24. Al-Khatib goes on to argue that the

Cairo accord is more 'a step toward reorganizing the occupation than a step toward ending the occupation.'.

10. Quoted in Murphy (1995), p. 36.

11. Usher (1995b), p. 22.

12. Even where the agreements might have appeared quite clear on an issue, the relationship between power and effective interpretation have undermined that clarity. (A typical example is Israeli spokesman Moshe Fogel's statement that the tax breaks and subsidies for Israeli's who were willing to resettle in the OT (announced in mid-December 1996) were justified under the agreements which allow for 'natural growth' in the settlements. Power, it appears, sets the de facto boundary of interpretation in this dubious case.).

13. Avi Shlaim recognized the paradox the current peace process created from Israeli Labor Party perspective: 'While the agreement needs a strong PLO to implement the Gaza–Jericho settlement, a strong PLO only reinforces the Palestinians' determination to fight for a state of their own.' *Journal of Palestine Studies* vol. XXIV, no. 4 (Summer 1995), p. 28.

14. The only power brought by the Palestinian side was the ability of the inhabitants of the OT to make occupation chaotic, costly and even dangerous for the Israelis. Ironically, the future power of the PA as granted from Israel is made contingent on their giving up this 'power' within their new base.

15. Al-Quds home page, n.d (ca. Aug. 1996).

16. Roy (1995a), p. 78.

17. Usher (1996), p. 24.

18. Elmusa and Butler (1995), p. 79.

19. Hobbes argued that the only reason for the individual to submit to authority was self-preservation. The legitimate sovereign order would be one in which basic needs – measured both in terms of material needs and physical security – were given. Palestinians still experience arbitrary threats to their personal security from the institutions which are in theory supposed to protect them; and, ironically, control over basic needs has become the tool with which the PA is enforcing political compliance. Certainly other states are in fact constrained by the interests of more powerful neighbors or global economic trends, but in no other case are the political authorities *de jure* subject to restrictions such as those imposed on the PA. This greatly inhibits Palestinian society's and the PA's ability to adapt to and plan for changing contingencies.

20. Ashrawi (1985), p. 261.

21. Huntington (1968), p.1.

22. Ibid., p. 1; (remarks in parenthesis added).

23. Brynen (1995b), p. 25.

24. Tamari (1995), p. 10.

25. Ibid., p. 10, Tamari goes on to identify a crisis of national identity as it is reflected in self-rule institutions. 'This crisis is reflected in the symbolic national icons, on the one hand, and in the regulation of the relationship between civil society and the formative institutions of power – what can be called the institutionalization of authority – on the other.'

26. *Webster's Dictionary*, p. 43. New York: 1993.

27. Ibid., p. 9.

28. Events referred to include Israel's opening of a tunnel under the Islamic holy sites in Jerusalem's old city, increased settlement activity (including talks of expanding the Jewish population on settlements in Gaza), exchanges of fire between Israeli and Palestinian forces, and recent Palestinian mass demonstrations that were roughly put down by Israeli troops in Jerusalem. The situation further highlights the inability of the PA to enforce even the status quo in negotiations toward a final settlement. Since the first draft of the manuscript was completed, developments related to the unilateral Israeli decision to expand settlements around Jerusalem (Har Homa) have made this question even more urgent.

29. Usher, Graham. 'Down to jobs for peace' *Al-Ahram Weekly* 12–18 September, 1996, p. 1.

30. Shikaki (1996a), p. 9.

31. Usher (1996), p. 31.

32. JMCC poll no. 15.

33. Usher (1996), p. 26.

34. Ibid., pp. 22–3.

35. It should be noted that support for policing exists in part because it provides much needed income for families, and in an environment where the rule of law is not consolidated but rather personalized, it becomes an imperative not to alienate any contacts one might have in the security apparatus. The following section on jurisdiction illustrates how the basis of law that is guiding the transition allows the PA to overlook issues of internal accountability; prioritizing accountability to the peace process.

36. See Article XI. Article IX, however, allows no other armed forces and no import or production of arms [paragraph 2–3]).

37. See Gaza–Jericho Agreement, Annex III, Article I, paragraph 2a. and 2b. and Article III, paragraphs 2 and 3; and, see Interim Agreement, Chapter 2, Article XIII, paragraph 2b2.

38. See Gaza–Jericho Agreement, Annex III, Article I, paragraphs 5–9. See Usher (1996a), pp. 21–22.

39. 'Agreement on Transfer of Powers and Responsibilities' Article VI, paragraph 5.

40. See also *Agreement on Gaza and Jericho Area:* Annex I, Art. VII, para. 6 and 9.

41. See for example 'Interim Agreement' Article XI, paragraph 1 and Article XVII, paragraph 1.

42. For a brief but interesting overview of how they could be manipulated, see Cossali and Robson (1986), p. 75.

43. Cossali and Robson (1986), p. 65.

44. Roy (1995a), p. 22.

45. Harlow, p. 33.

46. Ibid., p. 34.

47. Cossali and Robson (1986), p. 71.

48. Conversation with Ron Wilkinson, UNRWA information officer, September 1995.

49. Beyer (1996), p. 25.

50. Ibid., p. 25.

51. Usher (1996), p. 32.

52. Shikaki (1996a), p. 10.

53. A PA statement on the events referred to 'suspicious attempts to distort the National Authority's image.' Amayreh (1996a). As of early February 1997, the number of deaths in PA custody had jumped to twelve.

54. Beyer (1996), p. 26.

55. Amayreh (1996a), np. The PA admitted later that the victim was killed by police fire.

56. Quoted in Usher (1996a), p. 28.

57. 'Arafat's bastard regime' *Middle East Realities*, 20 May 1996.

58. LAWE press releases of 12-30 June 1996. It is worth noting that al-Sarraj was also moved for trail in security courts in spite of the fact that no security related charges were brought against him, which indicates that the PA continues to manipulate a confusing array of judicial institutions to get the outcomes it desires in legal matters. In a more recent incident, Dr al-Sarraj (along with several other Palestinian activists and academics) was prevented from attending an academic conference in Oslo, Norway (22–24 November1996) when the PA, apparently enforcing an Israeli request, denied Sarraj the documents to travel to Oslo. After intervention by the Norwegian organizers, Sarraj did make it to the conference. Others, including Bir Zeit professor Ali al-Jarbarwi, were stopped in Ben-Gurion airport by Israeli authorities and prevented from making the trip. These incidents highlight the degree to which the PA is being used as a tool to enforce old Israeli policies of denying basic rights to Palestinians.

59. The statement of the court was as follows: 'We find that the detention of the plaintiffs in Ramallah prisons since March 1996 and until now has happened without any legal reason and took place in the absence of procedures and in contravention of the rule of law, which gives us the power to accept this case and to find the arrest of the plaintiffs illegal. Release them immediately.' [case No. 96/25] Source: Birzeit Human Rights Record No. 17 (April–Sept. 1996). It is this ruling to which Arafat responded that he 'was not a puppet of the court.'.

60. LAWE press releases of August 18 and 20.

61. Ibid.

62. LAWE press release, 26 March 1996.

63. Hilal (1995), p. 17.

64. Shikaki (1996b), p. 22.

65. Ibid., p. 21.

66. Usher (1996), pp. 21–34.

67. Shehadeh (1994), p. 22.

68. See Gaza–Jericho Agreement, Annex II, Article IIb, paragraph 31.

69. Shehadeh (1994), p. 21.

70. Ibid., p. 24.

71. Andoni (1996), p. 5.

72. Shikaki (1996b), p. 17.

73. Interim Agreement, Article II, paragraph 2.

74. Personal interviews with Gazans – 21–25 January 1996. A personal anecdote reflects a couple of the various attitudes toward elections and their context. On the day after the Palestinian national elections, the author was invited in to *iftar* (the breaking of the fast during Ramadan, the Muslim holy month of fasting) with a family in Gaza City. After our meal, a discussion about politics ensued between the father of the family, (an elderly lawyer who had been forced out of Kuwait in 1990 and in 1995 ran a small stationary shop), his son, and myself. (The mother of the family left for work soon after dinner). While the son felt that the elections were important in establishing a precedent, he felt that ultimately the exercise had been meaningless in terms of executing any expression of the popular will. He emphasized ideology in his choices at the polls and had not voted for any family members at all; his father, on the other hand, had voted for family members second only to Dr Haydar Abd al-Shafi. In a political situation with very little substantive content and where the rule of law is uncertain at best, one had best have contacts in visible and/or influential places.

75. Shikaki (1996a), p. 9. Gaza's historical experience with elections has probably not encouraged its people to have much faith that they might lead to manifestations of popular will. Usually, it has been countries pointed to as democratic which have stepped in to undermine democracy in Gaza. Israel annulled municipal elections in 1976 when it became apparent that pro-PLO candidates were victorious. The British similarly annulled elections in Gaza in the mid-1940s. Such cases illustrate that elections can be used as a front – i.e. it appears that power and rights emanate from popular will until popular will runs counter to the wishes of other actors who have the power to assert their interests regardless of popular will or the institutional and ritual facades which are set up to disguise the real nature of the situation. One can only wonder what would have happened if Arafat had not won the elections.

76. JMCC poll no. 13.

77 For a comprehensive discussion see Andoni (1996), esp. pp. 8–12. This was also discussed extensively in the *Jerusalem Post* in the run-up to the elections.

78. Shikaki (1996b), p. 21.

79. JMCC poll no. 18 (Dec. 1996) suggests that about a quarter of the population feels that the Palestinian Legislative Council (PLC) represent the aspirations of the Palestinian people well, while about another 50 per cent feel that the Council represents the aspirations of the people, but to no effect. About 15 per cent reported negative attitudes toward the PLC. A lack of information about the PLC is suggested by the JMCC poll no. 16 in August, when 44.9 per cent of respondents noted that they felt they did not have enough information about the PLC, and 39 per cent reported that they were not informed at all.

80. Beyer (1996), p. 25; (There has since been one PLC resolution implemented).

81. Ibid., p. 22. ' … based on our exit poll, we concluded that the most important primary selection criterion for the selection process was political affiliation, followed by the character of the candidate himself … only thirdly did family or clan considerations figure. However, as suggested in Chapter 2 below, there is not always a distinction between these first and third factors.

82. Andoni (1996), p. 15. (emphasis added).

83. Those interested in reviewing the literature on the 'democracy = peace' argument

might consider starting with the following articles: Doyle, Michael. 'Kant, Liberal Legacies, and Foreign Affairs' *Philosophy & Public Affairs* vol. 12, no. 4 (Fall 1983); Gates, Knutsen and Moses. 'Democracy and Peace: A More Skeptical View' *Journal of Peace Research* vol. 33, no. 1, 1996 pp. 1–10.

84. See Gaza Center for Rights and Law report entitled 'Freedom of Expression Under the Palestinian National Authority' dated 16 September 1995.

85. In one episode, the leading Jerusalem daily *Al-Quds* was closed by Arafat and its editor arrested for failing to put good news about a recent Arafat speech on the front page.

86. Amayreh (1996a), n. p.

87. In this regard, Ahmad S. Khalidi issues a blunt call for realism that is duly noted here: 'No matter what image the Palestinians have of themselves—in particular the self-image of the large and vociferous Palestinian intelligentsia—the truth is that Palestinian society is fundamentally no different from the Arab societies that surround it ... [T]he kind of regime that will initially emerge from these conditions will in many ways replicate other regimes that have sprung from similar conditions. To expect a full-blown democracy is an ahistorical exercise in wishful thinking ... ' Khalidi (1996), p. 21. While a useful caution, given the limited but genuine advances in organizational democracy within the universities, professional organizations and municipalities of the OT (leading to expectations of democracy as well), Khalidi's statement might actually be more relevant of the environment within which the PLO elite have formed their conception of politics.

88. For a persuasive argument in this regard, see Byrne (1996b).

89. Usher (1996), p. 33.

90. It has been consistently repeated by the Israeli leadership that concessions toward greater autonomy were premised upon Arafat's success at crushing unrest in the areas under his police control.

91. There are several cases which indicate an increasing trend toward speculative humiliation of Palestinians at the expense of the powerlessness of the PA. A *B'tselem* report issued in late December 1996 documented that Israeli soldiers were breaking into Palestinian homes in the Hebron area and forcibly strip searching the women. While scores of women and girls were subject to such treatment in front of male soldiers (and while male family members and neighbors were forced to watch as well) only one man was strip searched, suggesting that the main purpose of the action was humiliation. The reader is encouraged to examine the reports of such organizations as B'tselem, Human Rights Watch, LAWE the Alternative Information Center, and other reports cited in this work.

92. *Muslim World News.* 'Israeli army ready to return to PA territories: officer' Nov. 27, 1996. The Israeli daily *Ha'aretz* is cited as the source for this report. On February 3, 1995, Sa'eb Erakat told Lindholm Schulz (1996) that, 'the Israelis are still seeking this kind of peace equation where they can still have settlements, continue [to be occupiers] and at the same time have peace. The Israelis are still thinking in the mentality of occupiers, not in the mentality of those who signed an agreement.' Cited in Lindholm Schulz (1996), p. 27.

Chapter Six

1. Ziad Abu-Amr clearly suggested the pragmatic interests that brought Palestinians out of the passive dependent *sumud* mode toward demands for immediate rights and accountability. Reflecting the optimism of the early days of the intifada, Abu-Amr goes so far as to argue that the uprising, 'has served as a catalyst in bringing Palestinian political thinking into maturity. There is a strong desire among Palestinians in the occupied territories for a settlement and compromise. Their pragmatic reading of the situation says that Israel is here to stay, but that Palestinians must have their equal rights.' Abu-Amr (1990): p. 3.

2. Lindholm Schulz (1996), p. 7. Indeed, demographic features offer insight into points of tension within the transition period, with age and place of origin seeming to offer significant variables.

3. All definitions of Arabic words are based on Hans Wehr. *Dictionary of Modern Written Arabic* Third Edition edited by J. M. Cowan. Ithaca, N.Y.: Spoken Language Services, 1976.

4. Comparisons might be made with the Arab revolt of 1936–1939 which seemed to leave the Palestinian grassroots exhausted, its traditional leadership decimated and/or discredited, and a leadership in exile (namely Haj Amin al-Husseini) who was perhaps too distanced from the events on the ground and too embittered with the British to see the relative possibilities offered by the British 'white paper' of 1939.

5. Why identify with a larger framework for restrictions at all? Freud (p. 69) asks a question which, phrased in various ways, has always troubled political thinkers: 'why love one's neighbour' when it provides no real benefit? 'In consequence of this primary mutual hostility of human beings, civilized society is perpetually threatened with disintegration ... instinctual passions are stronger than reasonable interests.' The utility of Freudian concepts to this case study of popular identification with authority is suggested by the perceived inability of the new order to balance the social and economic restrictions placed by the new order on libidinal gratification with fundamental economic and personal security. This is especially true from the perspective of the young – the most libidinally active segment of the population – thus reinforcing generational divisions in the relationship with authority.

6. Freud, p. 91.

7. Punamaki-Gitai (1990), p. 43.

8. 'Political Detainees in the Russian Compound in Jerusalem' in Augustin, p. 188.

9. Al-Jarbarwi (1996), p. 31.

10. Mahmoud Zahar, Hamas, interviewed by Lindholm Schulz (1996) on 11 January 1995. Lindholm Schulz (1996), p. 38.

11. Ibid., p. 37. Interview with Bassam Jarrar, 19 Oct. 1994.

12. Punamaki-Gitai (1990), p. 37.

13. Punamaki-Gitai (1990), p. 4.

14. Giacamen et al. (1993), p. 129.

15. Ibid., p. 124.

16. Ibid., p. 120.

18. Freire, pp. 568, 569.

19. Punamaki-Gitai (1990), p. 34. 'The clinical finding that avoidance and denial may be helpful only in a limited time frame, and might extract a price later on shows how the criteria for effectiveness can change over time.' Ibid., p. 42.

20. Freire, p. 568. During a visit to Gaza in early 1997, the author was struck by the prevelance of malicious gossip and 'finger pointing.'.

21. Punamaki-Gitai (1990), p. 9. Many observers have argued that long term exposure to political violence tends to encourage individuals to accept violence as an appropriate method for resolving conflicts generally. Such arguments should however be considered cautiously as very few are empirically verified (Ibid., p. 18).

22. Punamaki-Gitai (1990), p. 10. Punamaki-Gitai's (1990) review of the literature suggests that exposure to political violence has a less severe disruptive impact on aggressiveness or morality than popular beliefs suggest. One must therefore ask questions about how individuals assimilated ideological or social factors which tended to legitimize the use of violence in certain situations and perhaps about the attitude of those who continue to use violence who see it as a way of protecting their position. On the other hand, the finding that violence does not seem to be inevitably legitimized through long term exposure might be important in understanding the prevalence of passive coping strategies toward dealing with the hardships and perceived injustices thus ideological disorientation which have accompanied the transition to self rule. Ibid., p. 18. Concurrently, however, the literature indicates that sometimes social cohesion increases under stress related to political violence, and sometimes it doesn't. In fact, the old 'myths of war' argument – that war situations in and of themselves enhance social cohesion – was not backed up by the empirical evidence.

23. Punamaki-Gitai (1990), p. 15. Generally, the 'protective function of social identification and support in times of war' tends to mitigate the negative impact of political violence on the individual psyche. (Or, it seems better said, such identification channels the stress in directions deemed appropriate by the group and thus enhances the chances for the group to identify with and contribute to the protection of the individual while the group pursues a collective strategy for survival.) Ibid., pp. 11–12.

24. Goulet (1992), p. 552.

25. JMCC polls numbered 17 (November 1996) and 18 (December 1996) respectively.

26. Giacamen et al. (1993), p. 119.

27. Punamaki-Gitai (1990), pp. 8, 40, 41.

28. Simmel (1964), p. 19.

29. While I tend to be supicious of his reference to 'authenticity', Freire offers an excellent insight into the tensions between the objective and subjective forces which inform political action: 'To deny the importance of subjectivity in the process of transforming the world and history is naive and simplistic. It is to admit the impossible: a world without men. This objectivistic position is as ingenious as that of subjectivism, which postulates men without a world. World and men do not exist apart from each other, they exist in constant interaction.' Freire, p. 561. Those who have few other options will often more easily accept the myths which promise to lift them from alienation and insignificance because it is the only choice; and in the absence of

meaningful political choices, the call for authenticity, for loyalty to the perceived limitations and dictates of tradition, becomes an ever more potent force in political society. As it did throughout the occupation, Gaza society continues to improvise on traditions as a mode of resistance. Traditions are also inevitably used as modes for the disguise of power. As authority is in the process of reconstitution, tensions inevitably arise as symbols are squeezed for interpretations of structural realities and structural reality is squeezed to conform to the imagined significance of symbols.

30. Goulet (1992), p. 553.

31. Ashrawi (1985), pp.167–8.

32. Punamaki-Gitai (1990), p. 42.

33. Almond and Powell (1978), pp.31–2.

34. Eickelman (1987), p. 136.

35. Brynen (1995a), p. 35.

36. Based on discussions with 'former activists' in Gaza and in East Jerusalem.

37. Punamaki-Gitai (1990), pp. 44, 47. Reporting on incidents in Netzarim in the Gaza Strip on Sept. 26, 1996 (during clashes between Israeli Soldiers and Palestinians), Reuter recorded that 'A Palestinian boy briefly joined the Gaza Strip gun battles on Thursday, picking up the rifle of a wounded Palestinian policeman and firing a Israeli soldiers, witnesses said. The policeman dropped the rifle after being shot in the neck. The boy, who looked to be about 12 to 14 years old, then took it from the ground and fired at Israeli troops until Palestinian policemen persuaded him to hand over the weapon.'

38. See Punamaki-Gitai (1990), p. 12. However, the ways in which the studies tend to evaluate responses as either representing psychological resilience or mental health problems tend to divide across whether the researcher deems activities based in apparent ideological commitment to be appropriate responses to a given situation or serve as cover for the release of stress or trauma disorders. This can be demonstrated in the two stages of the intifada; one of ideologically committed resistance supported by identifiable social structures and one which used the old rhetoric to cover what were in fact socially destructive and self interested behaviours.

39. Cossali and Robson (1986), p. 103.

40. Punamaki-Gitai (1990), p. 36.

41. Personal interview with Palestinian human rights field worker in Gaza, September 1995.

42. Punamaki-Gitai (1990), p. 16.

43. Hammami (1993), p. 299. Zureik reiterates many of the points made in this section, see esp. pp. 47–8.

44. Ibid., p. 305.

45. Ibid. However, it should be noted that especially in Gaza, freedom of movement was restricted for all by non-traditional forces, and the low employment figures in part reflect the shortage of employment in general; the low incidence of home production for sale by women [10%] should also be considered in the lack of markets – this would be due not only to the generally poor economic situation but the fact that there is a limited number of activities conducive to home production and thus only a limited number of individuals could participate in this home economy unless

supply were to vastly outstrip any possible demand).

46. At the same time, however, the author also heard the argument that because women were in Gaza while men were becoming familiar with attitudes over the border in Israel, women actually tended to be more conservative on average, and more likely to come in daily contact with the demands and influences of the growing Islamist trend in Gaza during the intifada.

47. Hammani, p. 300.

48. Quoted in Moghadam (1993).

49. See Abdul Jawwad (1990), p. 73.

50. Ibid., p. 65, 66.

51. Ibid., p. 66.

52. See Ibid., p. 72.

53. Kandiyoti (1991), p. 14.

54. JMCC polls 16 (August 1996), 17 (November 1996), and 18 (December 1996). With respect to personalities, Arafat was most trusted by just under 50 per cent of respondants, with Haydar Abd-al Shafi getting the primary trust of just under 10%, Hamas leader Ahmad Yassin receiving consistently around 3% with Hanan Ashrawi (1985) coming in a close fourth. Fatah numbers swung from a low of 34% in August 1996 to a high of 41.7% in October 1996. Hamas, the only other faction to register significant support, recieved between 6 and 10% of people's primary trust. Poll 16 suggests that Arafat's approval rating is much higher in Gaza (72.3%) than in the West Bank (47.1%).

55. This claim is of course by its nature anecdotal; during a recent visit to Gaza, most of the people I spoke with either complained about gossip and 'backstabbing' or offered gossip themsselves. This atmosphere has left many people demoralized.

56. JMCC poll no. 16, August 1996. Significantly, 76.9% of Gazans feel that there has been an improvement as opposed to 50.3% of West Bankers. Just under 20% of Palestinians in the OT reported no change in their feelings of personal security. Such perceptions should be evaluated against conditions toward the end of the intifada when the Israeli Defence Forces (IDF) carried out mass arrests in Gaza and torture and even extra-judicial killings were rampant. In almost every Gazan household visited by the author, the inhabitants had stories of the IDF coming to the door to arrest or punish young men in the home. Giacamen et al., using the data collected in the FAFO survey, notes that 1 in 3 housholds had a member arrested by Israeli authorities and demonstrated a correlation between this and general psychic stress (p. 126). Clashes in the street were commonplace. British and Danish nurses working in Gaza hospitals as part of a European Union funded project told the author of incidents where Israeli soldiers had broken into hospital operating rooms to shoot and kill patients who had been brought in during street clashes with the soldiers. For the thoughtful perspective of an Israeli who spent time in Gaza as an on-duty IDF reservist, see Shavit. Ominously, however, an Islamic Jihad leader has said that the 'Palestinian police are 'worse than the Israelis' in their treatment of prisoners.'—'Jihad: More suicide attacks soon' *The Jerusalem Post* Sept. 22, 1996, p. 1.

57. Of course, it reflects conditions of extreme economic distress as well, but noteworthy is the mitigating factors which have created a breakdown in social solidarity

and moral restraint as well. The anecdote in Chapter 4 concerning the repayment of loans offers a case in point. During Palestinian elections in 1996, rising crime was a prominent issue as evidenced by the agendas and concerns on various campaign posters in Gaza.

58. Tamari (1990), p. 32.

59. Roy (1993), p. 28.

60. Tamari (1990), p. 38.

61. Hammami (1995), p. 58.

62. Peretz (1991), pp. 17–35.

63. Brown, D. 'The new beat' *The Guardian*, 25 June 1994, pp. 23–7.

64. This was noted a case worker with the Gaza Center for Rights and Law during an interview in Sept. 1995.

65. Roy (1994), pp. 90–1.

66. Roy (1994).

67. Roy (1994), pp. 87–8.

68. During the intifada, wearing this garb in public was conspicuously unsafe, according to the aid worker who first related this anecdote (it was later corroborated by both Palestinians and aid workers who had spent considerable time in Gaza). According to one story, a female aid worker who had gone into the street wearing a cap and sunglasses had been shot by a shebab who had mistaken her for an Israeli agent (I did not corroborate this particular story, however). Paulo Freire has made a provocative observation in this regard: 'the oppressed find in the oppressor their model of manhood.' Freire (1992), p. 558.

69. Information gathered in conversations with various activists in and inhabitants of Gaza.

70. When 12 Hamas protestors were shot and killed, and over 200 injured, by PA security forces.

71. For comprehensive documentation and a summary of these events as they played themselves out in Gaza, see: Palestinian Center for Human Rights, *The Clashes of September 1996: Investigation into the Causes and Use of Force, Series Study (7),* (Gaza: Mansour Press, 1996).

72. JMCC poll no. 17 of October 1996 suggests that close to 60% of Palestinians felt that the PA used these events to the benefit of the Palestinian cause, while over 90% of Palestinians approved of the action taken by the Palestinian police, which was reflected in higher approval ratings for the security forces in that month (44% reporting feeling that security forces performance wsa good as opposed to closer to 30% in other JMCC polls).

73. This was a turnaround from a month earlier, Immanuel continued, when 'people seemed too depressed to answer [Arafat's call for] a march on Al-Aksa mosque, which would have meant a march on Israeli checkpoints. (That failure had cost him credibility)' (np).

74. It is worth noting that the stock of militant activists and martyrs of resistance seems to remain very high in Gaza. *Al-Akbar,* an Islamic activist newletter, reprted on 12 Dec. 1996 that 40,000 people showed up at a rally marking the anniversery of Yahyia Ayash, (a.k.a. 'the engineer' – a bomb maker reputedly responsible for making

bus bombs).

75. Immanuel, np.

76. This Palestinian Center for Public Opinion poll – cited in *Muslim World News*, 1 Oct. 1996 – was based on the responses of 500 residents of the West Bank in late September during the height of the clashes. This finding should be considered carefully, however, as a JMCC poll later in October 1996 shows only 20.6% support for 'intensifying the struggle' while 44.4% called for intensifying the negotiations. In this poll, 28.3% responded that 'there is no need for further negotiations' which might conceal various attitudes.

77. Reported in *Muslim World News*, Oct. 4, 1996.

78. *Al—Akbar* 'PA Courts' Internet press release dated Dec. 30, 1996.

79. Brynen (1995b), p. 23. It should be noted that polling data on Palestinian opinion seems to be relatively volatile, reflecting the ups and downs of the peace process and dramatic events generally. Furthermore, opinion as to how to address problems can change quickly as the objective conditions on the ground change quickly. The uncertainty and unpredictability of the current situation also mean that there is no real rational and objective framework within which to evaluate policies and events.

80. After the bombing, collective punishment was meeted out to the bombers family and the inhabitants of the village of Surif near Hebron (which is still under Israeli control) where he lived. During the IDF imposed curfew under which the inhabitants were not allowed to go out and obtain food and other supplies. Beatings and provocations were reported. Furhtermore, two Israeli soldiers were accused of breaking into a Palestinian home where one raped a woman. The IDF admitted that 'indecent acts' had occured. See LAWE press release of March 31, 1997.

81. Roy (1994), p. 89.

82. Roy (1995b), p. 79.

83. Author's observations and discussions with local informants confirm this perception.

84. Dar Al-Haq interview with Sheik Yassin #1 (*Al-Akbar* IAP www page spring 1996).

85. Shikaki (1996a), p. 12.

86. CNN World News, April 7, 1997. (It is important to remember that when trying to analyse what this means, one should know more specifically what question(s) was(were) asked.

87. See Hovsepian (1995) or Ajami (1992). Ajami (1992) notes of the Arab Nationalist elites of the 1950s and 1960s that 'the case they had made against the ancient regime was the standard case made by broadly middle-class nationalists against older, more narrowly based political regimes: that they were embarrassingly weak and compromised, prone to collaboration, disconnected from the aspiring social classes, and easily torn to shreds by outsiders.' There are similar claims being made against the new elites in Gaza.

88. For example, 'Egyptian Islamic writer Dr Hilmi Muhammad Qa'ud attributes the outbreak of the intifada to the disappointment of the Palestinian people in their outside organizations, after they had been disappointed in an effective support from other Arab nations.' Abu-Amr (1994a), p. 61.

89. Abu-Amr (1993) p. 7.

90. Cossali and Robson (1986), pp. 98, 144.

91. Ibid., pp. 13, 14.

92. Abu-Amr (1993), p. 11. In most countries of the Middle East, shop keepers and middle class merchants form the backbone of the Muslim Brotherhood. The leadership of Hamas is also of largely middle class origin.

93. Brynen (1995a), p. 37.

94. Locke and Stewart, p. 14. See also Cossali and Robson (1986), p. 111 and, for a more graphic description of events, p. 134.

95. Abu-Amr (1994a), p. 14.

96. Ibid., p. 35.

97. Ibid., pp. 40–3.

98. Abu-Amr, (1994a), p. 56.

99. Abu-Amr (1993), p. 14. The Muslim brotherhood was able to gain control of the waqf, which controls 10% of all real estate in the occupied territories and 'employed scores of people from clerics to gravediggers.' Ibid., p. 8.

100. Al-Jarbarwi (1994), p. 136.

101. Abu-Amr, (1993), p. 13.

102. Al-Jarbarwi (1994), p. 136.

103. Ibid., p. 137.

104. Abu-Amr (1994a)p. 70.

105. Discusion with UNRWA information officer Ron Wilkinson. Gaza City, Sept 29,1995.

106. Abu-Amr (1994a), p. 37.

107. Abu-Amr (1993), p. 13.

108. Usher (1995d), p. 65.

109. Abu-Amr (1993), p. 14.

110. Hajjar (1993), p. 12; and, Al-Jabarwi (1994), p. 135.

111. Abu-Amr(1994a), p. 50.

112. Abu-Amr (1993), p. 17.

113. Hajjar (1993), p. 11.

114. Abu-Amr (1994a), pp.37–40.

115. See Lindholm Schulz (1996), p. 9.

116. Abu-Amr (1994a), p. 43.

117. Ibid., pp. 44–6, 48.

118. Ibid., p. 48.

119. Usher (1996), p. 30.

120. *Palestine Times* no. 62 – (August 1996).

121. *Palestine Times* no. 67 – (February 1997).

122. 'Jihad: More suicide attacks soon' *The Jerusalem Post*, Sunday, September 22, 1996, p. 1.

123. *Muslim World News*, 13 Oct. 1996.

124. Roy (1995c), p. 68.

125. While it is beyond the scope of this paper to present the evidence in detail, the author would like to emphasize the developments in the second half of 1996 which

highlighted the threats to the security of Palestinians posed by settler violence and the unwillingness of Israeli authorities to deal effectively with and demonstrate good faith by prosecuting those in the IDF and the settlements who were responsible for killing and maiming Palestinians and/or destoying Palestinian property.

126. It must be remembered that the resistance of the Palestinian grassroots has been about more than recognition or cultural rights. Recognition was merely a stepping stone on the way to greater control over the economic and political destiny of one group, Palestinians, whose rights were being violated and denied to the profit of another group.

127. Freire (1992), p. 558.

Chapter Seven

1. Cited by Owen (1994), p. 14.

2. For a very useful discussion of this issue, see Ian Lustick (1993), 'The Quiescent Palestinians: The System of Control over Arabs in Israel' in Nakleh, Khalil and Elia Zureik (eds). *The Sociology of the Palestinians* (London: Croom Helm, 1980) pp. 64–83. The conceptual framework outlined by Lustick (1993) might be usefully applied to the situation under PA rule today.

3. A major obstacle to sustainable stability through neo-patrimonial methods is that ideologically grounded popular movements have considerable support and do exert influence on Palestinian life in the OT. The Islamists are the primary example of this. Because individuals affiliated with this ideology are likely to identify their primary social and political obligations outside of the sectoral bases upon which the corporatist state lies, they are not likely to be as prone to co-optation. At the same time, constraints of the economic and political environment suggest to these groups that there are few reasons for competing for power within the institutions that exist. As they do not see that the existing political institutions offer the tools by which they might pursue their goals, they take their political conflicts outside the framework that exists to institutionalize political competition.

4. Even among the minority of Palestinians who oppose the peace process, a plurality (37%) see no other option than 'waiting.' CPRS Public Opinion Poll #30 shows that 27% of those opposed to the peace process prefer 'armed struggle,' while 16% prefer a resort to the 'Intifada.' CPRS public opinion polls are available on the WWW at: <http://bertie.la.utexas.edu/research/mena/CPRS/SRU/polls_list.htm>.

5. Hanf and Sabella (1996), p. 169.

6. Ibid. p. 67.

7. See Byrne, (1996b).

8. Usher (1996b), p. 1.

9. JMCC poll no. 18, Q. 1; December 1996. Interestingly, more Gazans describe themselves as optimistic than pessimistic (17% vs. 14.9%) while in the West Bank the opposite was the case (18.4% pessimistic as opposed to 12.4% optimistic).

10. Usher (1996b), p. 1.

11. Indeed, the dynamics of autonomy suggest that a return to intifada might raise

the specter of Palestinian civil war in the OT.

12. See CPRS Public Opinion Poll #30 showing that 18% of Palestinians in the OT would accept such a resolution. CPRS WWW address in footnote 4 above.

13. 'Hamas makes new call for armed resistance' *Middle East Times,* 22–28 September 1996, p. 6.

14. This even seems to have gone so far that the PA workload is extremely reduced if Arafat is out of Palestine. For a very revealing article on this issue that utilizes Palestinian sources, see Rubinstein, Danny 'A growing popular disaffection' *Ha'aretz English Internet edition* Friday, 28 November 1997. The problems with this situation seem more immediate if reports of Arafat's ill health are to be taken seriously. For a Palestinian perspective on the succession issue, see Khalid Amriyeh, 'On who would succeed Arafat' *Palestine Times* December 1997.

15. Al-Husari (1997), pp. 70–1.

16. 'Council says ministries chaotic' *Palestine Report* vol. 2, no. 50 (23 May 23 1997), p. 4. Moreover, even the suicide bomb phenomenon – which was unknown in Palestine before 1993 – should be seen in the context of an increase in suicide rates amongst Palestinians generally over the same period and reflecting the hopelessness of the new order (and thus not, as is often argued, any cultural tendency).

17. For a thorough overview of public opinion with regard to corruption in the PA, see Center for Palestine Research and Studies (CPRS) Public Opinion Poll #28; available via WWW at address in footnote 4 above.

18. Al-Husari (1997), p. 70. In this interview, Bishara offers a brief but stinging critique of this new class and the clientist system which has emerged in the autonomy.

19. It is in the contrast between the historical construction of legitimacy and the consolidation of narrower interests, between the actual powers of the Israeli state and the implied powers of Palestinian autonomy, between the genuine desire for peace and its imposition through a paradigm of repression, and between the expected economic rights implied by the notion of national sovereignty and the economic realities of self rule that contradictions within the current transition process are manifest. The nationalist discourse usually assumes political legitimacy without having to respond to more specific demands of accountability or to operate with regard to real and effectively functioning institutions in society. Current tensions in Palestinian society reflect inconsistencies in the powers granted to, and the demands made on, the institutions, structures and affiliations associated with the current provisional regime.

20. Hawkins, p. 89.

21. The 'Basic Law', which articulates broad principles with regard to future constitutional arrangements, is a step in this direction. However, it remains superseded by the powers and responsibilities articulated in the Interim Agreement. These have ironically been used to justify and demand behaviour by the PA that is inconsistent with the rule of law, and establish precedent that might be difficult to overcome in the future.

22. Even if not reflecting the kinds of processes that might coalesce in a sovereign order, the power embodied within limited autonomy certainly backs up administrative functions and represents a rudimentary apparatus of rule from which such processes

might eventually arise.

23. The role of overt political activism in building and protecting these lines of accountability are important, but are ultimately unsustainable – given that most people prefer to absorb themselves in personal concerns (e.g. survival, leisure and relationships, unless those opportunities are denied them) – without the creation of a structural environment in which rights, boundaries and obligations are reconfirmed via productive participation in daily life.

24. This is based on a formulation by Clifford Geertz in, 'After the Revolution: The fate of Nationalism in the New States', *The Interpretation of Cultures*. New York: Basic Books, 1973, p. 235.

Bibliography

I. Books

Abed, George T. *The Palestinian Economy: Studies in Development Under Prolonged Occupation* (London: Routledge, 1988).

Abu-Amr, Ziad (1994a). *Islamic Fundamentalism in the West Bank and Gaza Strip* (Bloomington: Indiana University Press, 1994).

Ajami, Fouad. *The Arab Predicament* (Cambridge: Canto, Cambridge University Press, 1992).

Almond, Gabriel and Bingham Powell. *Comparative Politics* (Boston: Little Brown, 1978).

Apter, David. *Re-thinking Development* (London: Sage Publications, 1987).

Ashrawi, Hanan. *This Side of Peace* (New York: Simon and Schuster, 1995).

Augustin, Ebba (ed.). *Palestinian Women: Identity and Experience* (London: Zed Books, 1993).

Cobban, Helena. *The Palestinian Liberation Organization: People, Power and Politics* (Cambridge: Cambridge University Press, 1984).

Cossali, Paul and Clive Robson. *Stateless in Gaza* (London: Zed Books, 1986).

Eickelman, Dale F. *The Middle East: An Anthropological Approach* (Englewood Cliffs, NJ: Prentice Hall, 1989).

Endresen, Lene C. and Geir Øvensen. *The Potential for UNRWA Data for Research on Palestinian Refugees: A study of UNRWA administrative data* (Oslo: FAFO, 1994).

Fischer, Stanley et al. *Securing Peace in the Middle East: Project on Economic Transition* (Cambridge, Mass: The MIT Press, 1994).

Freud, Sigmund. *Civilization and its Discontents: the standard edition* (New York: W.W. Norton & Company, 1989).

Gresh, Alain. *The Struggle Within: Towards and Independent Palestinian State* (London: Zed Books, 1985).

Gilen, Signe et al. *Finding Ways: Palestinian Coping Strategies in Changing Environments* (Oslo: FAFO, 1994).

Gowers, Andrew and Tony Walker. *Behind the Myth: Yasser Arafat and the Palestinian Revolution* (London: W. H. Allen, 1990).

Hanf, Theodor and Bernard Sabella. *A Date with Democracy: Palestinians on Society and Politics. An empirical survey.* (Freiburg: Arnold Bergstaesser Institue, 1996).

Hiltermann, Joost. *Behind the Intifada: Labor and Women's Movements in the Occupied Territories* (Princeton: Princeton University Press, 1991).

Huntington, Samuel. *Political Order in Changing Societies* (New Haven: Yale University Press, 1968).

JMCC. *The Palestinian Council* (East Jerusalem: Jerusalem Media and Communications Center, October 1996).

——*Public Opinion Polls On Palestinian Attitudes Toward Politics: nos. 1–18 1993–1996* (East Jerusalem: Jerusalem Media and Communications Center, January 1997).

Kalaf, Issa. *Politics in Palestine: Arab factionalism and social disintegration, 1939–1948* (Albany: State University of New York Press, 1991).

Kandiyoti, Deniz (ed.). *Women, Islam and the State* (Philadelphia: Temple University Press, 1991).

Kimmerling, Baruch and Joel S. Migdal. *Palestinians. The making of a people* (Cambridge: Harvard University Press, 1994).

Lustick, Ian S. *Unsettled States, Disputed Lands: Britain and Ireland, France and Algeria, Israel and the West Bank–Gaza* (Ithaca and London: Cornell University Press, 1993).

Moghadam, V. *Modernizing Women: Gender and Social Change in the Middle East* (Cairo: The American University in Cairo Press, 1993).

Punamaki-Gitai, Raija-Leena. *Political Violence and Psychological Responses* (Tampere Peace Research Institute: Research Report No.41, 1990).

Robinson, Glenn E. *Creating Space: Organization, Ideology, and Leadership in the Palestinian Intifada* (unpublished PhD dissertation, University of California Berkeley, 1992).

Roy, Sara (1995a). *The Gaza Strip: The Political Economy of De-development* (Washington D.C.: Institute of Palestine Studies, 1995).

Rubenberg, Cheryl. *The Palestine Liberation Organization: Its Institutional Infrastructure* (Bellmont: Institure of Arab Studies, IAS Monograph Series, no. 1, 1983).

Schwedler, Jillian. *Toward Civil Society in the Middle East: A Primer* (Boulder and London: Lynne Rienner, 1995).

Sharabi, Hisham, *Neopatriarchy : A Theory of Distorted Change in Arab Society* (Oxford: Oxford University Press, 1988).

Simmel, Georg. *Conflict and the Web of Group Affiliations* (translated by Kurt H. Wolff and Reinhardt Bendix) (New York: The Free Press, 1964).

World Bank. *Developing the Occupied Territories: An Investment in Peace* (Washington D.C.: World Bank, 1993).

Zureik, Elia, *Palestinian Refugess and the Peace Process* (Washington D.C: Institute for Palestine Studies, 1996).

Øvensen, Geir. *Responding to Change: Trends in Palestinian Household Economy* (Oslo: FAFO, 1994).

II. Articles

Abdul Jawwad, Islah. 'The Evolution of the Political Role of the Palestinian Woman's Movement in the Uprising,' in Michael Hudson (ed.) *The Palestinians: New Directions* (Washington D.C.: Center for Contemporary Arab Studies, 1990): pp. 63–77.

Abu-Amr, Ziad. 'The Gaza Economy' in Abed, George T. *The Palestinian Economy: Studies in Development Under Prolonged Occupation* (London: Routledge, 1988).

—— 'The Politics of the Intifada' in Michael Hudson (ed.) *The Palestinians: New Directions* (Washington D.C.: Center for Contemporary Arab Studies, 1990): pp. 3–23.

—— 'Hamas: A Historical and Political Background' *Journal of Palestine Studies* vol. XXII, no. 4 (Summer 1993): pp. 5–19.

—— (1994b). 'The View from Palestine: In the Wake of the Agreement' *Journal of Palestine Studies* vol. XXIII, no. 2 (Winter 1994): pp. 75–83.

—— 'Report From Palestine' *Journal of Palestine Studies* vol. XXIV, no. 2 (Winter 1995): pp. 40–7.

Al-Jarbawi, Ali. 'The Position of the Palestinian Islamists on the Palestine–Israel Accord' *The Muslim World* vol. LXXXIV, no. 1–2 (Jan.–April 1994): pp. 127–54.

—— 'Palestinian Politics at a Crossroads' *The Journal of Palestine Studies* vol. XXV, no. 4 (Summer 1996): pp. 29–39.

Amayreh, Khalid (1996a). 'Arafat besieged by domestic trouble' in *Palestine Times* no. 63 (September 1996): n.p. [http://www.ptimes.com].

—— 'Hamas regains popularity among Palestinians' in *Palestine TImes* no.67 (January 1997): n.p. [http://www.ptimes.com].

Andoni, Lamis. 'PLO at the Crossroads' *Journal of Palestine Studies* vol. XXI, no. 1 (Autumn 1991): pp. 54–65.

—— 'The Elections: Democracy or One Party Rule' *Journal of Palestine Studies* vol. XXV, no. 3 (Spring 1996): pp. 5–16.

Bergman, Ronen and David Ratner. 'The Man Who Swallowed Gaza' *Ha'aretz*, Weekend Supplement (April 4, 1994).

Beyer, Lisa. 'Peace in Flames' *Time International* vol. 148, no. 15 (7/10/1996): pp. 23–7.

Brynen, Rex (1995a). 'The Dynamics of Palestinian Elite Formation' *Journal of Palestine Studies* vol.XXIV, no. 3 (Spring 1995): pp. 31–43.

—— (1995b). 'The Neopatrimonial Dimension of Palestinian Politics' *Journal of Palestine Studies* vol. XXV, no. 1 (Autumn 1995): pp. 23–36.

Byrne, Aisling (1996a). 'Hammered from both sides' *News From Within* (June1996): n.p. [http://www.aic.org]

—— (1996b). "Manufacturing consent' in post-Oslo Palestine' *News From Within* (December 1996): n.p. [http://www.aic.org].

Connel, Dan. 'Palestine on the Edge: crisis in the national movement' *MERIP* (194/195) vol. 25, no. 3–4 (May–June/July–Aug 1995): pp. 6–9

Davidi, Asher. 'Israel's Economic Strategy for Palestinian Independence' *MERIP* (184) vol. 23, no. 5 (Sept. –Oct. 1993): pp. 24–6.

Ehteshami, Anoushiravan and Emma C. Murphy. 'Transformation of the Corporatist State in the Middle East' [Unpuplished paper presented at the 'Conference on Citizenship and the State in the Middle East' (Nov. 22–24, 1996) in Oslo, Norway].

Eickelman, Dale F. 'The Political Economy of Meaning' *American Ethnologist* vol. 6 (1979): pp. 386–93.

—— 'Introduction: Self and Community in Middle Eastern Societies' *Anthropological Quarterly* vol. 58, no. 4 (Oct. 1985): pp. 135–40.

Elmusa, Sherif S. 'When the Well Springs of Identity Dry Up: Reflections on Fawzi Turki's *Exile's Return*' *Journal of Palestine Studies* vol. XXV, No. 1 (Autumn 1995): pp. 96–102.

Elmusa, Sharif S. and Mahmud El-Jafari. 'Power and Trade: The Israeli–Palestinian Economic Protocol' *Journal of Palestine Studies* vol. XXIV, no. 2 (Winter 1995): pp. 14–32.

Freire, Paulo. 'The Pedagogy of the Oppressed' in Charles K. Wilbur and Kenneth P. Jameson. *The Political Economy of Development and Under-development*, fifth edition (Singapore: McGraw Hill, 1992): pp. 556–75.

Giacamen, Rita; Camilla Stoltenberg and Lars Wieseth. 'Chapter 4: Health' in Marianne Heiberg and Geir Øvensen. *Palestinian Society in Gaza, West Bank and Arab Jerusalem: A survey of living conditions* (Oslo: FAFO, 1993): pp. 99–130.

Goulet, Denis. "Development" ... or Liberation?' in Charles K. Wilbur and Kenneth P. Jameson. *The Political Economy of Development and Under-development* (fifth edition) (Singapore: McGraw Hill, 1992): pp. 547–55.

Hammami, Rema. 'NGOs: the professionalisation of politics' in *Race and Class* vol. 37, no. 2 (Oct.–Dec. 1995): pp. 51–64.

—— 'Chapter 10: Women in Palestinian Society' in Marianne Heiberg and Geir Øvensen. *Palestinian Society in Gaza, West Bank and Arab Jerusalem: A survey of living conditions* (Oslo: FAFO, 1993): pp. 283–312.

Hareide, Henrik. 'Geographical Reflections on the Formation of a Palestinian National Identity' [Unpuplished paper presented at the 'Conference on Citizenship and the State in the Middle East' (Nov. 22–24, 1996) in Oslo, Norway].

Hass, Amira. 'Gaza's Workers and the Palestinian Authority' *MERIP* (194/195) vol. 25 no. 3–4 (May–June/July–Aug 1995): pp. 25–8.

Heiberg, Marianne. 'Chapter 3: Housing' in Heiberg, Marianne and Geir Øvensen. *Palestinian Society in Gaza, West Bank and Arab Jerusalem: A survey of living conditions*. (Oslo: FAFO, 1993): pp. 81–98.

Hilal, Jamil M. 'The PLO: crisis in legitimacy' *Race and Class* vol. 37, no. 2. (Oct.–Dec. 1995): pp. 1–18.

—— 'PLO institutions: The Challenge Ahead' *Journal of Palestine Studies* vol.XXIII, no. 1 (Autumn 1993): pp. 44–60.

Hovsepian, Nubar. 'Competing Identities in the Arab World' *Journal of International Affairs* vol.49, No.1 (Summer 1995): pp. 1–24.

Immanuel, Jon. 'Arafat Wins Back Lost Popularity' *The Jerusalem Post* (Sept. 29, 1996).

Khalidi, Ahmad S. 'The Palestinians' First Excusion into Democracy' *Journal of Palestine Studies* vol. XXV, no. 4 (Summer 1996): pp. 20–8.

Kuttab, Daoud. 'The West Bank and Gaza Strip: Current Developments in the Peace

Process' *Journal of Palesinian Studies*. vol. XXII, no. 1 (Autumn 1992): pp.100–7.

—— 'Report From the Occupied Territories' *Journal of Palestine Studies* vol. XXIII, no. 1 (Autumn 1993): pp. 80–9.

—— 'PA Election: it's a Fatah affair' *The Jerusalem Post* (Jan. 5, 1996): p.7.

Lesch, Ann M. 'Transition to Palestinian Self Government' *Journal of Palestinian Studies*. vol. XXII, no. 3 (Spring 1993): pp. 46–56.

Lindholm Schulz, Helena. 'Palestinian Identities and Self Government: The problematic transition' [Unpublished paper presented at the 'Conference on Citizenship and the State in the Middle East' (Nov. 22–24, 1996) in Oslo, Norway].

Marx, Emanuel. 'Palestinian Refugee Camps in the West Bank and Gaza Strip' *Middle Eastern Studies* vol. 28, no. 2 (April 1992): pp. 281–94.

Moughrabi, Fouad. 'A Year of Discovery' *Journal of Palestine Studies* vol. XXVI, no. 2 (Winter 1997): pp. 5–15.

Murphy, Emma. 'Stacking the Deck: The Economics of the Israeli–PLO Accords' *MERIP* (194/195) vol. 25 no. 3–4 (May–June/July–August 1995): pp. 35–9.

Muslih, Mohammad. 'Palestinian Civil Society' in Jillian Schwedler. *Toward Civil Society in the Middle East? A Primer* (Boulder and London: Rienner, 1995): pp. 65–6.

Nakleh, Khalil. 'Anthropological and Sociological Studies of Arabs in Israel: A Critique' *Journal of Palestine Studies* vol. VI, no. 4 (Summer 1977): pp. 41–70.

Nakleh, Emile. 'The West Bank and Gaza: Twenty Years Later' *Middle East Journal* vol. 42, no. 2 (Spring 1988): pp. 209–26.

Olmsted, Jennifer. 'Thwarting Palestinian Development' *MERIP* (201) vol. 26, no. 4 (Oct.–Dec. 1996): pp. 11–13.

Owen, Roger. 'Reflections on the Meaning and Consequences of the Gulf Crisis' in Dan Tschirgi (ed.), *The Arab World Today* (Boulder and London: Lynne Rienner Publishers, 1994): pp. 13–20.

Peled, Yoav. 'From Zionism to Capitalism' *MERIP* (194/195) vol. 25, no.3–4 (May–June/July–Aug. 1995): pp. 13–19.

Peretz, Don. 'The Impact of the Gulf War on Israeli and Palestinian Political Attitudes' *Journal of Palestine Studies* vol. XXI, no.1 (Autumn 1991): pp. 17–35.

—— 'Palestinian Authority, Israeli Rule: From Transitional to Permanent Arrangement' *MERIP* (201) vol. 26, no. 4 (Oct.–Dec. 1996): pp. 2–6.

Roy, Sara. 'Gaza: The New Dynamics of Civil Disintegration' *Journal of Palestine Studies*. vol. XXII, no. 4 (Summer 1993): pp. 20–31.

—— 'The Seed of Chaos, and of Night: The Gaza Strip after the agreement' *Journal of Palestine Studies* vol. XXIII, no. 3 (Spring 1994): pp. 85–98.

—— (1995b). 'Alienation or Accomodation' *The Journal of Palestine Studies* vol. XXIV, no. 4 (Summer 1995): pp. 73–82.

—— (1995c). 'Civil Society in the Gaza Strip' in Jillian Schwedler. *Toward Civil Society in the Middle East?* (Boulder and London: Lynne Rienner, 1995): pp. 67–8.

—— 'U.S. Aid to the West Bank and Gaza Strip: The Politics of Peace' *Middle East Policy* vol. IV, no. 4 (October 1996): pp. 50–76.

Sayigh, Rosemary. 'Palestinians in Lebanon: (dis)solution of the refugee problem' *Race and Class* vol. 37, no. 2 (Oct.–Dec.1995): pp. 27–42.

Shadid, Mohamed and Rick Seltzer. 'Political Attitudes of Palestinians in the West

Bank and Gaza Strip' *Middle East Journal* vol. 42, no. 1 (Winter 1988): pp.16–32.
Sharabi, Hisham, 'The Neopatriarchal Discourse: Language and Discourse in Contemporary Arab Society' in *Theory, Politics and the Arab World: Critical Responses* 1988: pp. 149–65.
Shavit, Avi. 'On Gaza Beach' in Ian Lustick. *Palestinians Under Israeli Rule* (New York and London: Garland Publishing, 1994): pp. 283–96.
Shehadeh, Raja. 'Transfers and Powers' *MERIP* (194/195) vol. 25 no. 3–4 (May–June/July Aug. 1995): pp. 29–34.
—— 'Questions of Jurisdiction: A Legal Analysis of the Gaza–Jericho Agreement' *Journal of Palestine Studies* vol. XXIII, no. 4 (Summer 1994): pp. 18–25.
Shikaki, Khalil (1996a). 'The Peace Process, National Reconstruction and the Transition to Democracy in Palestine' *Journal of Palestine Studies* vol. XXV, no. 2 (Winter 1996): pp. 5–20.
—— (1996). 'The Palestinian Elections: An Assessment' *Journal of Palestine Studies* vol. XXV, no. 3 (Spring 1996): pp. 17–22.
Tamari, Salim. 'Revolt of the Petite Bourgeoisie: Urban Merchants and the Palestinian Uprising' in Michael Hudson (ed.). *The Palestinians: New Directions* (Washington D.C.: Center for Contemporary Arab Studies, 1990): pp. 24–43.
—— 'Fading Flags: The Crisis of Palestinian Legitimacy' *MERIP* (194/195) vol. 25, No. 3–4. (May–June/July–August 1995): pp. 10–12.
Taylor, Mark. 'The Economics of Defeat' *Race and Class* vol. 37, no. 2 (Oct–Dec 1995): pp. 100–6.
Usher, Graham (1994b). 'The Islamic Movement and the Palestinian Authority' *MERIP* (189) vol. 24, no. 4 (July–August 1994): pp. 28–9.
—— (1995a). 'Palestinian Trade Unions and the Struggle for Independence' *MERIP* (194/195) vol. 25, no. 3–4. (May–June/July–Aug. 1995): pp. 20–4.
—— (1995d). 'What Kind of Nation? The Rise of Hamas in the Occupied Territories' *Race and Class* vol. 37, no. 2 (Oct.–Dec. 1995): pp. 65–80.
—— (1996a). 'The Politics of Internal Security: The PA's New Intelligence Services' *Journal of Palestine Studies* vol. XXV, no. 2 (Winter 1996): pp. 21–34.
—— (1996b). 'Down to jobs for peace' *Al-Ahram Weekly* (12–18 Sept., 1996): p.1.
Whitbeck, John V. 'The Palestinian state already exists' *Middle East International* no. 529 (July 15, 1996): pp. 19–20.

III. Interviews

Abd al-Shafi, Haydar (interview with), 'The Oslo Agreement' *Journal of Palestine Studies* vol. XXIII, no.1 (Autumn 1993): pp. 14–19.
Abed, George T. (interview with), 'Developing the Palestinian Economy' *Journal of Palestine Studies* vol. XXIII, no.4 (Summer 1994): pp. 41–51.
Al-Husari, Ruba. 'Bridging the Green Line: The PA, Israeli Arabs, and Final Status: An Interview with Azmi Bishara' *The Journal of Palestine Studies* vol. XXVI, no. 3 (Spring 1997), pp. 67–80.
Elmusa, Sherif and Linda Butler. 'Moving beyond Oslo: An Interview with Haydar

'Abd al-Shafi' *Journal of Palestine Studies.* vol. XXV, no. 1 (Autumn 1995): pp. 76–85.

Gassner-Jaradat, Ingrid. 'Political Negotiations on the Palestine Refugee Question: Interview with Salim Tamari' *MERIP* (201) vol. 26, no. 4 (October–December 1996): pp. 7–9.

Hajjar, Lisa. 'The Islamist Movement in the Occupied Territories: An interview with Iyad Barghouti' *MERIP* (183) vol. 23, no. 4 (July–August 1993): pp. 9–12.

Harlow, Barbara. 'There is Not Even a Basic Understanding About What Laws Apply Here: Interview with Usama Halabi' *MERIP* (194/195) vol. 25 no. 3–4 (May–June/July–Aug 1995): pp.33–4.

Hawkins, Julia. 'Guarded Optimist on the Peace Process: An Interview with Hanan Ashrawi' *The Journal of Palestine Studies* vol. XXVI, no. 3 (Spring 1997), pp. 81–91.

Naim, Mona. 'An Interview with Mahmoud Darwish' *MERIP* (194/195) vol. 25 no. 3–4 (May–June/July–August 1995): pp. 18.

Rabbani, Mouin. 'The Standard Colonial Pattern: An Interview with Noam Chomsky' *Race and Class* vol. 37, no. 2 (Oct.–Dec. 1995): pp. 93–7.

Shaath, Nabil (interview with). 'The Oslo Agreement' *Journal of Palestine Studies* vol. XXIII, no. 1 (Autumn 1993): pp.5–13.

Usher, Graham (1994a). 'An Interview with Salah Abd al-Shafi' *MERIP* (186) vol. 24, no. 1 (Jan.–Feb. 1994): p. 11–13.

—— (1995b). 'An Israeli Peace: Interview with Ilan Pappé' *Race and Class* vol. 37, no. 2 (Oct.–Dec. 1995): pp. 19 26.

—— (1995c). 'Bantustanization or Bi-nationalism: An Interview with Azmi Bashara' *Race and Class* vol. 37, no. 2 (Oct.–Dec. 1995): pp. 43–50.

Zahar, Mahmud (interview with). 'Hamas: Waiting for Secular Nationalism to Self Destruct' *Journal of Palestine Studies* vol. XXIV, no. 3 (Spring 1995): pp. 81–8.

V. Agreements

Agreement on Preparatory Transfer of Powers and Responsibilities (Erez: Aug. 29, 1994).

Israeli–Palestinian Agreement on the West Bank and Gaza Strip [Washington, 28 September, 1995] and Declaration of Principles on Interim Self Government Arrangements [Washington DC, 13 September, 1993] (East Jerusalem: JMCC, Occasional documents series, no. 7, August 1996).

Palestinian Authority and Government of Israel Joint Statement (Taba: Aug. 11, 1995): 'Documents and Source Materials' *Journal of Palestine Studies* vol. XXV, no. 1 (Autumn 1995): pp. 147–8.

Index